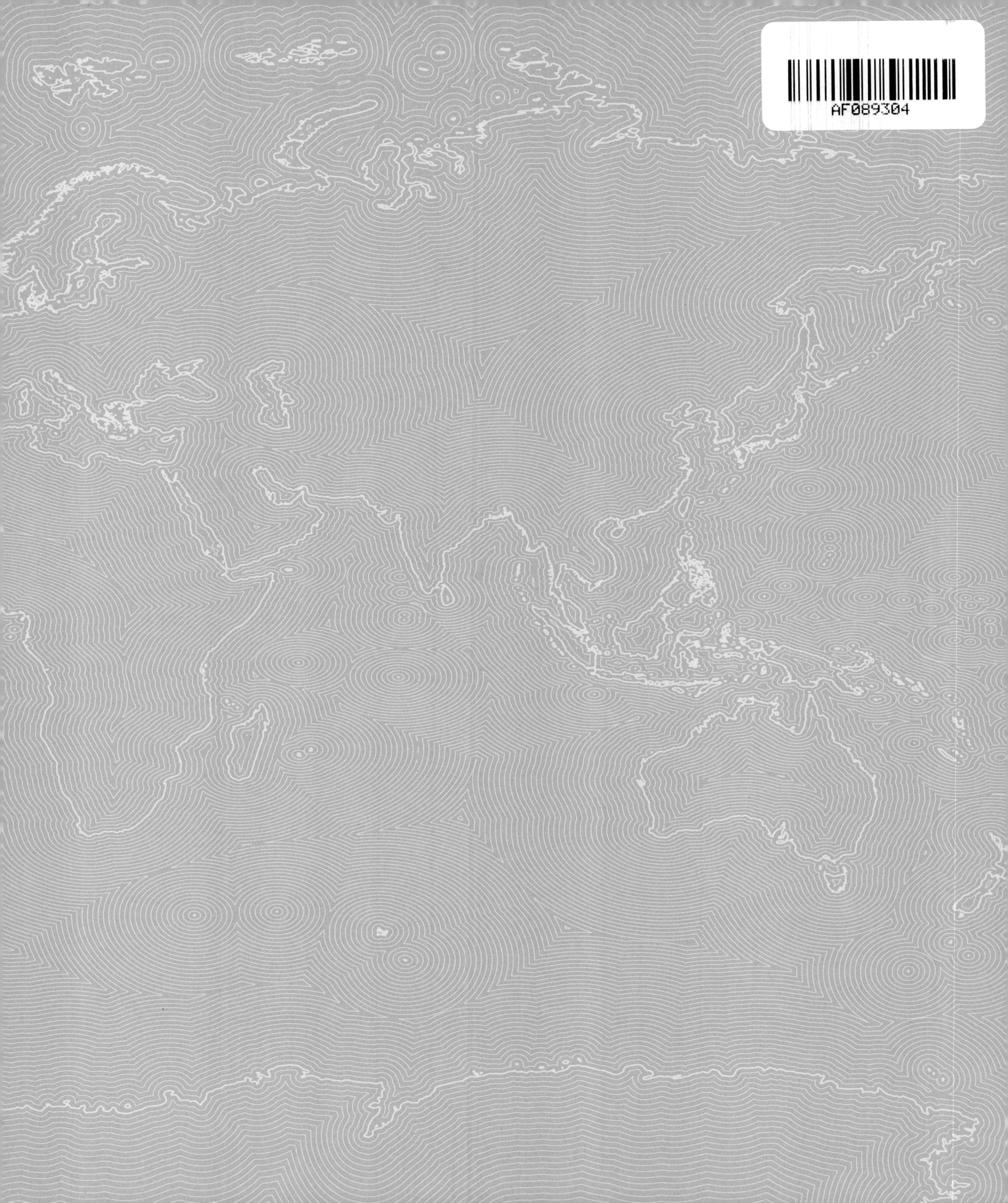

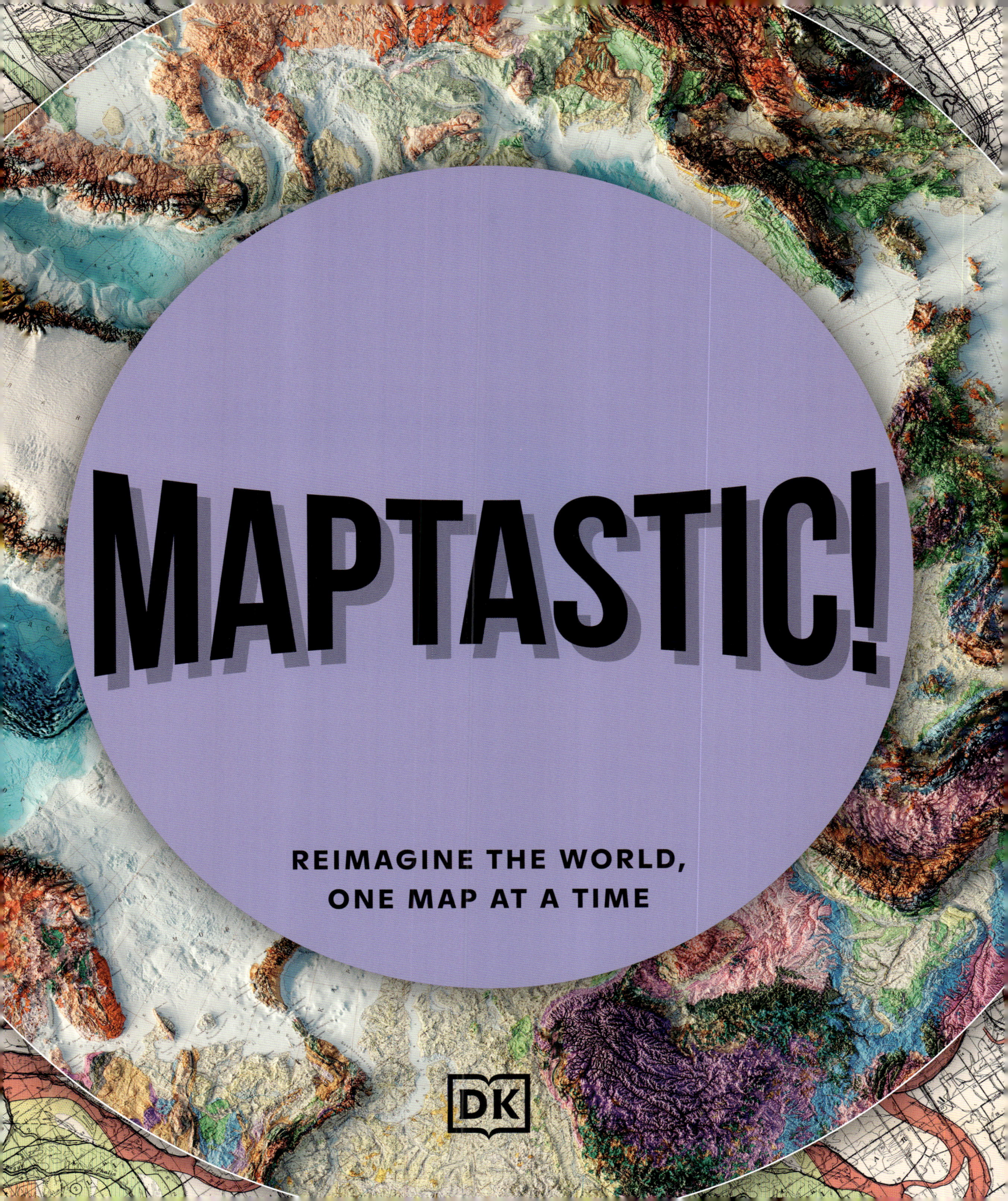

MAPTASTIC!

REIMAGINE THE WORLD, ONE MAP AT A TIME

DK

Senior editor Ben Morgan
Senior designer Smiljka Surla
Managing editor Rachel Fox
Managing art editor Owen Peyton Jones
Editors Rebecca Fry, Lizzie Munsey, Ed Pearce
Designers Emma Clayton, Jim Green, Victoria Gordon-Harris, Rhys Thomas
Production editor Dragana Puvacic
Production controller Leanne Burke
Jacket design Elle Ward
Cartographers James Macdonald, Simon Mumford
Illustrator Peter Bull
Picture research Myriam Meguarbi
Publisher Andrew Macintyre
Art director Mabel Chan

Authors
Rebecca Fry, Clive Gifford, Ben Morgan,
Isabel Thomas, Justine Willis

The authorised representative in the EEA is
Dorling Kindersley Verlag GmbH. Arnulfstr. 124,
80636 Munich, Germany

Copyright © 2025 Dorling Kindersley Limited
A Penguin Random House Company
10 9 8 7 6 5 4 3
007–350757–September/2025

All rights reserved.
No part of this publication may be reproduced, stored in or introduced into a retrieval system, or transmitted, in any form, or by any means (electronic, mechanical, photocopying, recording, or otherwise), without the prior written permission of the copyright owner. DK values and supports copyright. Thank you for respecting intellectual property laws by not reproducing, scanning or distributing any part of this publication by any means without permission. By purchasing an authorised edition, you are supporting writers and artists and enabling DK to continue to publish books that inform and inspire readers.
No part of this publication may be used or reproduced in any manner for the purpose of training artificial intelligence technologies or systems. In accordance with Article 4(3) of the DSM Directive 2019/790, DK expressly reserves this work from the text and data mining exception.

A CIP catalogue record for this book
is available from the British Library.
ISBN: 978-0-2417-5389-7

Printed and bound in the UK
www.dk.com

THE PHYSICAL WORLD	6
Flat Earth	8
The Pacific is how big?	10
How big is Australia?	12
Top of the world	14
Ice flows	16
Under the ice	18
Longest mountain range	20
Shifting seas	22
Sea of change	24
Air and water	26
Where the rain goes	28
Rivers in the desert	30
Carved by time	32
Meandering Mississippi	34
Hidden landscapes	36
Hidden landslides	38
Lava flows	39
Hurricane tracks	40
Tornado Alley	42
Ring of fire	44
Mount Taranaki	46

THE HUMAN WORLD	48
Where is everyone?	50
How many countries?	52
What names mean	54
Curious names	56
Endonyms of the world	58
Who's across the ocean?	60
Who's on the opposite side?	62
Where's the money?	64
How many Switzerlands fit in Brazil?	66
Coral cities	68
Cities by design	70
Sky highways	72
Ocean highways	74
Internet highways	76
Longest journeys	78
What's the time at the poles?	80

WORLD OF ANIMALS — 82

Where the wild things aren't	84
Where sheep live	86
Where swallows fly	88
Where eagles roam	90
Ships of the desert	92
Deadly animals	94

SPACE — 96

Earth at night	98
Lost in space	100
Meteorite map	102
Destination Moon	104
Lunar rock	106
Martian rock	108
Solar system	110
Cosmic eye	112
Earth from space	114

HISTORY — 116

Roman treasure	118
The Book of Roger	120
The world in 1375	122
A world of wonders	124
A New World	126
America's birth certificate	128
Attack on Vienna	130
Here be dragons!	132
Shipwrecks	134

REFERENCE — 136

Rock solid North America	138
Rock solid South America	140
Rock solid Africa	142
Rock solid Europe	144
Rock solid Australia	146
Rock solid Asia	148
Types of map	150
Map projections	152
Reading maps	154
Index	156
Acknowledgments	160

Contents

Flat Earth

MAKING 2D MAPS OF A 3D PLANET

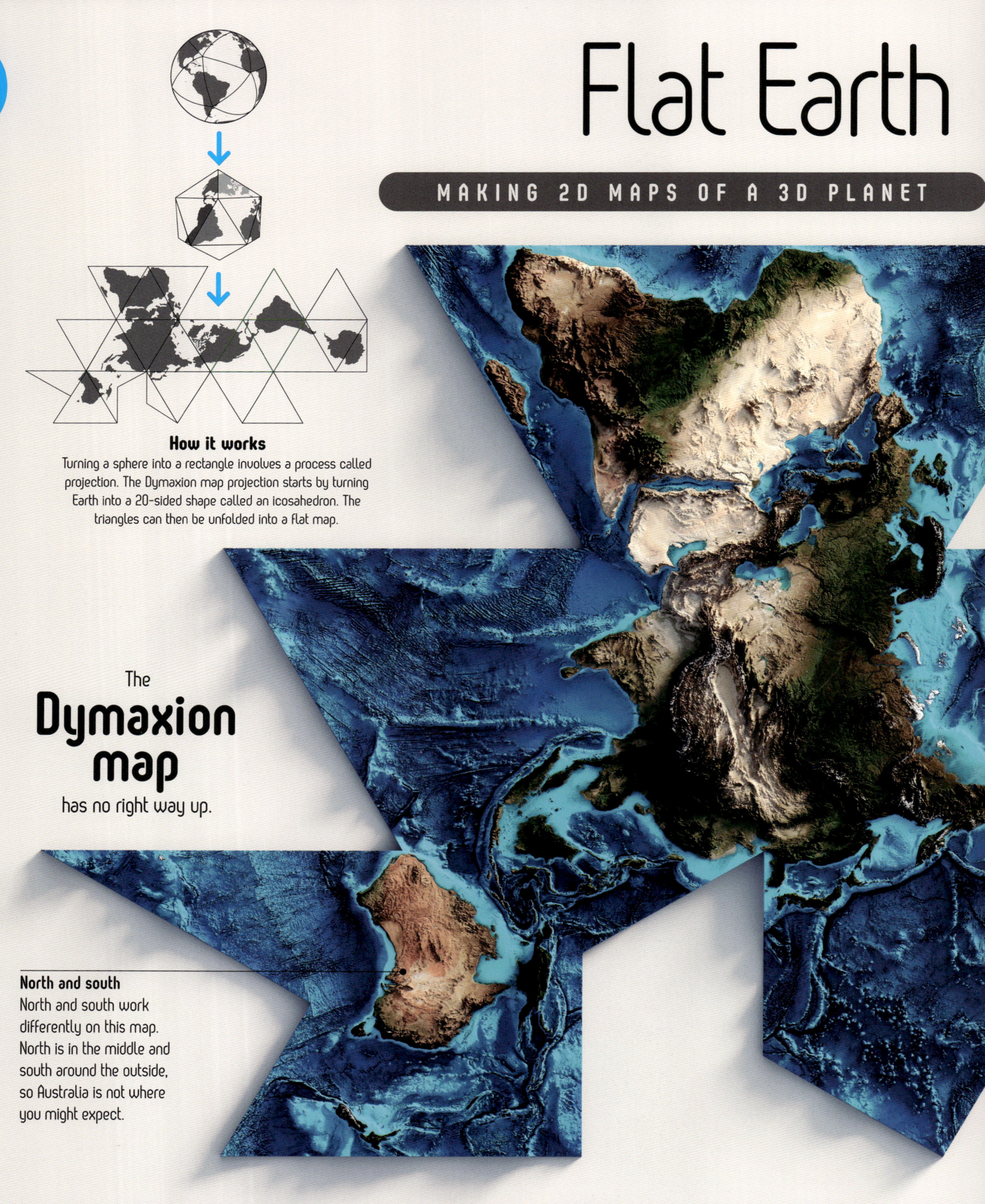

How it works
Turning a sphere into a rectangle involves a process called projection. The Dymaxion map projection starts by turning Earth into a 20-sided shape called an icosahedron. The triangles can then be unfolded into a flat map.

The **Dymaxion map** has no right way up.

North and south
North and south work differently on this map. North is in the middle and south around the outside, so Australia is not where you might expect.

PHYSICAL WORLD

We live on a spherical world, but maps in books are flat 2D rectangles. This gives map makers a problem – how do you convert a sphere into a rectangle without distorting it? The answer is you can't. Rectangular maps stretch and squeeze Earth's surface, making some areas look bigger than they really are. Countries near the poles get stretched the most. However, this version – the Dymaxion map, created by US architect Buckminster Fuller – does a better job of preserving the true size and shape of each continent.

One island
The map reveals that all the world's continents are almost connected, forming what the map's creator called "one island Earth".

Greenland
Far closer to its true size here, on some maps Greenland can appear as large as Africa.

South Pole
Rectangular maps stretch Antarctica into a long strip, but here we see its true shape and size.

Sideways look
Although the continents are the right size and shape, they are not the usual way round.

Water world

We call our planet Earth because we live on land, but aliens would probably call it Water. Liquid water covers 71 per cent of Earth's surface, which is actually very odd. Of the 300 or so planets and moons in our solar system, liquid water has been found only on the surface of our world.

NORTH AMERICA

AFRICA

The Pacific is how big?

The biggest geographical feature on Earth is, without question, the Pacific Ocean.

It covers nearly a third of Earth's surface and is greater in area than all the world's continents and islands put together. At its widest point, the Pacific spans 19,800 km (12,300 miles) from Indonesia to Colombia. That's a shade under halfway round the world and more than five times wider than the Moon.

The Pacific Ocean is **21 times** greater in area than Australia.

THE SIZE OF EARTH'S BIGGEST OCEAN

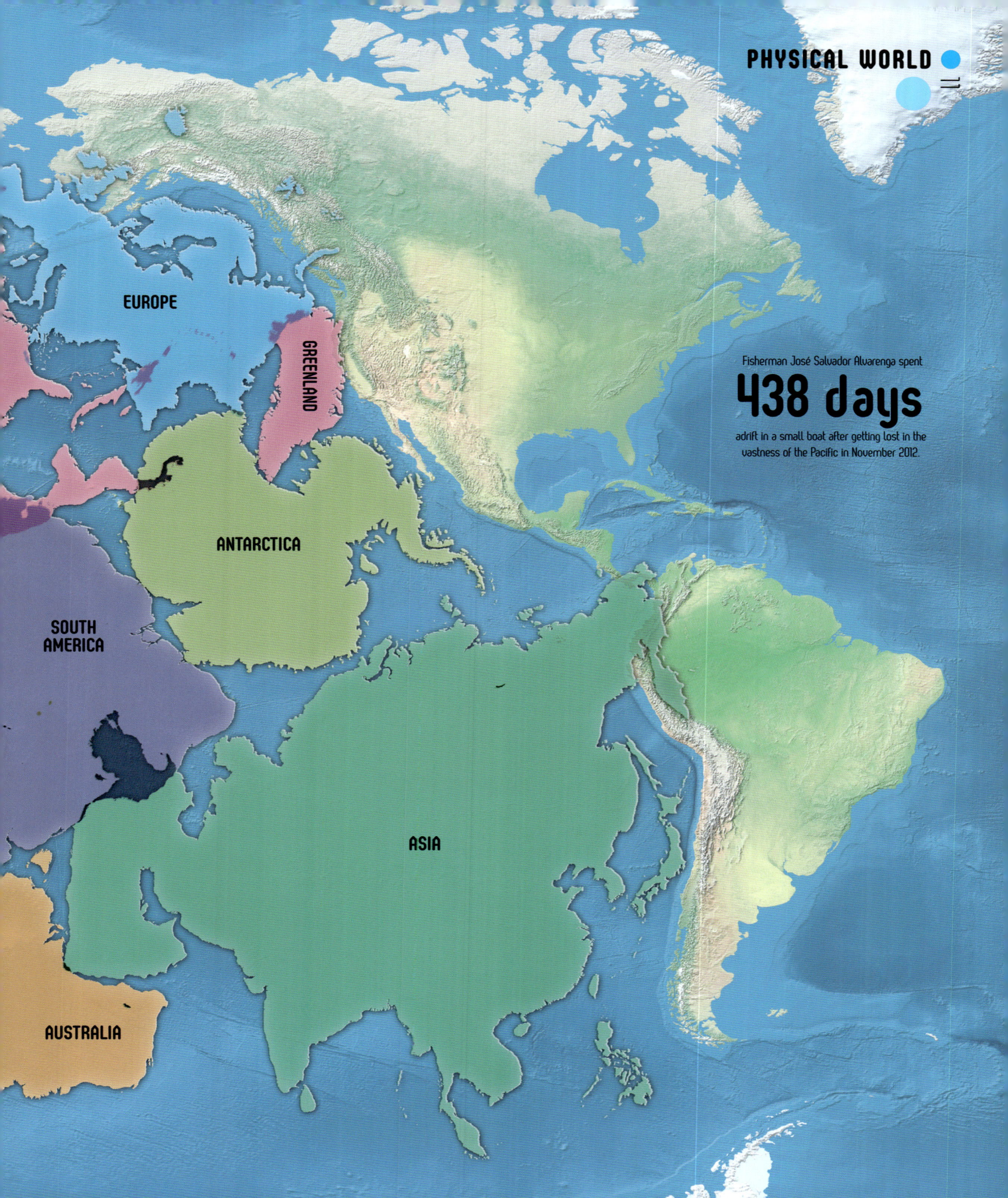

How big is Australia?

MAPPING AUSTRALIA'S TRUE SIZE

Australia is so big we call it a continent as well as a country. As this map shows, it would swallow the whole of the Mediterranean Sea if you put one on top of the other.

Australia is entirely surrounded by ocean, with no land borders, but it's too big to be called an island. The world's largest official island, Greenland, is only a quarter of the size. Australia sits atop its own tectonic plate – one of the jigsaw pieces that make up Earth's crust. This has kept it separate from other continents for more than 30 million years, which is why its marsupial animals are so different from animals elsewhere. Despite its great scale, Australia isn't the largest country. That honour goes to Russia, which is more than twice as big.

MEDITERRANEAN SEA

AUSTRALIA

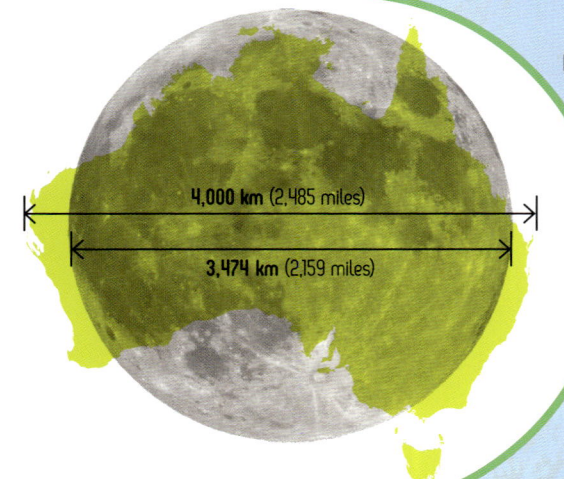

Over the Moon
Measuring 4,000 km (2,485 miles) from west to east at its widest point, Australia is more than 500 km (310 miles) wider than the Moon. People in Australia see the same side of the Moon as people in the northern hemisphere, but it's the other way up and crescent moons curve the opposite way.

4,000 km (2,485 miles)
3,474 km (2,159 miles)

One of the longest structures in the world is the

dingo fence

that stretches 5,614 km (3,488 miles) across Australia to protect sheep from dingos (wild dogs).

PHYSICAL WORLD
13

The interior of Australia is a hot, dusty wilderness called the outback, with 10 deserts and very few people. Most Australians live on the coast.

Compared to Europe

With a total area of 7.7 million sq km (3 million sq miles), Australia could swallow all of Europe except Russia. The distance from the Australian city of Perth in the west to Sydney in the east is similar to the distance from Lisbon to Kiev in Europe – a 41-hour drive without loo breaks.

Australia's largest cattle ranch is almost **as big as Belgium.**

PHYSICAL WORLD

Divided ocean
Running across the floor of the Arctic Ocean from Iceland is a deep gash – a rift between two of the huge tectonic plates that make up Earth's crust. The plates are moving apart here, and molten rock is welling up between them from Earth's interior and hardening to form new ocean floor.

Life on ice
Sea ice is important to a wide range of Arctic animals, including polar bears and several seal species. Polar bears jump and swim between chunks of ice while hunting for seals nesting in ice caves.

Poles apart
Near the centre of the Arctic Ocean is Earth's North Pole – the northernmost place in the world and the point around which the planet rotates. But this isn't where compass needles point. The magnetic north pole drifts slowly around the Arctic region due to changes in Earth's molten iron core, which generates the planet's magnetic field.

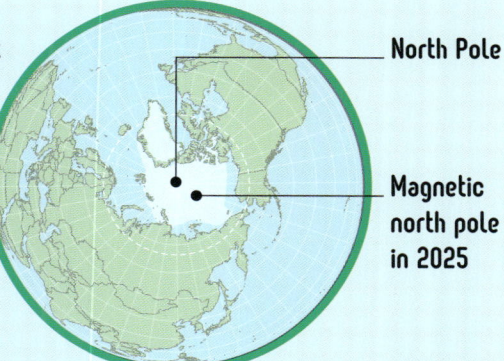

North Pole

Magnetic north pole in 2025

Top of the world

This top-down map of Earth's North Pole offers an unusual view of the Arctic Ocean stripped of ice, revealing a hidden split in Earth's crust.

The world's smallest and shallowest ocean, the Arctic is almost completely encircled by land and partly covered with floating ice all year round round. This ice-free view was made by combining elevation data with a Russian geological map of 1966 to create a 3D image. The colours show rocks of different geological eras.

MAPPING THE ARCTIC OCEAN

ICE SPEED (METRES PER YEAR)
1   10   100   1000

If the ice melted
The movement of Antarctica's ice is a natural part of Earth's water cycle, but climate change is speeding things up. If all the ice melted, sea levels would rise 60 m (200 ft) and great swathes of land would disappear underwater (blue areas above). Fortunately, scientists think that's very unlikely. However, Antarctica's small western ice sheet might melt, raising sea levels by around 5 m (16 ft).

River of ice
Even solid ice can't resist the force of gravity. Over time, it flows downhill like a river in slow motion. This photo shows a glacier snaking between mountains on the coast of Antarctica. At the bottom are icebergs that broke off the glacier and became trapped in sea ice over winter.

Ice flows

Antarctica looks frozen in time, but its vast blanket of ice is always moving. Creeping by just a few millimetres a day, the ice spreads outwards and flows towards the sea. Using satellite data, scientists mapped its speed and discovered hundreds of high-speed channels, like a network of rivers. Warmed by geothermal heat, these ribbons of softer ice speed up and merge as they near the coast, forming gigantic glaciers and then ice shelves that extend across the sea.

ANTARCTICA'S SLOW-MO WATERWAYS

PHYSICAL WORLD

Megabergs

Antarctica's ice flows fastest where it juts out over the sea. Giant ice shelves surround the continent, covering an area six times the size of the UK. At their edges, gargantuan icebergs tumble into the sea. The biggest-ever "megaberg" was 335 km (208 miles) long and 97 km (60 miles) wide, which is larger than Belgium.

Ice flows faster in the purple and red zones.

It can take
100,000
years for a snowflake to travel from the South Pole to the sea.

Under the ice

MAPPING A HIDDEN CONTINENT

Antarctica – one of the world's seven continents – has been hidden under ice for 34 million years. The ice sheets that cover Antarctica are nearly 5 km (3 miles) thick in places, but scientists can peer through them. Using radar transmitters, which emit radio waves that bounce off the underlying rock, scientists have mapped the hidden world below. Radar surveys have revealed five mountain ranges, 675 lakes, and countless river valleys and canyons. The vast weight of the ice – 25 million gigatonnes – has pushed 38 per cent of the land below sea level. If the ice disappeared, much of the continent would be underwater.

Mount Kirkpatrick, Antarctica's tallest mountain, is 4,528 m (14,856 ft) high.

The Antarctic Peninsula is the warmest part of Antarctica and is home to many penguins and seabirds.

Prehistoric life
Antarctica has been at the South Pole for 100 million years, but it wasn't always covered in ice. About 90 million years ago, there were lush rainforests and dinosaurs, and temperatures reached a balmy 25°C (77°F) in summer. Scientists think the climate was warmer then because CO_2 levels in the atmosphere were higher than today.

Ice depth
Radar surveys reveal that Antarctica's ice sheets have an average depth of about 2 km (1.2 miles). Many of the continents' research stations are as high as ski resorts due to the thick ice.

PHYSICAL WORLD

Antarctica is considered one of the world's **driest deserts** because it gets so little rain and snow.

Buried peaks

Many of Antarctica's mountains are buried under ice, with only the peaks poking out. The Gamburtsev Range, which is almost as tall as the Alps, is hidden entirely and only visible in radar images. Antarctica also has dozens of volcanoes, including Mount Erebus (right), which has a lake of lava at the summit.

At 3,300 km (2,050 miles) long, the Transantarctic Mountains form the world's fourth longest mountain range.

The Ross Ice Shelf is a shelf of floating sea ice about the size of France.

Hidden under 4 km (2.5 miles) of ice is Lake Vostok, one of the world's largest freshwater lakes.

Mount Erebus is the world's southernmost active volcano and erupts 1–10 times a day.

Longest mountain range

MAPPING THE OCEAN FLOOR

The length of the mid-ocean ridge system is

65,000 km.

For most of history, people had no idea what lay below the sea. That changed in 1977, when this revolutionary map was published.

US geologists Marie Tharp and Bruce Heezen spent over 20 years mapping the sea floor, using soundings from ships. They discovered submarine landscapes as spectacular as any on land. But most amazing was the discovery of the "mid-ocean ridge system" – the world's longest mountain range, which snakes through every ocean. This vast seam in Earth's crust helped prove that it is broken into moving tectonic plates – a theory once considered preposterous.

Sound waves reflect off the ocean floor.

How deep is the sea?
Ships can measure the distance to the sea floor by using sonar machines. These emit pulses of sound and time how long the echoes take to bounce back. The longer they take, the deeper the sea floor must be.

The map that changed the world
Heezen travelled on US navy research ships, collecting data for the map. As a woman, Tharp wasn't allowed on navy ships at the time. She used the data to draw the map by hand, translating endless lists of numbers into plains, canyons, and underwater mountains.

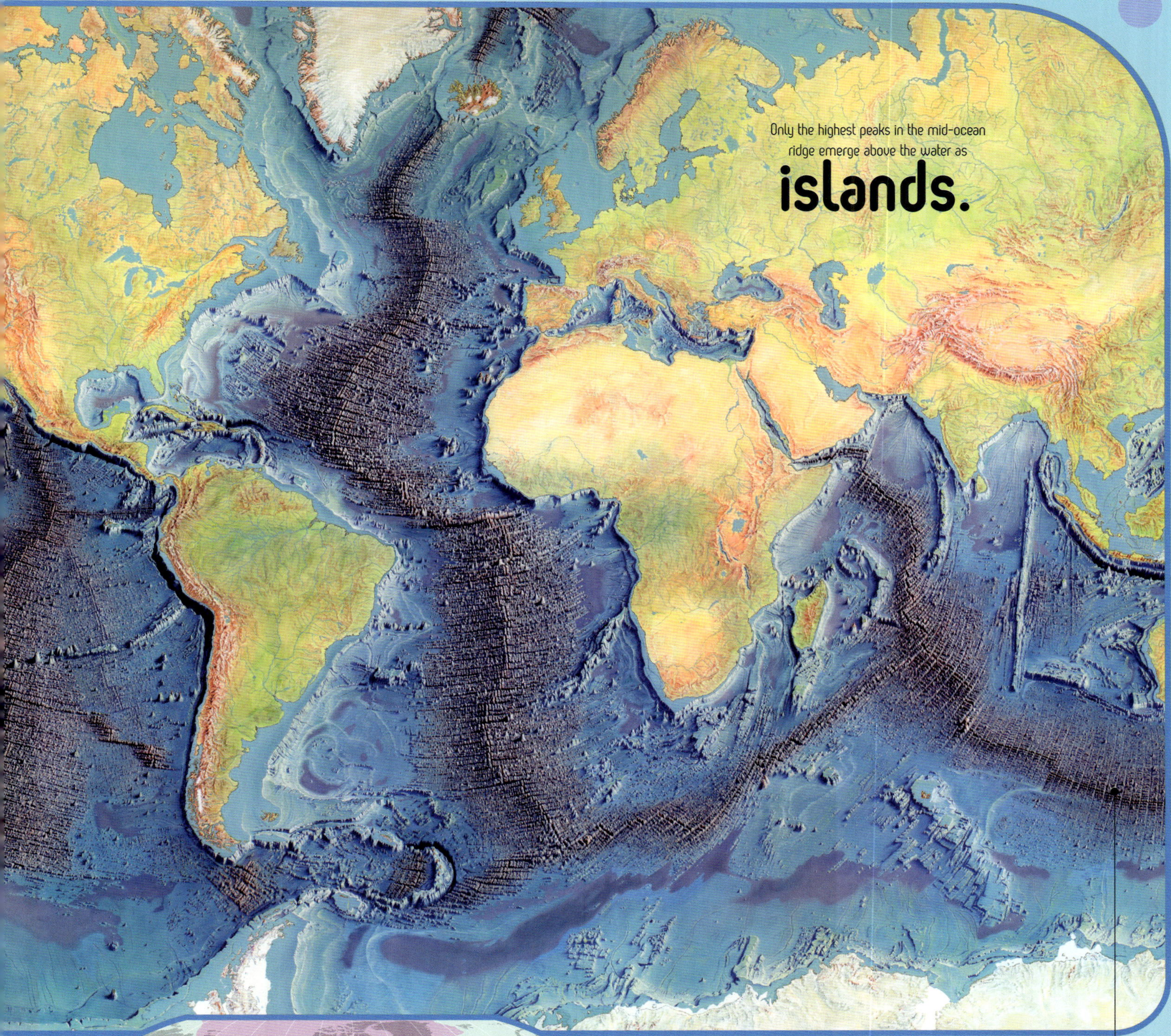

PHYSICAL WORLD

Only the highest peaks in the mid-ocean ridge emerge above the water as **islands.**

Mid-ocean ridge

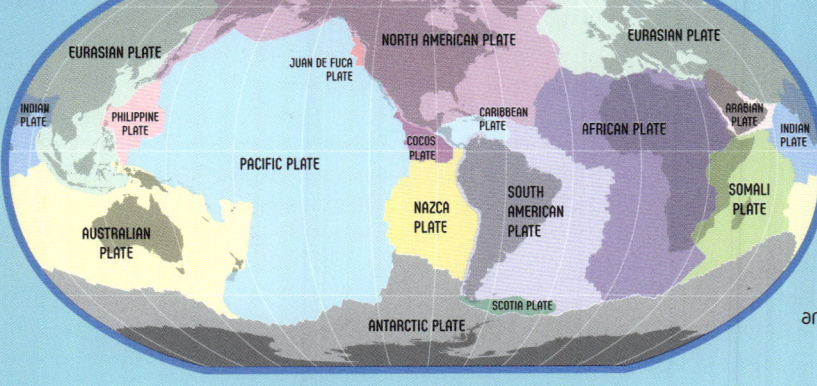

Moving plates
The new ocean map led scientists to rethink our planet's past, present, and future. It became clear that Earth's crust is constantly changing. As we now know, it is divided into a jigsaw of tectonic plates that slowly drift and collide, changing the shapes and positions of continents.

Shifting seas

Oceans are never still. Their surfaces spiral with currents, which carry huge amounts of heat energy from the hot, sun-soaked equator to the freezing poles. Satellites help scientists map these currents. This NASA visualization based on satellite data highlights the Gulf Stream, a persistent current that transports heat from the Gulf of Mexico across the Atlantic to Europe. Without this flow of warmth, western Europe would be bitterly cold.

MAPPING OCEAN CURRENTS

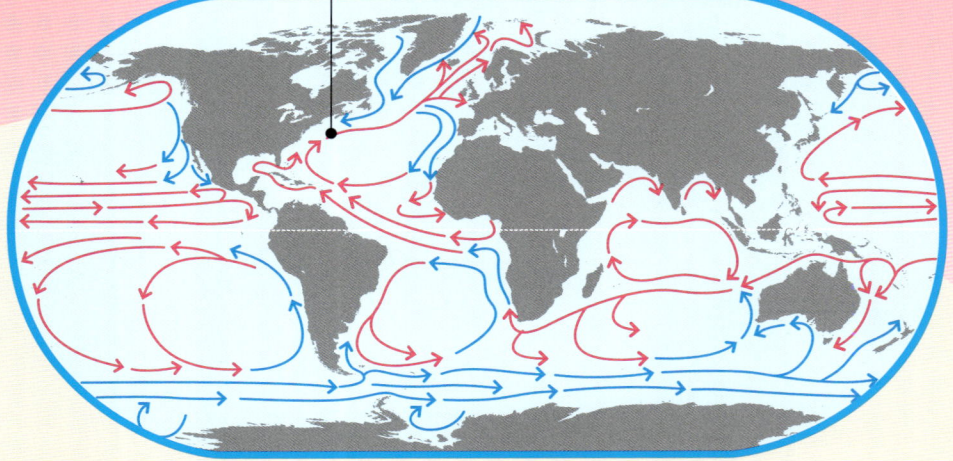

Major currents turn clockwise in the northern hemisphere and anticlockwise in the southern hemisphere.

Surface currents
Surface currents only flow in the top 100 m (300 ft) or so of the ocean. They are driven by the wind and carry both water and heat. The largest surface currents rotate in huge loops called gyres, set spinning by Earth's rotation.

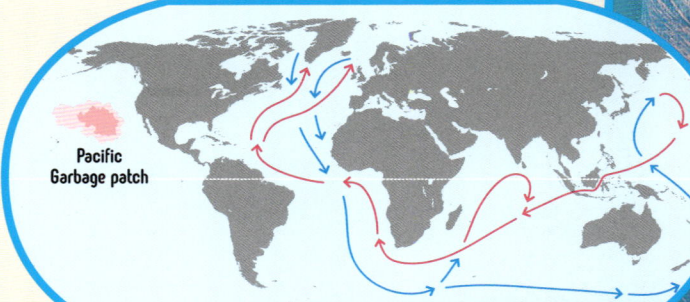

Pacific Garbage patch

Garbage patch
Gyres in the Pacific Ocean trap floating plastic waste from the Americas and Asia in two "great garbage patches". Much of this plastic waste is so tiny we cannot see it, but it is big enough to harm marine life.

CLOSE-UP OF MICROPLASTICS

Deep currents
Cold currents flow along the deep sea floor at about the speed that a tortoise walks. They are driven by cool, dense water that sinks in the polar oceans. The deep currents flow in a single giant cycle known as the global conveyor belt. Water takes around 1,000 years to complete one loop of this cycle.

PHYSICAL WORLD

23

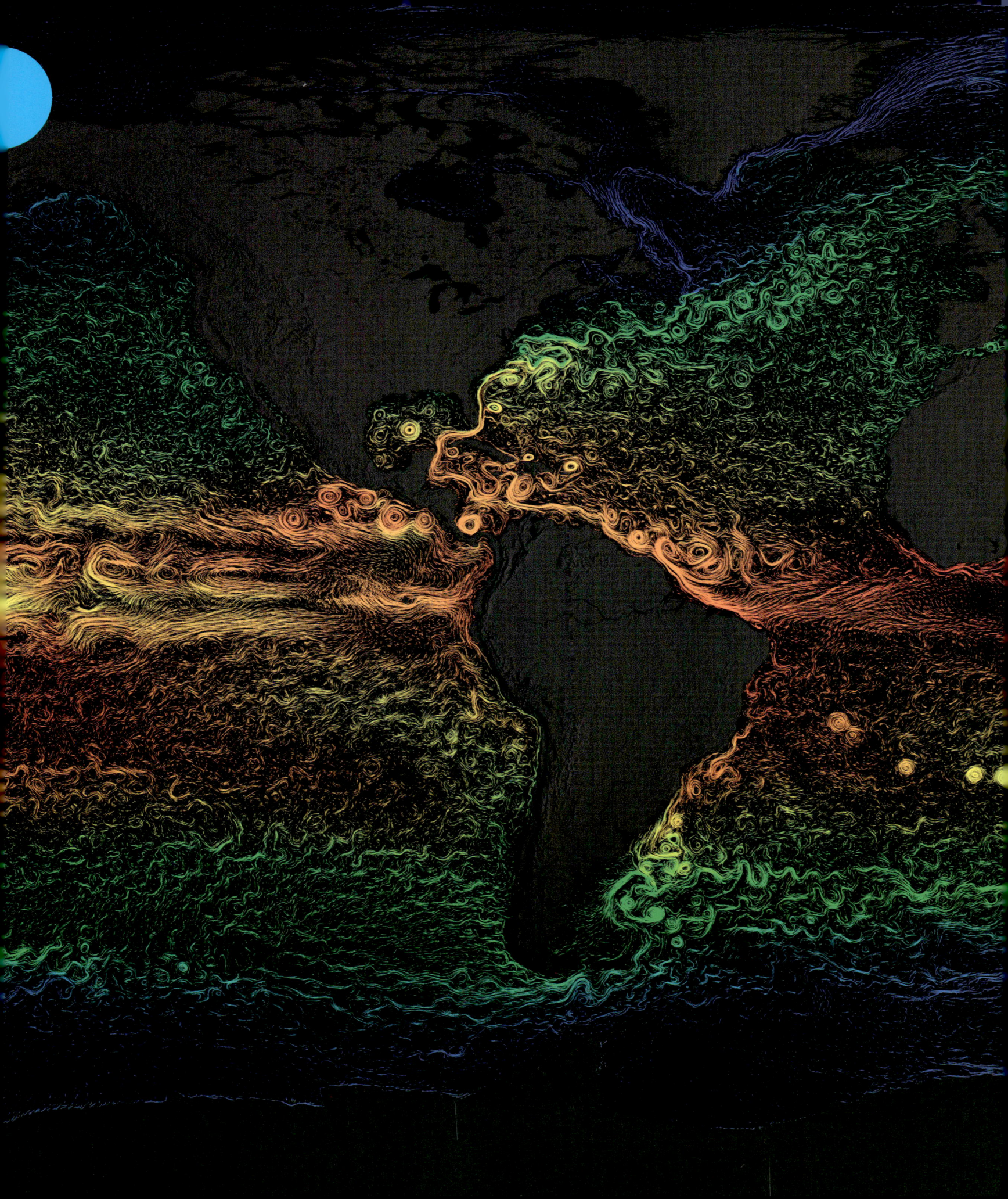

Sea of change

The Sun heats Earth unevenly, warming the tropics more than the poles. The imbalance creates swirling sea currents that redistribute heat across the globe. This NASA image – a blend of satellite data and computer model data – shows swirls of warm water travelling down Africa's east coast before drifting westwards across the Atlantic like smoke rings. These "Agulhas rings" are up to 400 km (250 miles) wide and can last for years.

Air and water

EARTH'S UNIQUE LIFE-SUPPORT SYSTEM

All Earth's air
Earth is covered by a thin blanket of air we call the atmosphere. If all the air in the atmosphere was removed and put in a sphere at normal air pressure, it would be only 2,000 km (1,240 miles) wide.

Thin blue line
Seen from space, Earth's atmosphere looks like a thin, glowing blue line. Only the bottom part of the atmosphere, where air is most dense, can support life. If Earth was the size of an apple, this life-support zone would be a tenth as thin as the apple's skin.

PHYSICAL WORLD

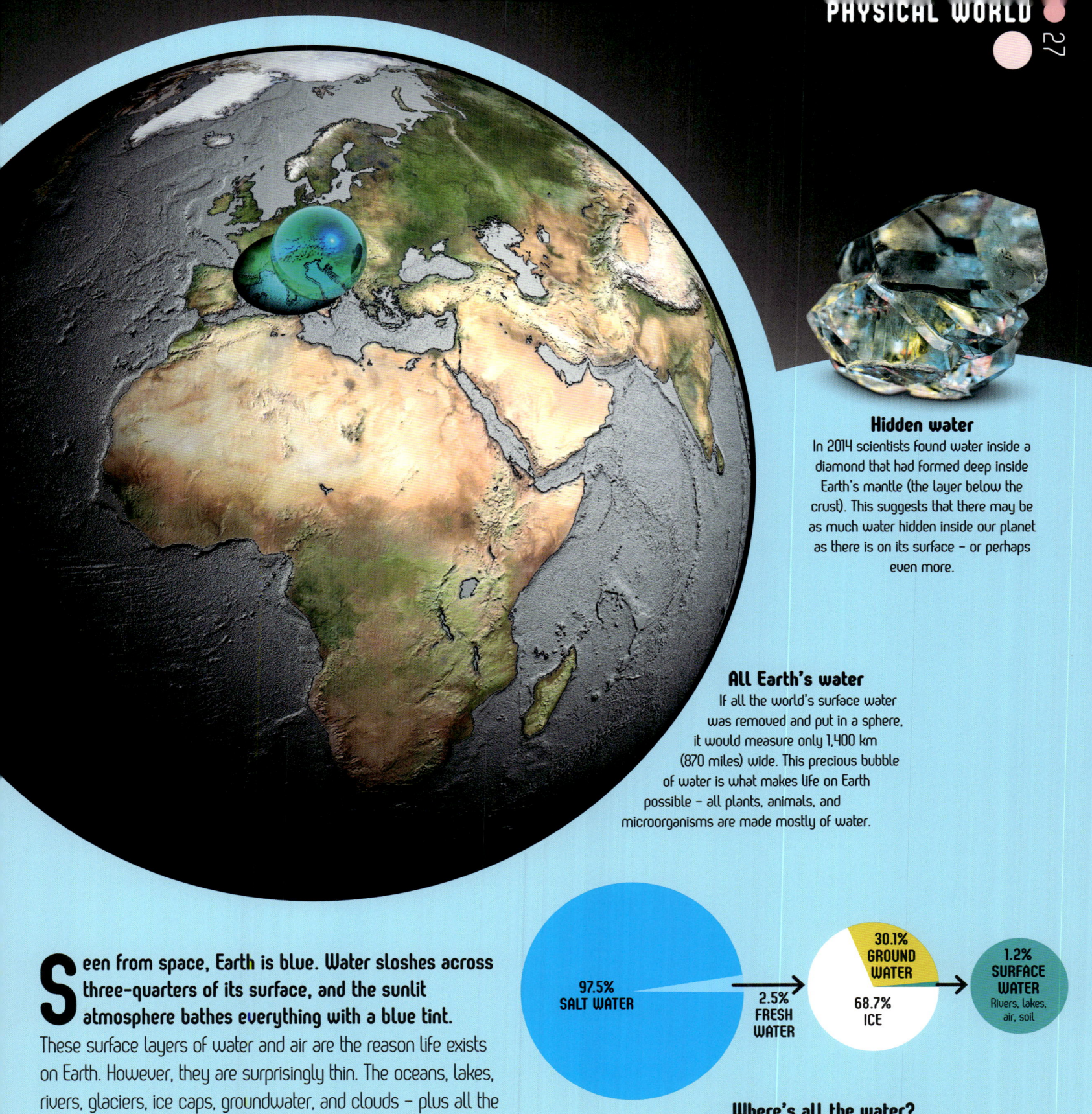

Hidden water
In 2014 scientists found water inside a diamond that had formed deep inside Earth's mantle (the layer below the crust). This suggests that there may be as much water hidden inside our planet as there is on its surface – or perhaps even more.

All Earth's water
If all the world's surface water was removed and put in a sphere, it would measure only 1,400 km (870 miles) wide. This precious bubble of water is what makes life on Earth possible – all plants, animals, and microorganisms are made mostly of water.

Seen from space, Earth is blue. Water sloshes across three-quarters of its surface, and the sunlit atmosphere bathes everything with a blue tint. These surface layers of water and air are the reason life exists on Earth. However, they are surprisingly thin. The oceans, lakes, rivers, glaciers, ice caps, groundwater, and clouds – plus all the water inside living things – make up a mere fiftieth of one per cent of Earth's mass. Earth's air takes up more space, but represents just a millionth of Earth's mass.

97.5% SALT WATER → **2.5% FRESH WATER** → **68.7% ICE**, **30.1% GROUND WATER** → **1.2% SURFACE WATER** Rivers, lakes, air, soil

Where's all the water?
The vast majority of Earth's water is salty and undrinkable. Most fresh water is frozen in ice caps and glaciers. The water we depend on is groundwater, as well as the tiny fraction of fresh water found in Earth's lakes and rivers.

Countries with no rivers

Some countries have hundreds of rivers, but a few have none. Much of the Arabian Peninsula is too dry for permanent rivers, though seasonal rivers fill up after storms. Some small island nations or very small countries have no rivers either.

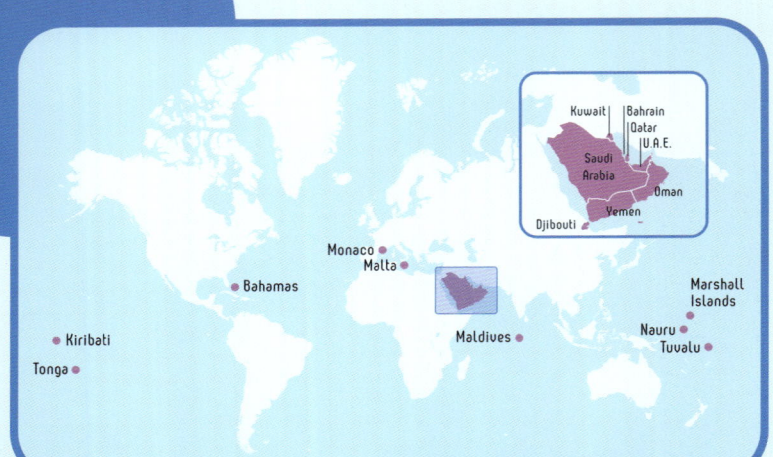

US river basins

Rainfall from a staggering 41 per cent of the continental USA drains into the Mississippi River (shown in deep green on the map). It funnels water from 31 states across the northern, eastern, western, and central USA into the Gulf of Mexico.

Where the rain goes

Humans divide the world in different ways, but water creates its own borders. This map highlights the world's largest drainage basin – an area of land where every drop of rain or snow flows towards the same place. The Amazon basin is a vast network of more than 1,100 rivers and streams that drain water from nine countries. These tributaries feed the mighty Amazon River, which winds more than 6,450 km (4,000 miles) across South America before pouring into the Atlantic Ocean. About 219,000 tonnes of water – enough to fill 88 Olympic swimming pools – flows from the river into the Atlantic Ocean every second.

MAPPING RIVER BASINS

PHYSICAL WORLD

29

Crocodiles

survive in some Saharan oases. They hibernate in caves or burrows during very dry spells.

Dry valleys

Dry river valleys, such as Wadi Mides in Tunisia, are found all over the Sahara. Desert plants can lie dormant in wadis for years, springing to life after rain and turning the valley floor green. Wadis provide shade and shelter for travellers, but they are dangerous places to camp: many people die of drowning after rainstorms fill wadis without warning.

River Niger

The Sahara has only two permanent rivers: the Niger and the Nile. The Niger loops up into the western Sahara before seeming to change its mind and head back south again. This vital supply of water in the desert nurtured some of Africa's oldest civilizations and ancient cities such as Timbuktu.

Rivers in the desert

Africa's Sahara desert is one of the world's driest places, but as this map shows, it is a maze of river valleys – nearly all of them bone dry. The network of ancient rivers was discovered by space shuttle surveys that used radar to measure ground height. Thousands of years ago, when the climate was wetter, water coursed through these veins. Some briefly fill with water once or twice a decade, but only after rare rainstorms.

MAPPING THE SAHARA'S ANCIENT WATERWAYS

PHYSICAL WORLD

Oases
Deep below the Sahara are vast reservoirs of water that filled up thousands of years ago in beds of absorbent rock. These reservoirs hold more water than all the world's lakes put together. In a few locations, where the ground is unusually low, water seeps to the surface to create patches of lush vegetation called oases, such as the oasis of Um El Ma in Libya.

The Nile
The only river to run right across the Sahara is the Nile, the world's longest river. It flows northwards from the tropical highlands of East Africa to the Mediterranean Sea, and its fertile riverbanks, which have been farmed since the Stone Age, supported the civilization of Ancient Egypt.

Sahara desert

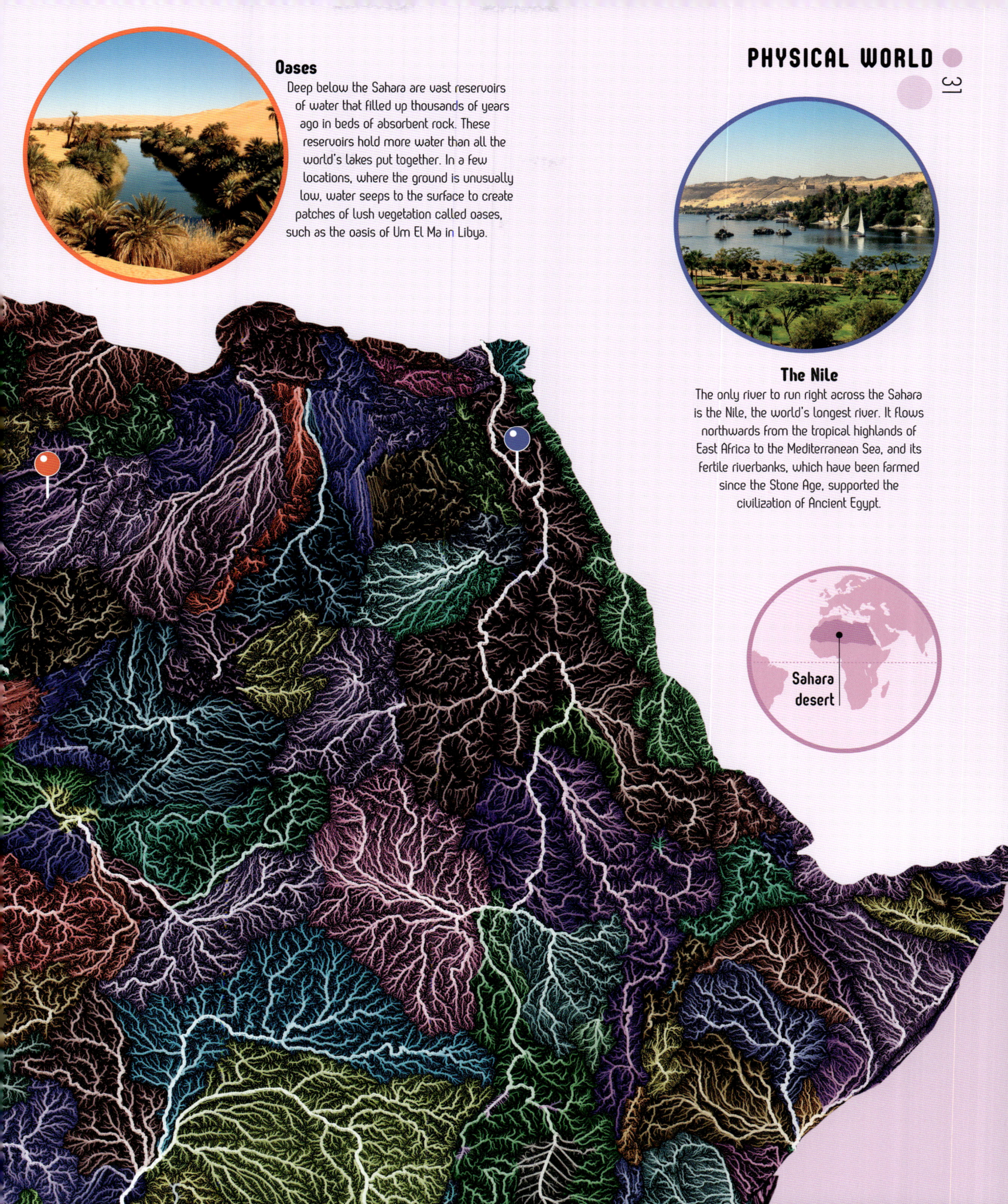

Carved by time

MAPPING THE GRAND CANYON

Over millions of years, rivers eat away at land through a process called erosion, creating valleys and canyons. This geological map shows how the USA's Colorado River eroded the most spectacular valley on Earth: the Grand Canyon. Over six million years, the river wore its way down through older and older layers of rock, carving ever deeper into Earth's past.

Hard rock

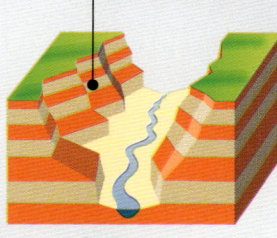
Soft rock

How it formed
The Grand Canyon is called a "stair-step" canyon because its walls have a series of steps. These formed because softer rock layers crumbled and washed away more quickly, while harder layers persisted.

The Grand Canyon
Rushing downhill and carrying tumbling boulders, the Colorado River cut a gash one mile deep in the Colorado Plateau. The horizontal rock strata formed earlier – by gradual deposition of sediments over half a billion years when the plateau was an ancient sea floor.

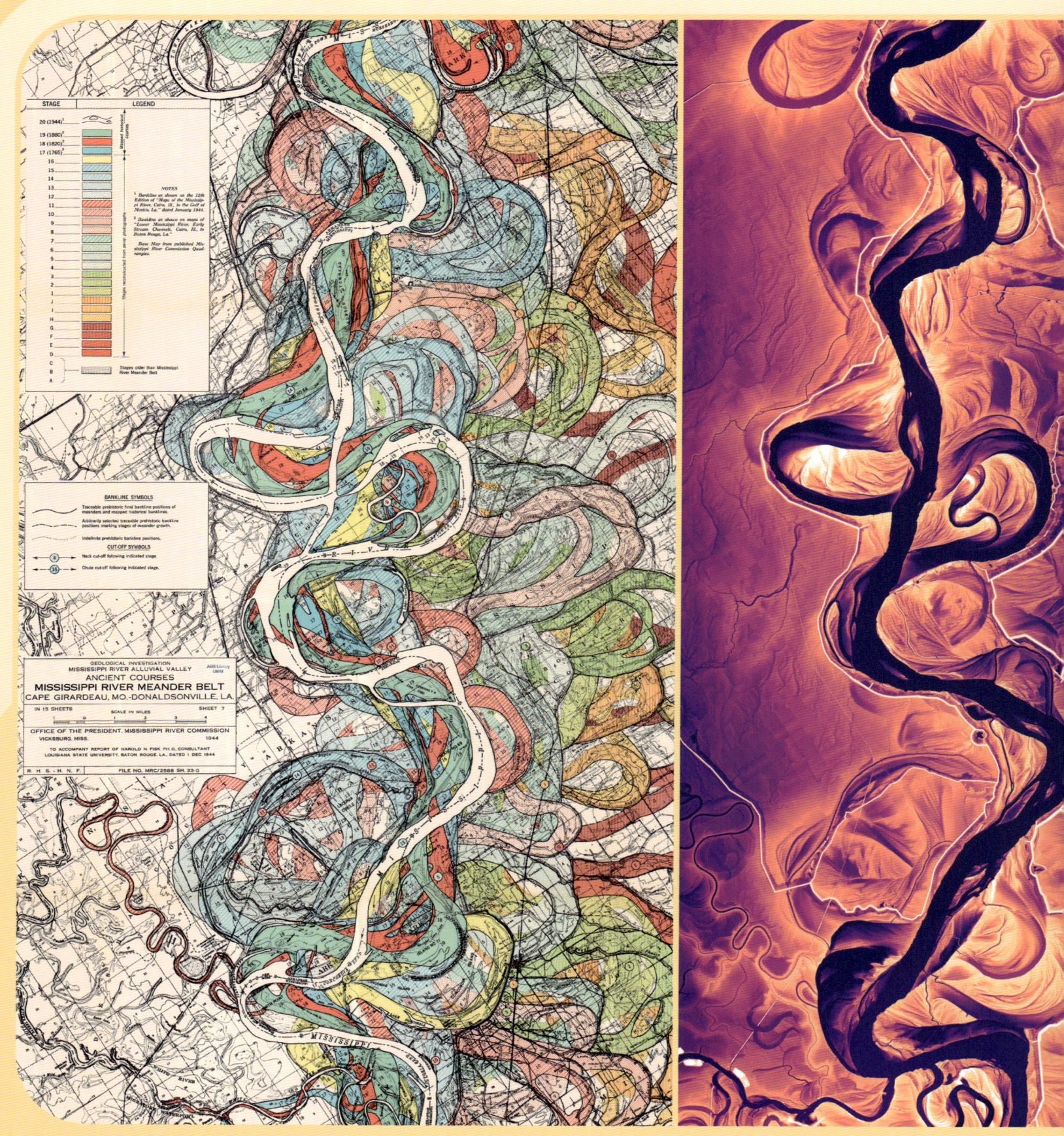

HAROLD FISK'S 1944 MAP OF THE MISSISSIPPI RIVER

LASER SURVEY MAP, 2019

PHYSICAL WORLD 35

Meandering Mississippi

HOW RIVERS SHIFT OVER TIME

Rivers may seem like permanent features of the landscape, but historical maps reveal that their paths are continually changing. These two maps show the Mississippi River at two points in time. The first was drawn by US geologist Harold Fisk in 1944. The second was made by a laser survey in 2019. Look carefully and you can see new islands in the modern image and changes in the bends. Both maps show something even more extraordinary: scars in the land where the river used to be. Fisk colour-coded these ghostly tracks by age, using clues from old maps and soil samples. His map records a pattern of change extending back centuries.

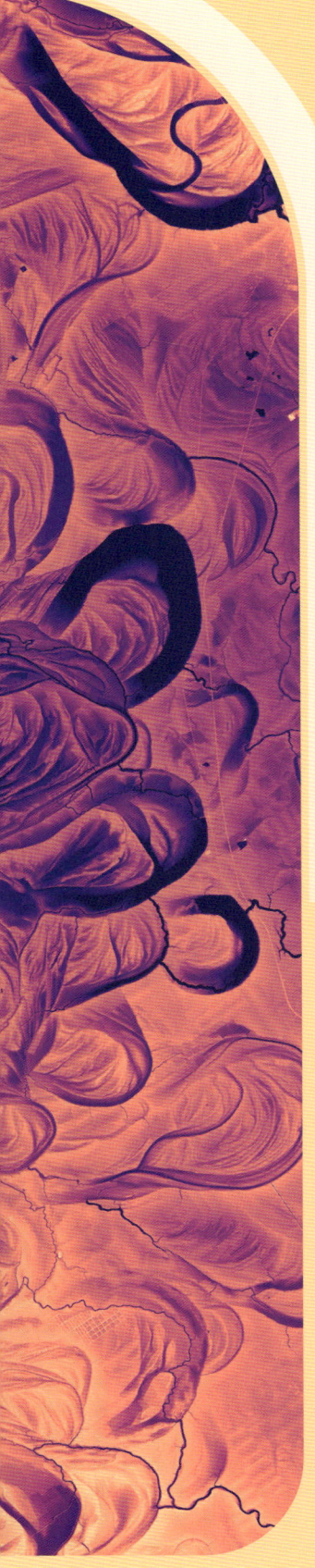

SATELLITE IMAGE

Oxbow lakes

Bends (meanders) in rivers widen over time because water flows faster at the outside of the bend, causing erosion of the riverbank. Meanwhile, slower water on the insides of bends allows mud to settle, forming new ground. Eventually a bend can cut itself off from the river entirely to leave a stranded loop – an oxbow lake.

The Mississippi River valley has more than

1,500

oxbow lakes.

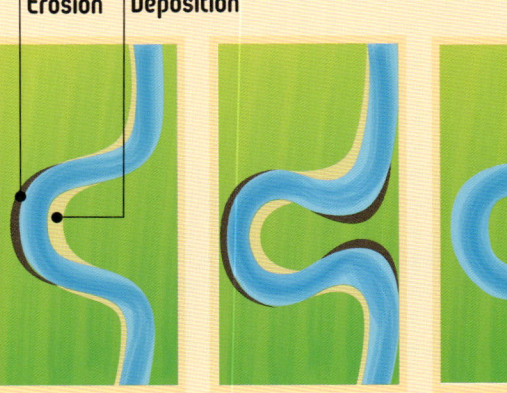

Erosion | Deposition

BENDS WIDEN | NECK CLOSES | OXBOW LAKE

Hidden landscapes

LASER SCANNING EARTH'S SURFACE

Photos of Earth from above capture everything from grass and trees to clouds, but sometimes we only want to see the ground.

Surveyors use a technique called LiDAR (light detection and ranging) to do exactly that. Lasers on a plane sweep the ground with pulses of light, capturing millions of distance measurements every second. The measurements are combined with location data to create a detailed, 3D map of Earth's surface. LiDAR maps remove vegetation to reveal features hidden from view – from lost cities in the jungle to landslides, lava flows, and scars left by ice-age glaciers.

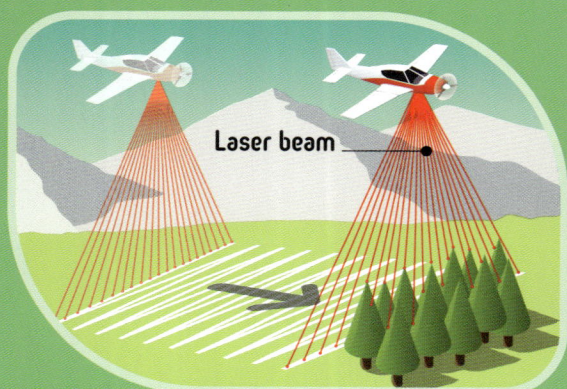

How it works
LiDAR systems calculate distance from the time it takes for lasers to reflect off something. If there are multiple reflections in a small area, the software filters out all but the slowest one, which is from the ground. This way, vegetation is stripped out.

Lost city
The ancient Mayan city of Ocomtún was discovered in 2023 using LiDAR. For 1,000 years or more, it was hidden in the jungle of southern Mexico. Pyramids, palaces, reservoirs, and even a ball games court were revealed.

Glacial scars
This LiDAR map of a sea inlet near Tacoma, USA, reveals hundreds of oval hills aligned in parallel. These are drumlins – mounds of rocky debris dumped, scraped, and moulded by giant glaciers sliding across North America in the ice age. The drumlins are almost invisible in satellite images.

PHYSICAL WORLD

37

Hidden landslides
Where forest covers the land, geologists can use LiDAR (light detection and ranging) to strip away vegetation and map the ground below. These two images show the same area of land around Cedar River east of Seattle, USA. A normal satellite image (below) shows only dense forest broken by the river and footpaths. In contrast, the LiDAR image reveals a series of landslides from an unstable slope.

Lava flows

West Crater is a dormant volcano in Gifford Pinchot National Forest, a beauty spot in Washington State, USA. The volcano last erupted around 8,000 years ago. This LiDAR image (below) reveals overlapping eruptions of thick, viscous lava that built up in layers, the surface stretching into deep wrinkles as the lava set. More than 14,000 people live within 30 km (19 miles) of the volcano, but geologists consider it low risk.

Hurricane tracks

MAPPING TROPICAL STORMS

Hurricanes are vast, rotating storms fuelled by heat energy from the ocean. They rarely form over land, and only develop over tropical and sub-tropical oceans, where the sea is warm. This map tracks the path of every hurricane from 2000 to 2024. Hurricanes travel west after forming before turning polewards, but they never cross the equator. Like the predictable trade winds that blow in cycles across the oceans, they follow curving paths due to Earth's rotation. Hurricanes rotate as they travel, with the fastest and deadliest winds whirling around the central eye.

Category 1
Wind speed 119–153 kph (74–95 mph). Minimal damage, weak trees fall, roof tiles blown off.

The largest hurricanes are **2,000 km** (1,200 miles) wide.

Hurricanes rarely form in the South Atlantic Ocean as the water is cold.

Typhoons

Hurricanes

Cyclones

What are they called?
These violent tropical storms are given different names depending on where on Earth they occur. In the North Atlantic and Northeast Pacific oceans, they are called hurricanes. In the Northwest Pacific Ocean they are known as typhoons. And in the South Pacific and Indian oceans they are called cyclones.

PHYSICAL WORLD

Category 2
Wind speed 154–177 kph (96–110 mph). Houses damaged, bigger trees snapped, rising seas.

Category 3
Wind speed 178–208 kph (111–129 mph). Major damage to homes, trees uprooted, some flooding.

Category 4
Wind speed 209–251 kph (130–156 mph). Roofs blown off, no water or electricity, major flooding.

Category 5
Wind speed more than 252 kph (157 mph). Catastrophic damage, massive flooding.

Hurricane scale
The strength of a hurricane is rated on the Saffir-Simpson scale, which is based on wind speed (although hurricanes also bring torrential rain). Category 5 hurricanes are rare, accounting for less than 10 per cent of all tropical storms globally.

Eye of the storm
Viewed from above, the hurricane's eye is clearly visible. This central area is relatively calm and has a ring of cloud around it, known as the eye wall, where the strongest winds occur. In Earth's northern hemisphere, the winds (and clouds) spin anticlockwise, while in the southern hemisphere, they spin clockwise.

40% of hurricanes that strike the USA make landfall in Florida.

Category 5
Category 4
Category 3
Category 2
Category 1
Tropical storm
Tropical depression

Tracking twisters
The map below shows the paths of all tornadoes reported in the USA since 1680, highlighting the huge number to affect the American Midwest, particularly in the states of Texas, Oklahoma, Kansas, Nebraska, Iowa, and Missouri. Each path is colour-coded according to the Enhanced Fujita (EF) scale.

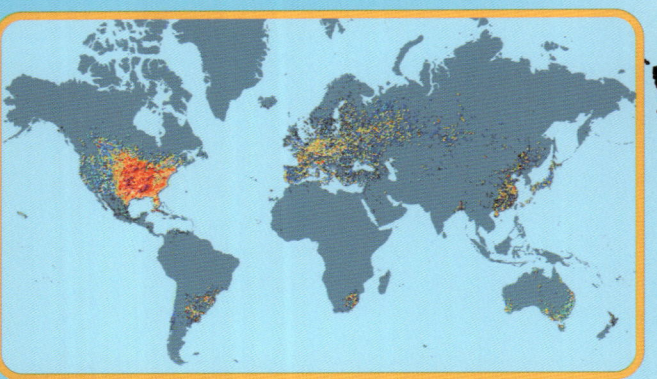

Hotspots and notspots
Although Tornado Alley gets by far the most tornadoes, this world map of reported tornadoes reveals hotspots in Europe, China, and other locations, while many places appear to get none. However, records of tornadoes come most often from densely populated areas, which shows there is bias in the data. In remote places where few people live, most tornadoes go unreported.

The USA gets around

1,200

tornadoes a year.

Tornadoes are whirling updraughts of raging wind that can flatten houses in seconds and send cars flying into the air.
The USA is plagued by more tornadoes than anywhere else. As this map shows, most hit the central and eastern states – an area known as Tornado Alley. This is where warm, moist air from the Gulf of Mexico mixes with cold, dry air from Canada and hot, dry air from the southwest. The collision of these three weather systems over flat land with nothing to block the wind creates the perfect conditions for tornado storm clouds.

Tornado Alley

TRACKING TORNADOES IN THE USA

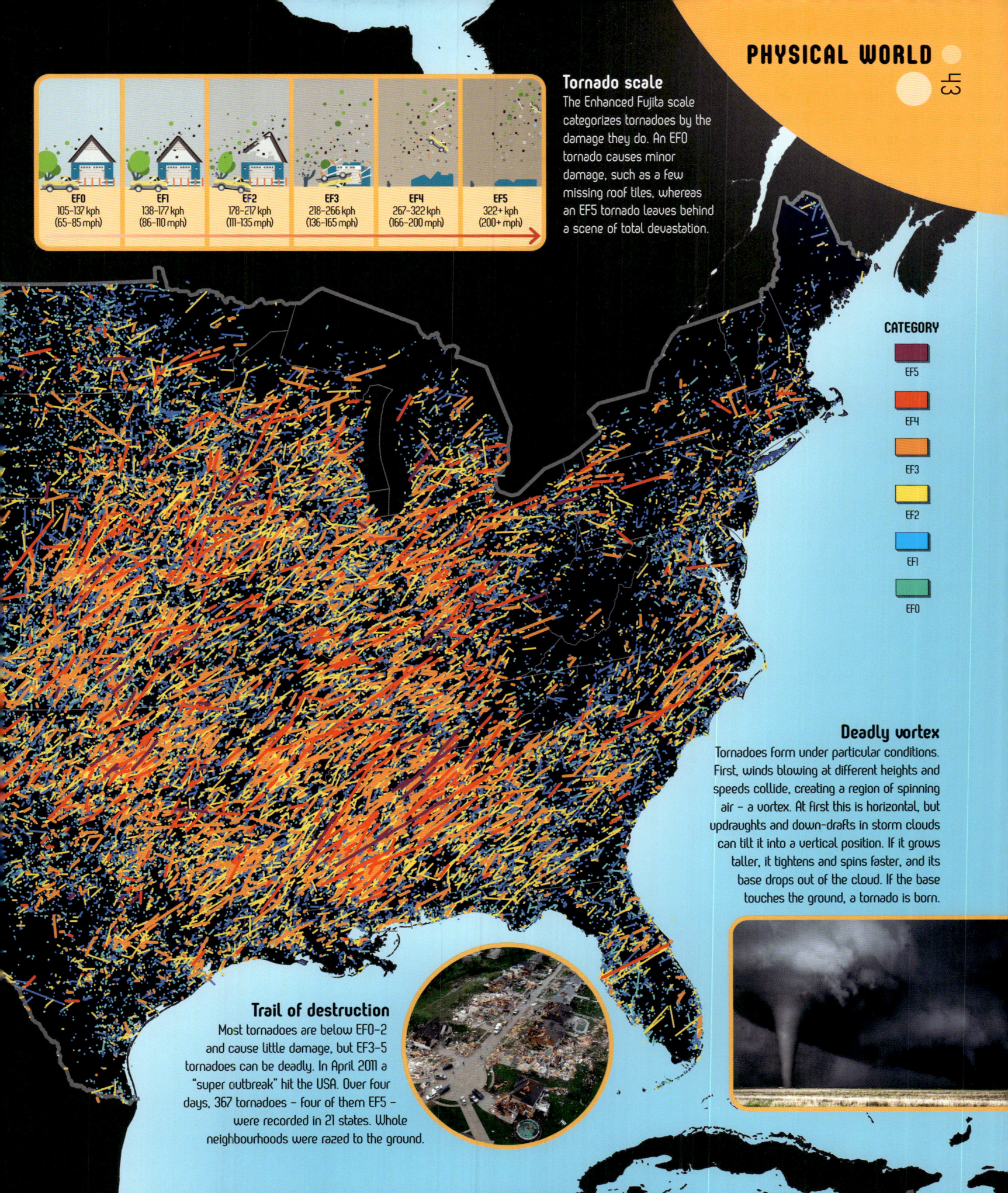

PHYSICAL WORLD

Tornado scale

The Enhanced Fujita scale categorizes tornadoes by the damage they do. An EF0 tornado causes minor damage, such as a few missing roof tiles, whereas an EF5 tornado leaves behind a scene of total devastation.

- EF0 105–137 kph (65–85 mph)
- EF1 138–177 kph (86–110 mph)
- EF2 178–217 kph (111–135 mph)
- EF3 218–266 kph (136–165 mph)
- EF4 267–322 kph (166–200 mph)
- EF5 322+ kph (200+ mph)

CATEGORY
- EF5
- EF4
- EF3
- EF2
- EF1
- EF0

Deadly vortex

Tornadoes form under particular conditions. First, winds blowing at different heights and speeds collide, creating a region of spinning air – a vortex. At first this is horizontal, but updraughts and down-drafts in storm clouds can tilt it into a vertical position. If it grows taller, it tightens and spins faster, and its base drops out of the cloud. If the base touches the ground, a tornado is born.

Trail of destruction

Most tornadoes are below EF0–2 and cause little damage, but EF3–5 tornadoes can be deadly. In April 2011 a "super outbreak" hit the USA. Over four days, 367 tornadoes – four of them EF5 – were recorded in 21 states. Whole neighbourhoods were razed to the ground.

75%
of the world's volcanoes are in the Ring of Fire.

Smoking mountain
Popocatépetl ("Smoking Mountain") in Mexico is one of the world's most dangerous volcanoes because so many people live around it. The volcano reawoke in 1994 after a 70-year sleep and hasn't stopped erupting since.

90%
of earthquakes happen in the Ring of Fire.

Shaken up
The tectonic plates that make up Earth's crust move slowly – about as fast as your fingernails grow. Where two plates collide they snag and cause a build-up of pressure. When they finally shift, the built-up pressure is released in a powerful burst of energy that can shake roads and buildings to pieces.

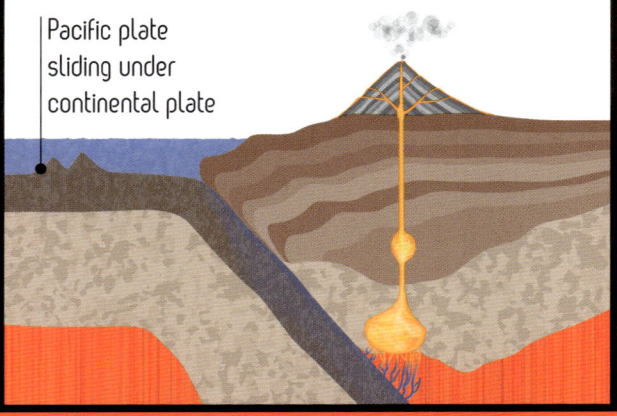

Pacific plate sliding under continental plate

How volcanoes form
Most volcanoes occur at "convergent boundaries", which is where two tectonic plates push together. The denser plate – almost always a sea floor – sinks under its neighbour. Water in the oceanic plate lowers the melting point of rock, causing magma (molten rock) to build up. The magma wells up to the surface and erupts to form a volcano.

PHYSICAL WORLD

Collision zone
This map shows all major earthquakes since 1923 (gold dots) and all the volcanoes that have erupted in the last 12,000 years (red dots). The Ring of Fire marks the collision zone between the tectonic plates that form the Pacific sea floor and the continental plates around it.

Ring of fire

Our planet may feel solid underfoot, but deep below the surface it's in motion. Every so often we are reminded of this inner turmoil by an earthquake or volcanic eruption.

There are about 1,900 active volcanoes on Earth, and most of them are found in a loop around the Pacific Ocean – the Ring of Fire. This is also where most earthquakes strike.

MAPPING VOLCANOES AND EARTHQUAKES

Mount Taranaki

Cartographers don't just map the world – they sometimes change it too. In 1881 a New Zealand cartographer created the perimeter for a new national park by placing a compass pin in a map and drawing a circle around the volcano Mount Taranaki. Today his handiwork is visible from space as an almost perfectly circular forest, interrupted only by later extension of the park to include the neighbouring Pouakai volcano.

Where is everyone?

MAPPING POPULATION

Our world is home to more than 8 billion people, but they aren't spread out evenly. This map of population density shows nothing but people. There are no borders or coastlines, but you can still see the shapes of continents from the pattern of human settlement. Most people live near coasts or rivers because of the need for water. Densely populated places are obvious, but just as interesting are the empty zones. Australia is revealed only by a few pinpricks – its coastal cities. The wildernesses of northern Canada, Siberia, the Amazon, and the Sahara are mostly empty too.

Canada

New York City

Monaco is the most densely populated country.

Sahara desert

Amazon rainforest

Rio de Janeiro

If people stood shoulder to shoulder, the

entire world population

could fit on the tiny island of Kauai in Hawaii.

7%

of all the people who have ever lived are alive today.

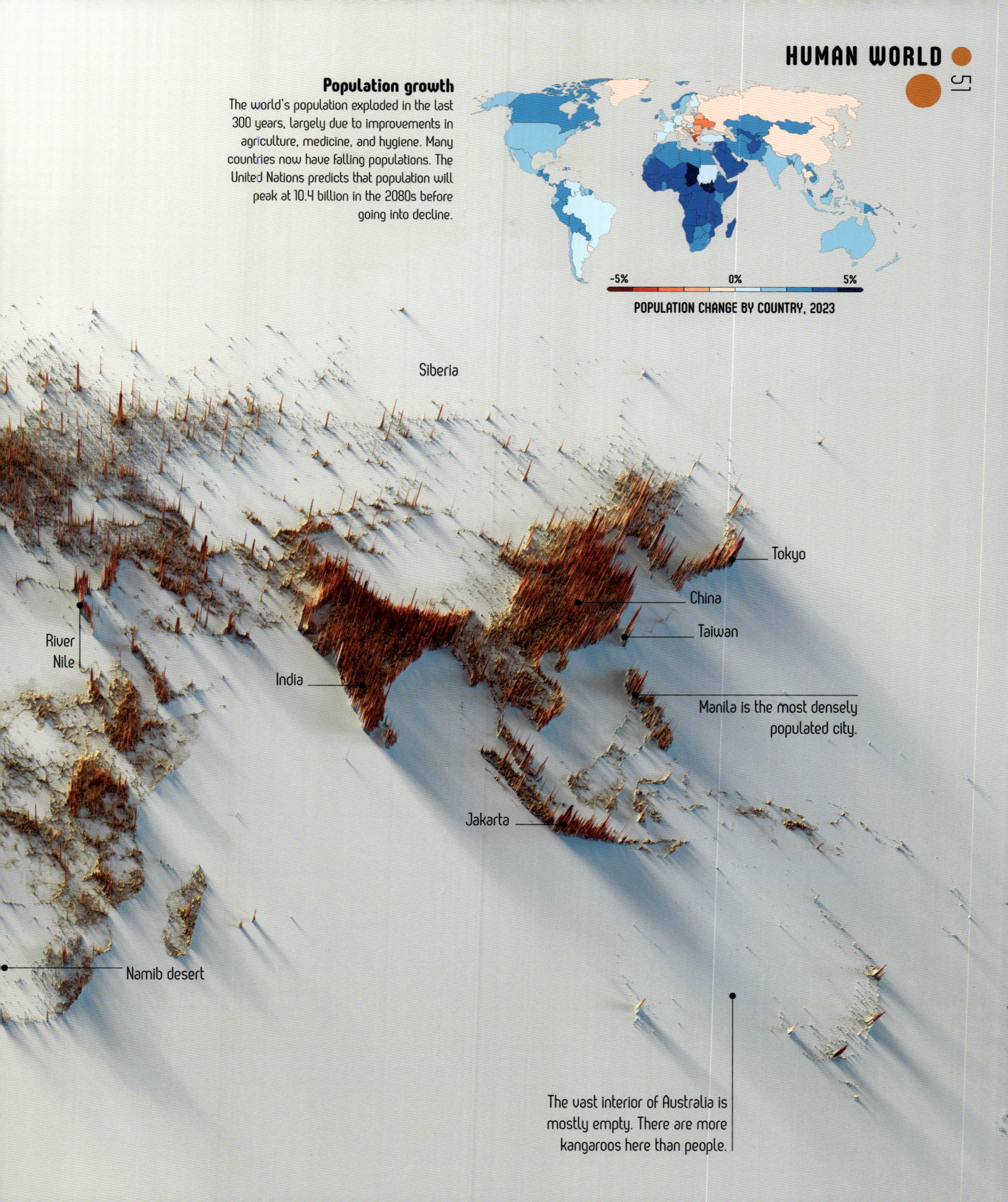

HUMAN WORLD 51

Population growth
The world's population exploded in the last 300 years, largely due to improvements in agriculture, medicine, and hygiene. Many countries now have falling populations. The United Nations predicts that population will peak at 10.4 billion in the 2080s before going into decline.

POPULATION CHANGE BY COUNTRY, 2023
−5%   0%   5%

Siberia

River Nile

India

Tokyo

China

Taiwan

Manila is the most densely populated city.

Jakarta

Namib desert

The vast interior of Australia is mostly empty. There are more kangaroos here than people.

Political maps show the world's countries, but how many countries are there?

It may be a simple question, but there's no simple answer. The United Nations recognizes 193 member states, but other definitions of country include states that aren't universally recognized (like Taiwan), dependent territories or islands governed by distant lands (like Greenland, governed by Denmark), and historical nations such as Scotland (which is part of the UK but has its own flag and parliament). More than 250 national flags exist, and more than 260 countries are listed by the USA's Central Intelligence Agency.

How many countries?

MAPPING POLITICAL BOUNDARIES

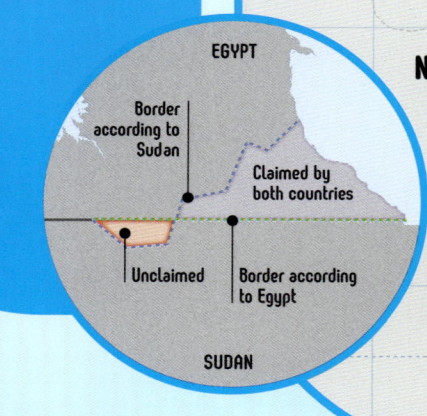

No-man's land
Not every patch of land belongs to a country. Some areas are shared, such as Antarctica. On the other hand, there is a 2,060 sq km (795 sq mile) patch of land in Africa that neighbouring countries refuse to claim as theirs. The cause was a border dispute more than a century ago that was never resolved.

Flying the flag
Although flags have been used as military emblems for millennia, their widespread use as national symbols dates back only to the 18th century. All are rectangular apart from Nepal's. Its double triangle represents the Himalaya Mountains and the nation's two religions. The only flag with people on it is Belize's. It shows two men under a mahogany tree.

HUMAN WORLD

53

Counting islands

How many islands are there on Earth? Nobody has a clue as there are too many small islands, islets, cays, and temporary sandbars to count. The country with the most is probably Sweden (right), which says it has 267,570 islands. Of these, 99 per cent are uninhabited. The world's largest island, Greenland, is 50 times larger than the country that owns it, Denmark.

More than 20 towns in the USA are called **Buffalo.**

There are more than 1,700 places called **San José.**

Southern lands

Australia's name comes from the Latin *australis*, meaning "southern". For centuries, cartographers added a mythical southern continent – Terra Australis – to world maps without having a shred of evidence that it existed. As it turned out, there were two southern continents waiting to be discovered by Europeans. They found Australia first, so it took the old Latin name. Antarctica got a newer name, from the Greek for "opposite the Arctic".

Curious names

Some places have names that might seem peculiar, from the US town that's actually called Peculiar to the village of No Name, whose paradoxical name proves it does have a name. Most curious place names are old words that sound quirky to our ears or that have acquired modern double meanings – like Sandwich in England or Batman in Turkey. Others are deliberate creations intended to amuse or attract attention. The map here includes just a tiny fraction of the world's many wonderful place names.

MAPPING UNUSUAL PLACE NAMES

CHARGOGGAGOGGMANCHAUGGAGOGGCHAUBUNAGUNGAMAUGG
3rd-longest place name (45 letters), USA

Massachusetts locals take pride in being able to pronounce this tongue twister. It means "lake divided by islands" in Algonquian.

Number names
A cluster of towns in the USA have numbers for names. Most are named after their post office district, but Hundred is named after resident Henry "Hundred" Church, who lived to 100 (but died at 109).

No Name
Legend has it that No Name in Colorado, USA, is so called because residents of the village wrote "no name" in a survey and their answer was officially logged in state records. The village is near to No Name Tunnel and a scenic hiking area called No Name Creek.

The US city **Truth or Consequences** is named after a 1940s game show.

Batman
The city of Batman in Turkey gets its ancient name from the nearby river. It isn't the only town to share a name with a famous superhero or supervillain. Other examples are the US towns of Tarzan in Texas and Frankenstein in Missouri.

HUMAN WORLD

Dull
The residents of Dull in Scotland are not ashamed to flaunt its unexciting name. The small village is proudly twinned with Boring in Oregon, USA, and Bland in New South Wales, Australia. The three call themselves the Trinity of Tedium.

Shortest names
The accolade of world's shortest name goes to no less than 30 places that have single-letter names. Thirteen of them are villages in Norway and Sweden. These get their name from the old Norse word Å (pronounced "or"), meaning river.

Finland's longest place name is thought to mean "the marsh where the hut belonging to Paul, son of Peter, son of Andrew, stands".

ÄTERITSIPUTERITSIPUOLILAUTATSIJÄNKÄ
5th-longest place name (35 letters), Finland

LLANFAIRPWLLGWYNGYLLGOGERYCHWYRNDROBWLLLLANTYSILIOGOGOGOCH
Second-longest place name (58 letters), Wales

Publicity stunt
To encourage tourists to stop at the train station, the residents of a Welsh village extended its name to 58 letters in 1869. It worked so well that Llanfairpwllgwyngyllgogerychwyrndrobwllllantysiliogogogoch still gets 200,000 visitors a year today. Translated from Welsh, the name means "St Mary's Church in the hollow of white hazel near the rapid whirlpool and the church of St Tysilio near the red cave".

TWEEBUFFELSMETEENSKOOTMORSDOODGESKIETFONTEIN
4th-longest place name (44 letters), South Africa

This farm in South Africa has the continent's longest place name. The name in Afrikaans means "the spring where two buffaloes were shot stone-dead with one shot".

World's longest name
The 85-letter name of this hill in New Zealand honours a local Maori chieftain: "the summit where Tamatea, the man with the big knees, the climber of mountains, the land-swallower who travelled about, played his nose flute to his loved one." Two alternative versions are even longer.

TAUMATAWHAKATANGIHANGAKOAUAUOTAMATEATURIPUKAKAPIKIMAUNGAHORONUKUPOKAIWHENUAKITANATAHU
World's longest place name (85 letters), New Zealand

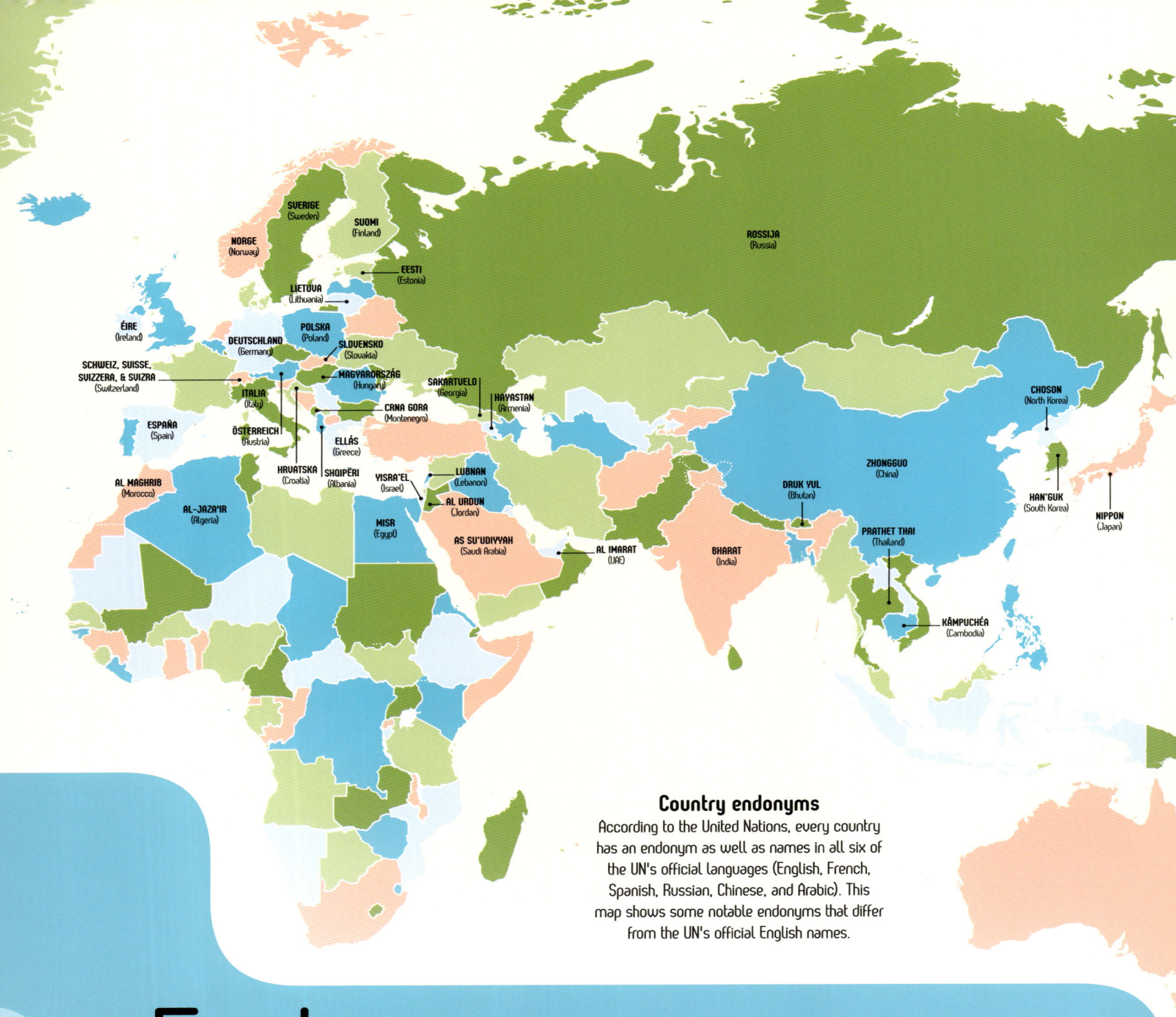

Endonyms of the world

Country endonyms
According to the United Nations, every country has an endonym as well as names in all six of the UN's official languages (English, French, Spanish, Russian, Chinese, and Arabic). This map shows some notable endonyms that differ from the UN's official English names.

You may be surprised to learn that the names you've been using for foreign countries are not their real names.
Every country has an "endonym" (the name it calls itself) and at least one "exonym" (a name used by foreigners). Often they're the same, but sometimes they are wildly different. Japan's real name, for example, is Nippon, and India is really called Bharat.

THE REAL NAMES OF COUNTRIES

HUMAN WORLD

KALAALLIT NUNAAT (Greenland)

Greece's
real name is Ellás.

Mount what?
It isn't just countries that have endonyms – landmarks like mountains and rivers have them too. Mount Everest got its famous exonym from Sir George Everest, a British geographer. But the people of Nepal (to its south) call it Sagarmatha, and the people of Tibet (to its north) call it Chomolungma.

Most of the countries in the Americas and Africa are colonial creations and so have no endonyms.

Exonyms
Top prize for the most exonyms goes to the country of Germany. Only one of its neighbours (Austria) uses its correct name. Germany has many exonyms because it sits at the crossroads of several different language zones. Further afield, it is also known as Doitsu in Japan and Deguo in China.

Who's across the ocean?

If you travelled due east or due west, what country would you reach after crossing the ocean? Countries that line up horizontally around the globe have the same latitude – a measure of how far north or south of the equator you are. Surprisingly, places with similar latitudes may not share similar climates. Tropical Miami with its hot, wet summers lines up with the bone-dry Sahara desert, while London, with its mild winters, shares a similar latitude to Calgary in Canada, which shivers below 0°C (32°F) for half the year.

FIND YOUR LATITUDE TWINS

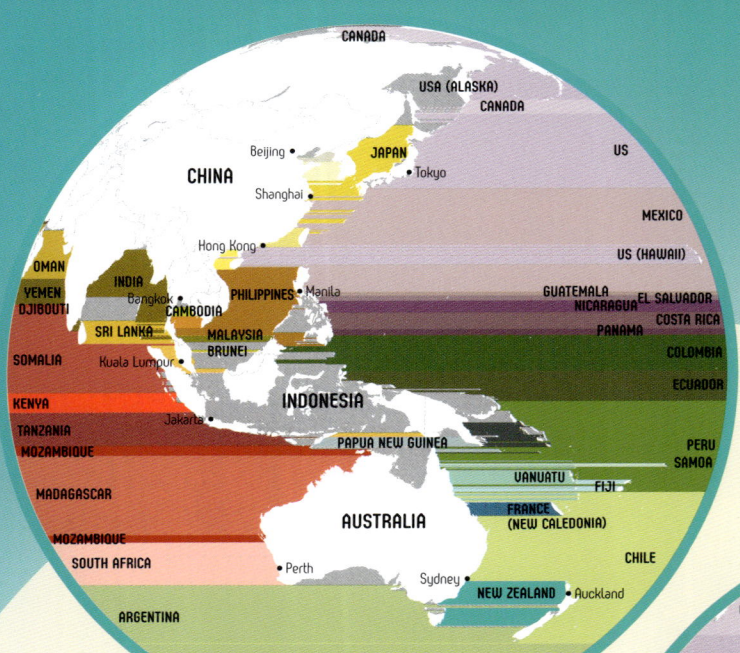

Between **Chile** and **Antarctica**, you could

sail west forever

without striking land.

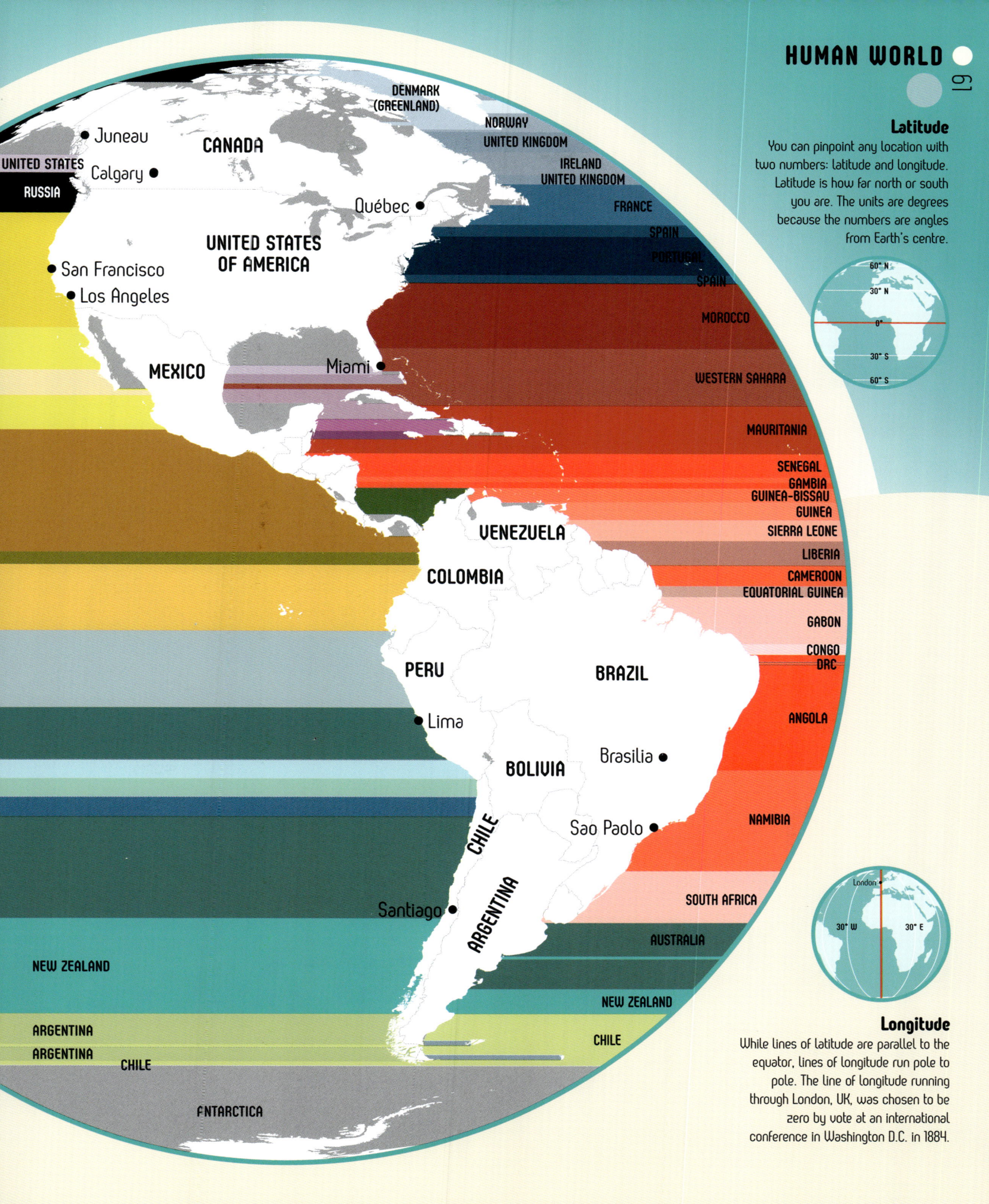

Foz,
Spain
Christchurch,
New Zealand

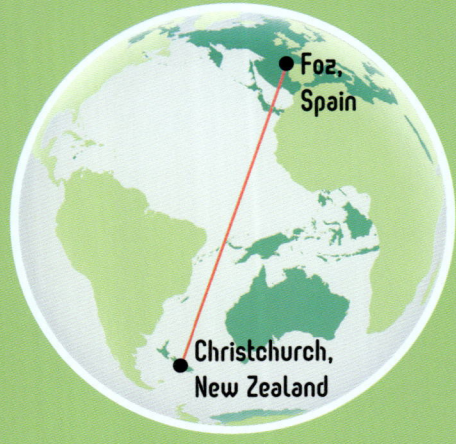

Point to point

The red line shows that the antipode of Christchurch in New Zealand is the town of Foz in Spain. Europeans sometimes use the nickname "antipodeans" for people from New Zealand and Australia because they come from the opposite hemisphere.

Imagine you dug a perfectly straight tunnel all the way through Earth's middle. The point you pop out is your antipode – the opposite side of the planet from where you are now. Your antipode is 12,750 km (7,920 miles) away, which is as far away as you can possibly get without going into outer space. This map shows the antipode of everywhere on Earth. What's on the other side of the planet from you?

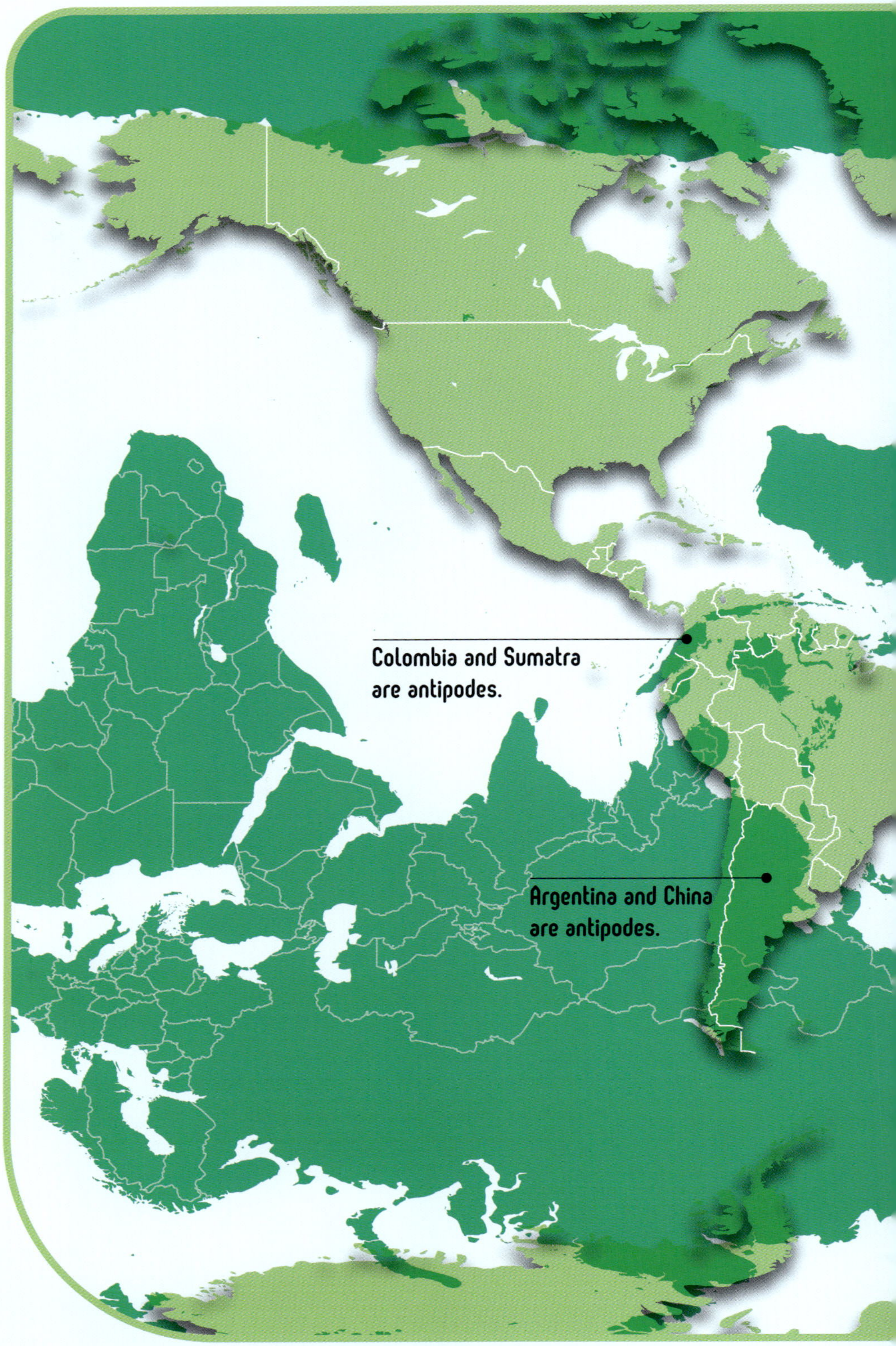
Colombia and Sumatra
are antipodes.
Argentina and China
are antipodes.

Who's on the opposite side?

A MAP OF ANTIPODES

Find your antipode

The map above is an ordinary world map (pale green) combined with an antipodal map (dark green). The antipodal map is a mirror image rotated 180 degrees so every point in the world lines up with its antipode. To find your antipode, locate your home in the pale green area. If there's an overlapping dark green area, your antipode is on land. If not, it's in the sea – as it is for most of Europe and North America.

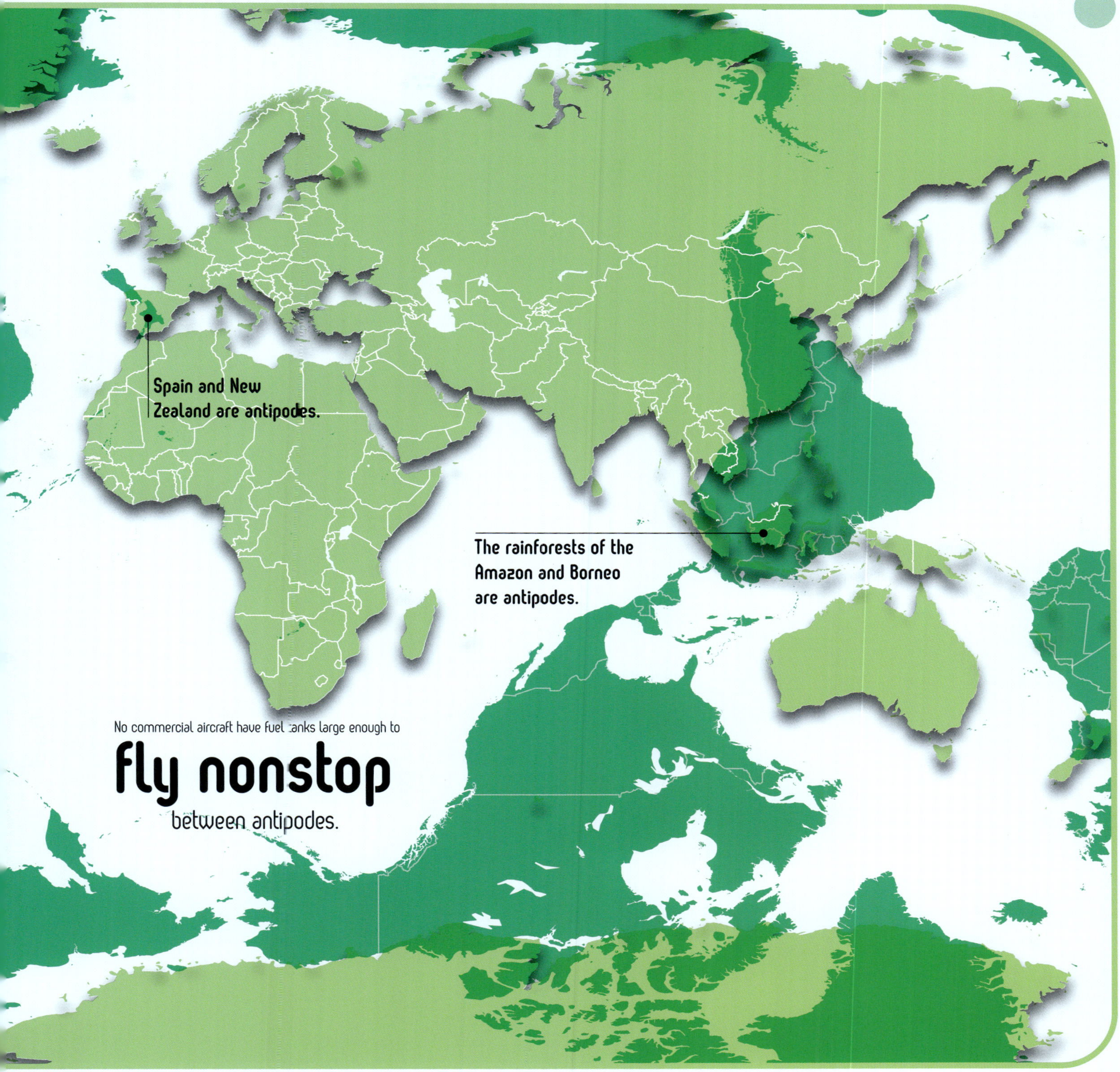

HUMAN WORLD

63

Spain and New Zealand are antipodes.

The rainforests of the Amazon and Borneo are antipodes.

No commercial aircraft have fuel tanks large enough to **fly nonstop** between antipodes.

When it's **noon** where you are, it's **midnight** at your antipode

Antipodes Islands
This cluster of remote volcanic islands in the South Pacific is called the Antipodes. They are so named because the British sailors who discovered them in 1800 were close to London's antipode, even though the Antipodes' antipode is actually in France. Their Maori name, *Moutere Mahue*, means deserted. Apart from shipwrecked sailors, nobody has ever lived here.

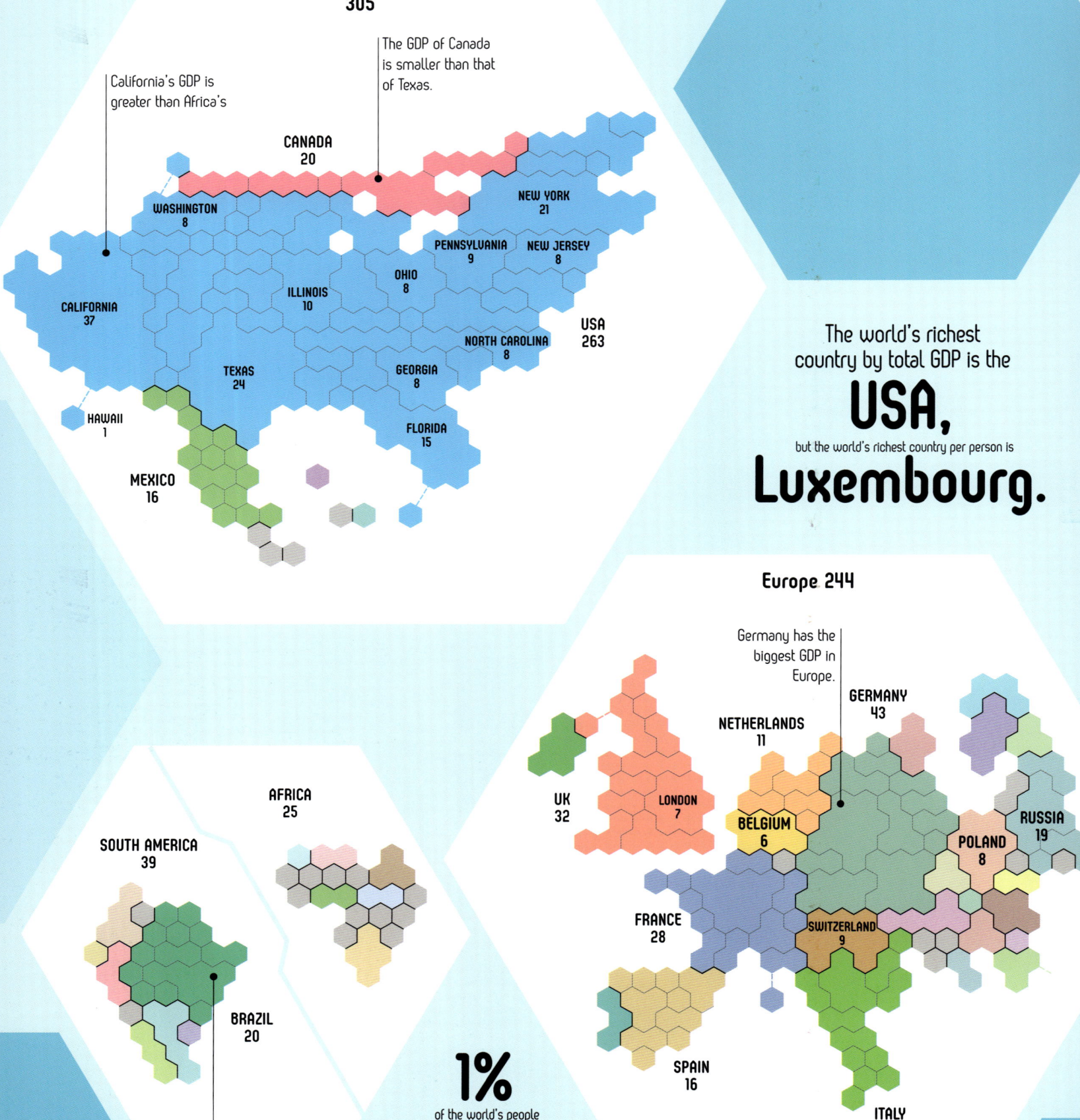

Where's the money?

MAPPING THE WORLD'S WEALTH

There's a lot of money in the world, but it isn't spread evenly around the planet or between its people.

One way of keeping track of global wealth is by looking at gross domestic product (GDP). GDP is a measure of how much is bought and sold over a particular period of time. This map divides the world's total GDP into 1,000 units and shows how these were shared out in 2024.

HUMAN WORLD

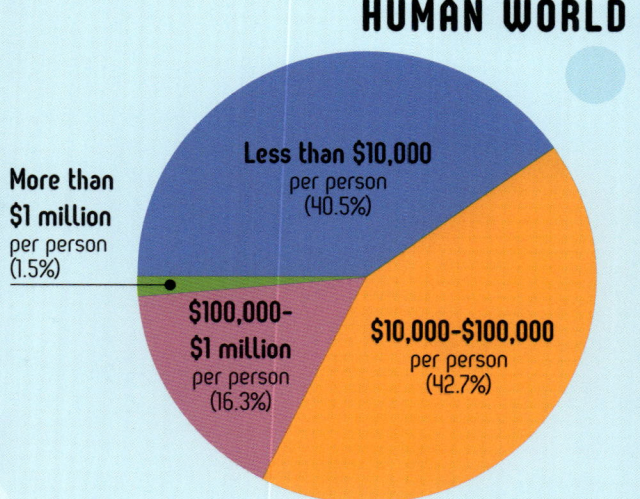

- Less than $10,000 per person (40.5%)
- $10,000–$100,000 per person (42.7%)
- $100,000–$1 million per person (16.3%)
- More than $1 million per person (1.5%)

Wealth inequality
In 2023, only 1.5% of the world's people had money and assets worth more than $1 million dollars. Between them, these millionaires held 47.5% of the world's total wealth.

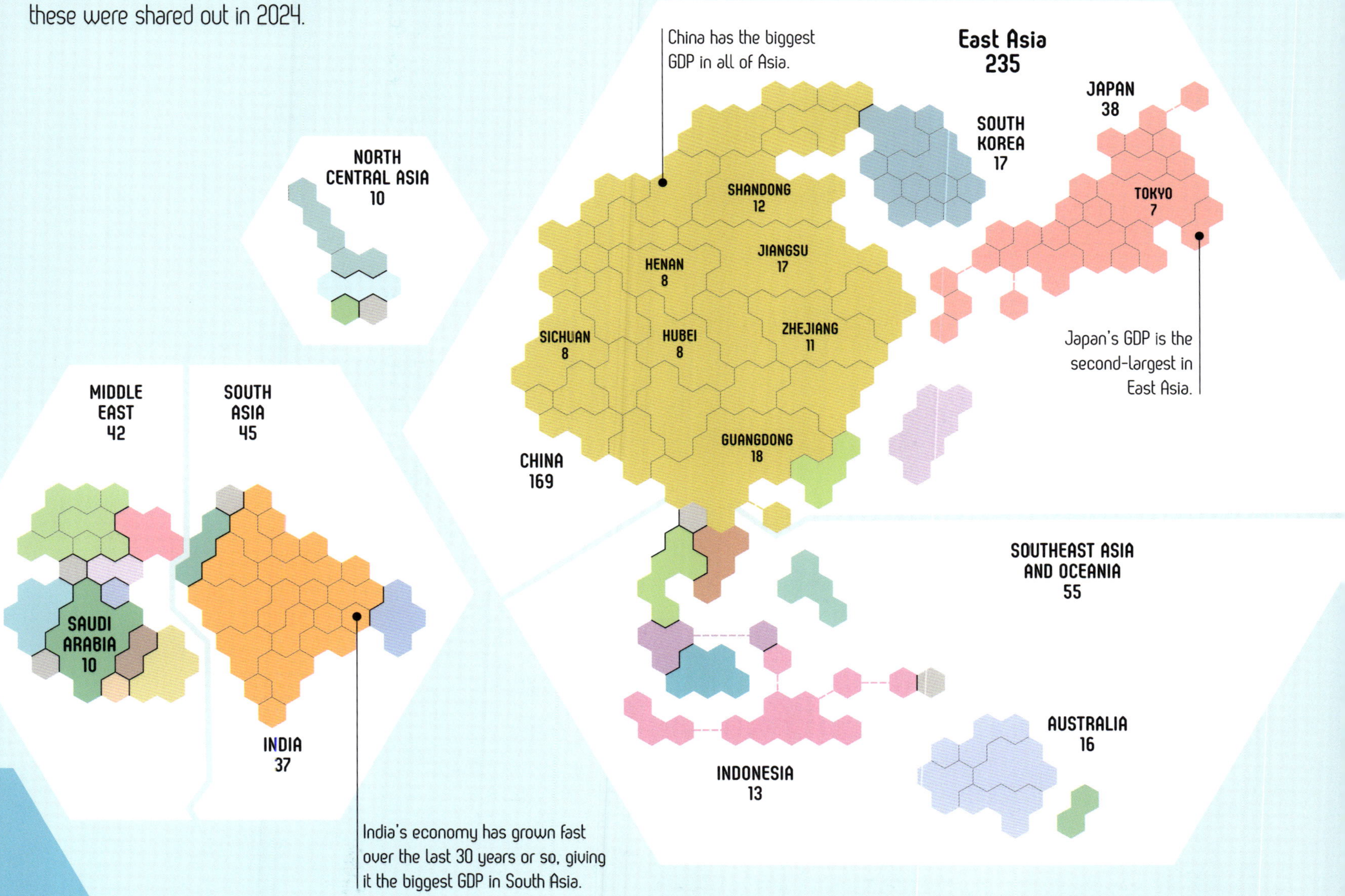

East Asia 235

China has the biggest GDP in all of Asia.

- NORTH CENTRAL ASIA 10
- MIDDLE EAST 42
  - SAUDI ARABIA 10
- SOUTH ASIA 45
  - INDIA 37
- CHINA 169
  - SHANDONG 12
  - JIANGSU 17
  - HENAN 8
  - SICHUAN 8
  - HUBEI 8
  - ZHEJIANG 11
  - GUANGDONG 18
- SOUTH KOREA 17
- JAPAN 38
  - TOKYO 7
- SOUTHEAST ASIA AND OCEANIA 55
  - INDONESIA 13
  - AUSTRALIA 16

Japan's GDP is the second-largest in East Asia.

India's economy has grown fast over the last 30 years or so, giving it the biggest GDP in South Asia.

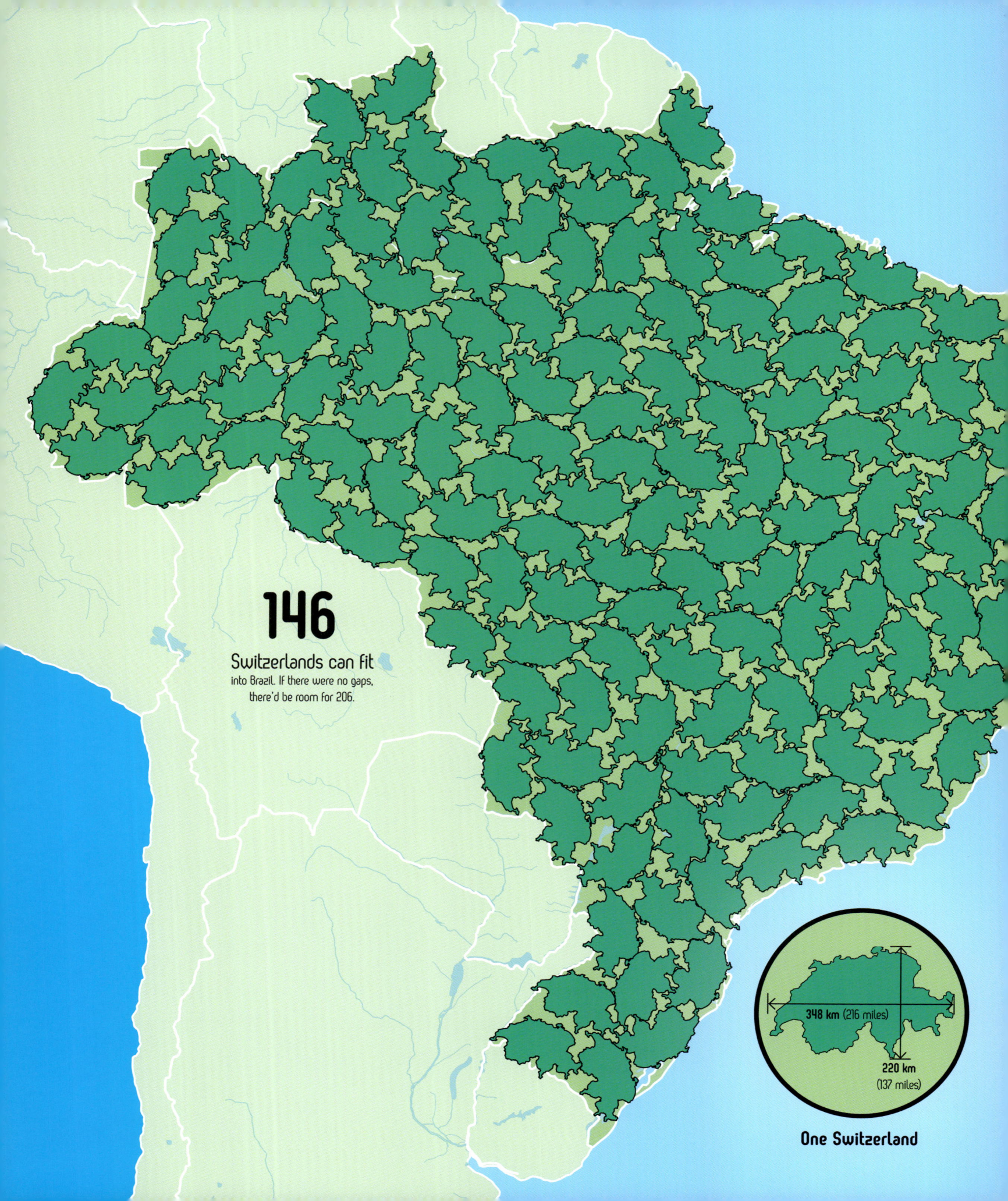

HUMAN WORLD

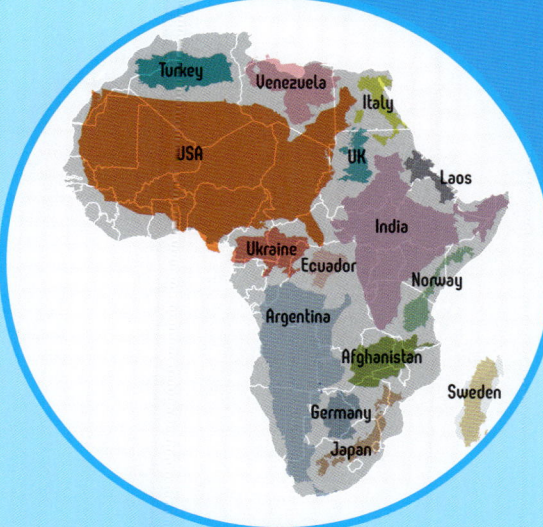

How big is Africa?
With a fifth of all the world's land, Africa could comfortably swallow three USAs, nine Indias, or 125 UKs. Africa's Sahara Desert alone is bigger than the continental USA.

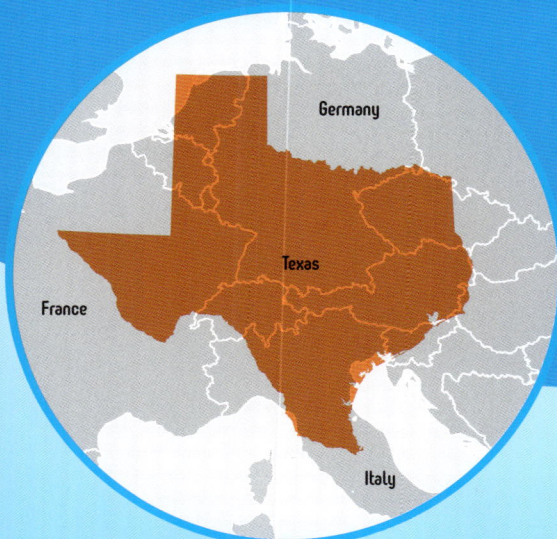

How big is Texas?
The US state of Texas is bigger than every country in western Europe and bigger than most countries in the world. It's about twice the size of Germany and five times bigger than England.

How many Switzerlands fit in Brazil?

COMPARING COUNTRY SIZES

How big is your country compared to others? You might be surprised to find out.

Traditional world maps show our round world as a rectangle, but this expands countries near the poles and shrinks countries near the equator. In reality, the countries of northern Europe are dwarfed by tropical giants like Brazil and Australia. Italy would fit into Peru more than 4 times, and the UK would fit into Argentina 11 times. The island nations of Japan and Indonesia look similar in size on maps, but Japan fits five times into the area taken by Indonesia's 17,000 islands.

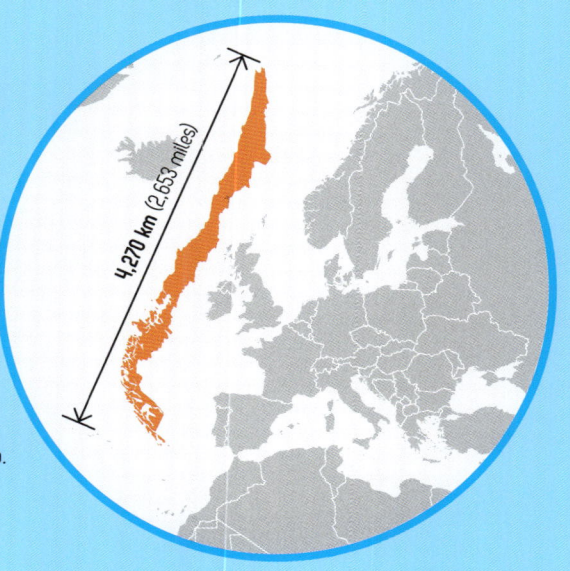

How long is Chile?
The world's longest country is Chile, which measures 4,270 km (2,653 miles) from end to end. That's more than enough to span the whole of Europe from north to south or to span the widest point in Australia.

Brazil could swallow the nation of Singapore
11,844 times.

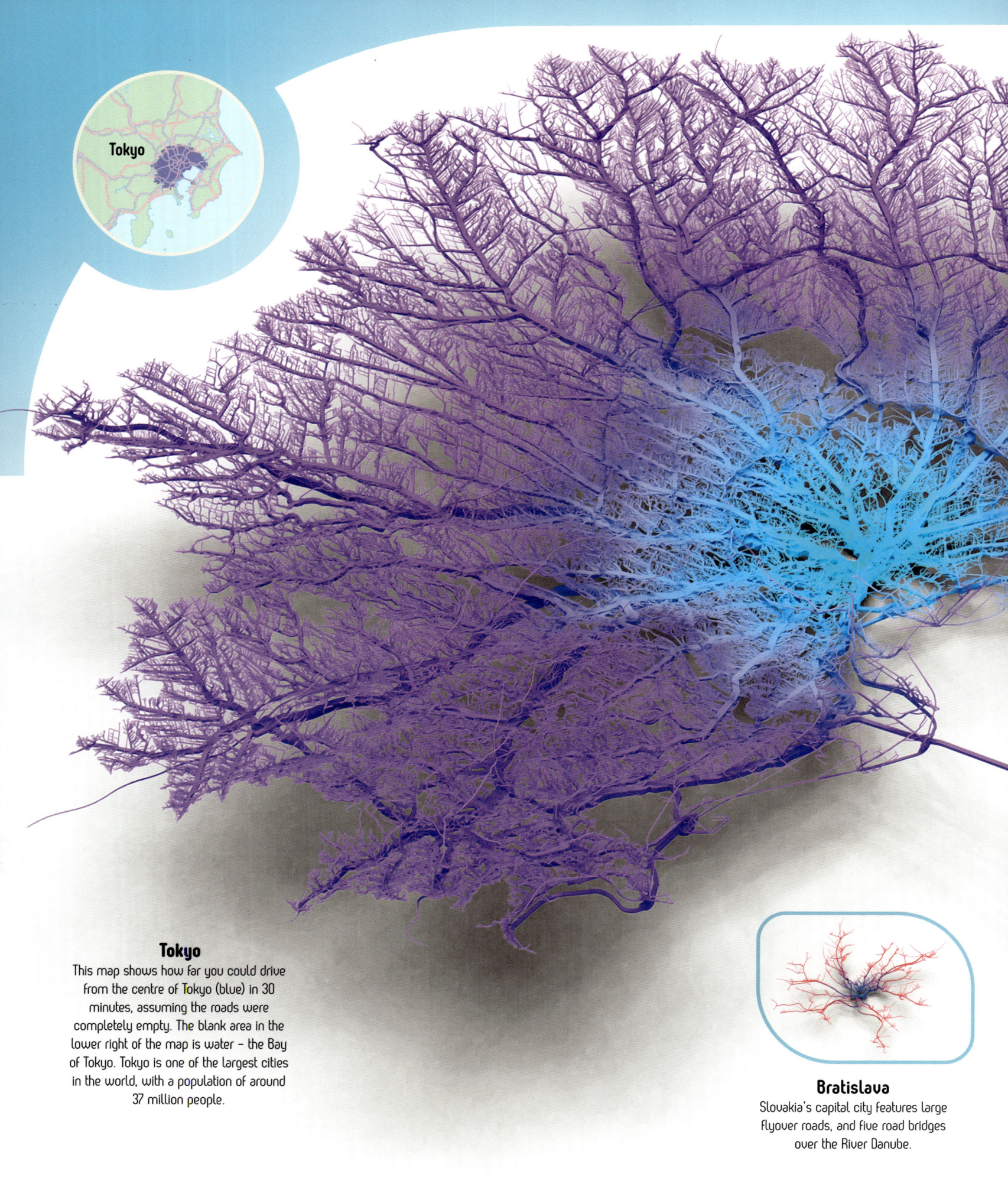

Tokyo
This map shows how far you could drive from the centre of Tokyo (blue) in 30 minutes, assuming the roads were completely empty. The blank area in the lower right of the map is water – the Bay of Tokyo. Tokyo is one of the largest cities in the world, with a population of around 37 million people.

Bratislava
Slovakia's capital city features large flyover roads, and five road bridges over the River Danube.

HUMAN WORLD

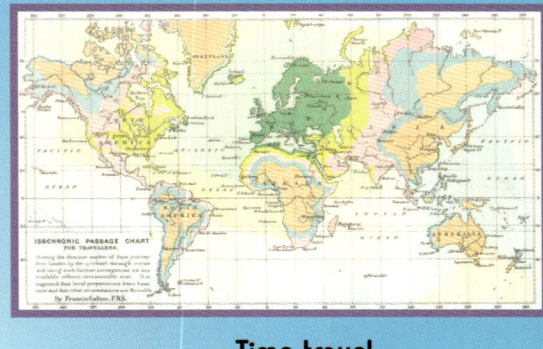

Time travel
This 1881 map by English scholar Francis Galton used colours to show how long it took to travel the world from London. Green shows journeys that took up to 10 days, yellow 10–20 days, pink 20–30 days, blue 30–40 days, and brown more than 40 days. Travel was a lot slower and more complicated in the 19th century.

Coral cities

Part bridge and part tunnel, the Tokyo Bay Aqua-Line includes the world's fourth-longest underwater tunnel.

This computer-generated artwork shows Tokyo's vast network of roads and highways. The branches spread outwards from the heart of the city, forming a shape similar to a coral. Maps like this tell a story of how road networks evolve. They help us see how vehicles, people, and freight flow through cities, much like blood flows through vessels in our bodies. The biggest roads, which carry heavy traffic, are known as arteries. In all these examples the city centres are shown in a contrasting colour.

MAPPING ROAD NETWORKS

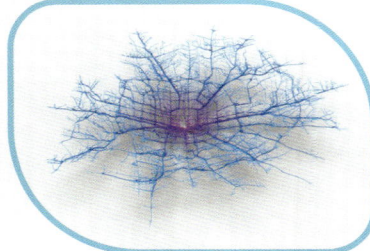

Beijing
Five ring roads circle Beijing, with expressways between the city centre and the suburbs.

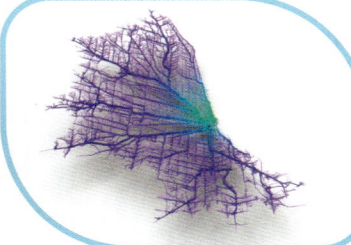

Chicago
A strict grid of roads run from north to south and east to west along the shores of Lake Michigan.

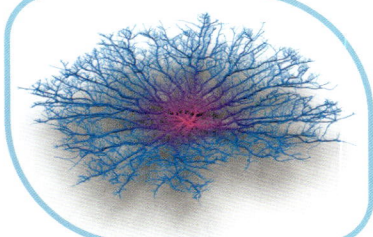

London
This incredibly dense network of roads has evolved over 2,000 years. The city is heavily congested.

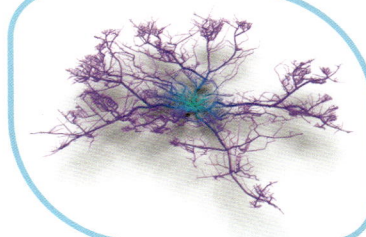

Amsterdam
The arteries branch where they flow into neighbouring settlements, such as Haarlem and Hoofddorp.

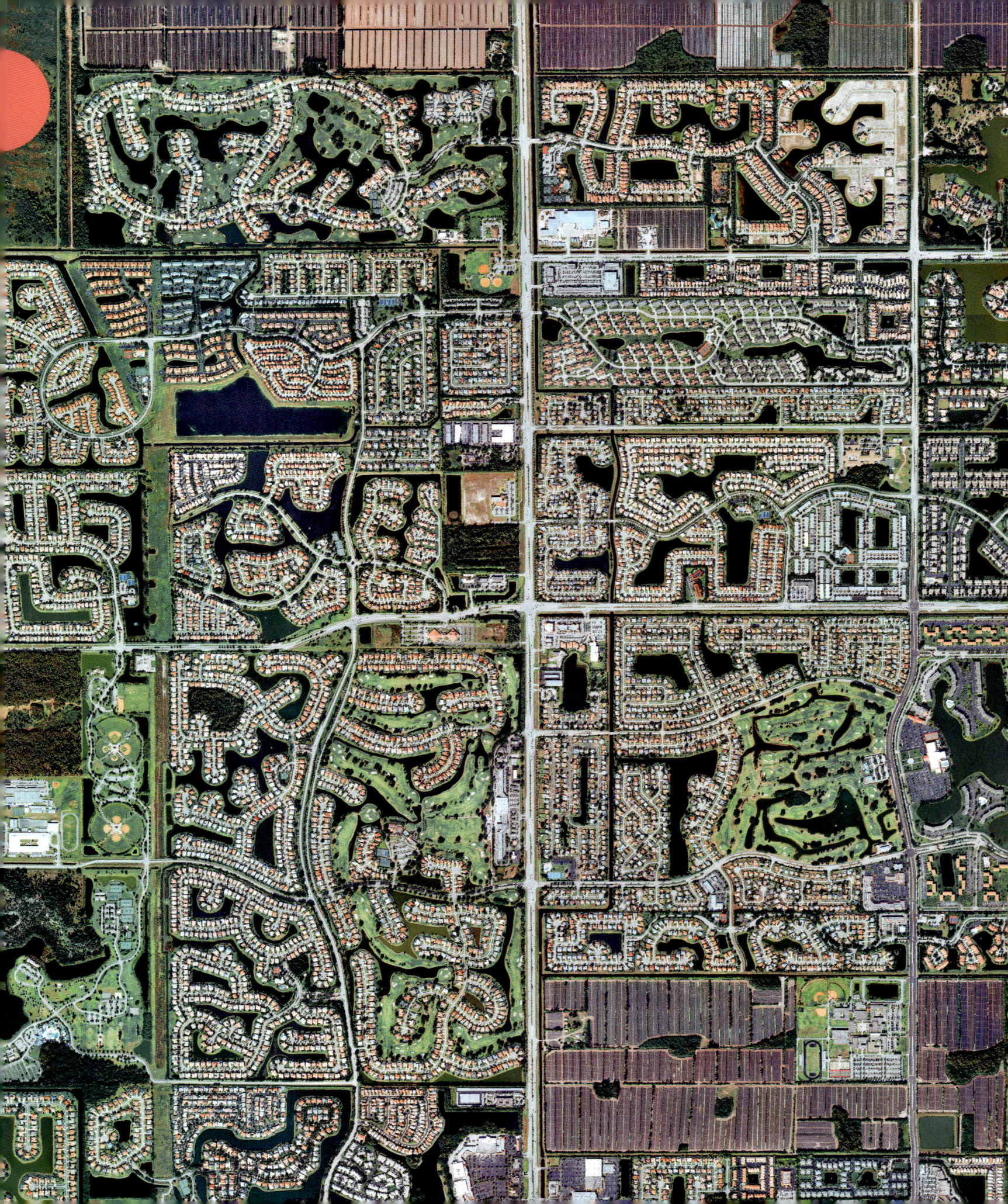

Cities by design

Some cities grow organically over centuries, but others are mapped in advance by designers and built in a matter of years. In 1903, Boca Raton in Florida, USA, was little more than swampland and pineapple farms with a population of 18. Today, more than 100,000 people live among its manicured parks and golf courses. Artificial waterways helped drain the land for development as well as giving waterfront views to the most desirable houses.

The world's shortest scheduled flight lasts

2 minutes

and runs between two islands in Scotland.

When all the world's commercial flights are mapped, a ghostly image of the continents emerges. The world's mega flight hubs in Europe, China, and North America shine most brightly. More than 4.5 billion passengers take to the skies every year. In 2023, a staggering 35.3 million commercial flights took off from more than 9,000 airports around the world. The aircraft flew 67,300 different routes, clocking up billions of kilometres in the sky. Commercial aviation is big business. If it were a country, it would be the world's 20th-richest.

Sky highways

FLIGHT ROUTES AROUND THE WORLD

Frequent fliers

In 2024, the busiest routes by number of passengers were all internal flights (flights within one country). The route from Jeju to Seoul in South Korea is the world's busiest, carrying around 38,000 people every day.

JEJU	14.1 MILLION A YEAR ✈	SEOUL
SAPPORO	11.9 MILLION ✈	TOKYO
FUKUOKA	11.3 MILLION ✈	TOKYO
HANOI	10.6 MILLION ✈	HO CHI MINH CITY
MELBOURNE	9.2 MILLION ✈	SYDNEY

HUMAN WORLD

RANK	CITY	COUNTRY	TAKE-OFFS AND LANDINGS
1.	Atlanta (ATL)	USA	755,818
2.	Chicago (ORD)	USA	720,582
3.	Dallas/Forth Worth (DFW)	USA	689,569
4.	Denver (DEN)	USA	657,569
5.	Las Vegas (LAS)	USA	611,806
6.	Los Angeles (LAX)	USA	575,097
7.	Charlotte (CLT)	USA	539,066
8.	Istanbul (IST)	Turkey	505,968
9.	New York (JFK)	USA	481,075
10.	Tokyo (HND)	Japan	464,910

Busiest airports

The world's busiest airport in 2023 was Atlanta in the USA, which had more than 2,000 arrivals and departures every day. The USA has more flights than any other country and is home to eight of the world's top ten busiest airports.

No-fly zones

Planes don't always take the most direct route. No-fly zones exist over areas of conflict to keep flights safe. Commercial planes also give the Himalayas and Tibetan Plateau a swerve. These areas have extremely high terrain, which stops airliners flying at the lower altitudes they need if they have engine or cabin pressure problems.

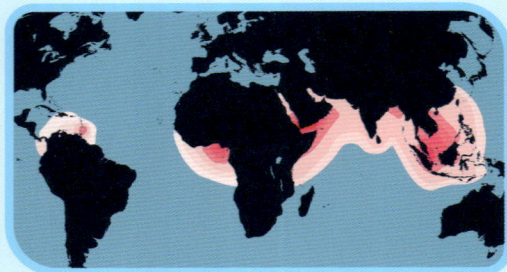

Pirate attacks

Pirates hijack merchant ships and either steal the cargo or hold the crew to ransom. About 13,000 attacks occurred between 1994 and 2024 (above). Almost half took place in East Asia and the Pacific Ocean. The Red Sea, the Horn of Africa, and the Caribbean are also piracy hotspots.

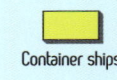 Container ships

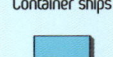 Bulker ships carrying raw materials

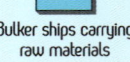 Tankers carrying liquids

 Gas bulk carrying gas

 Vehicle carriers

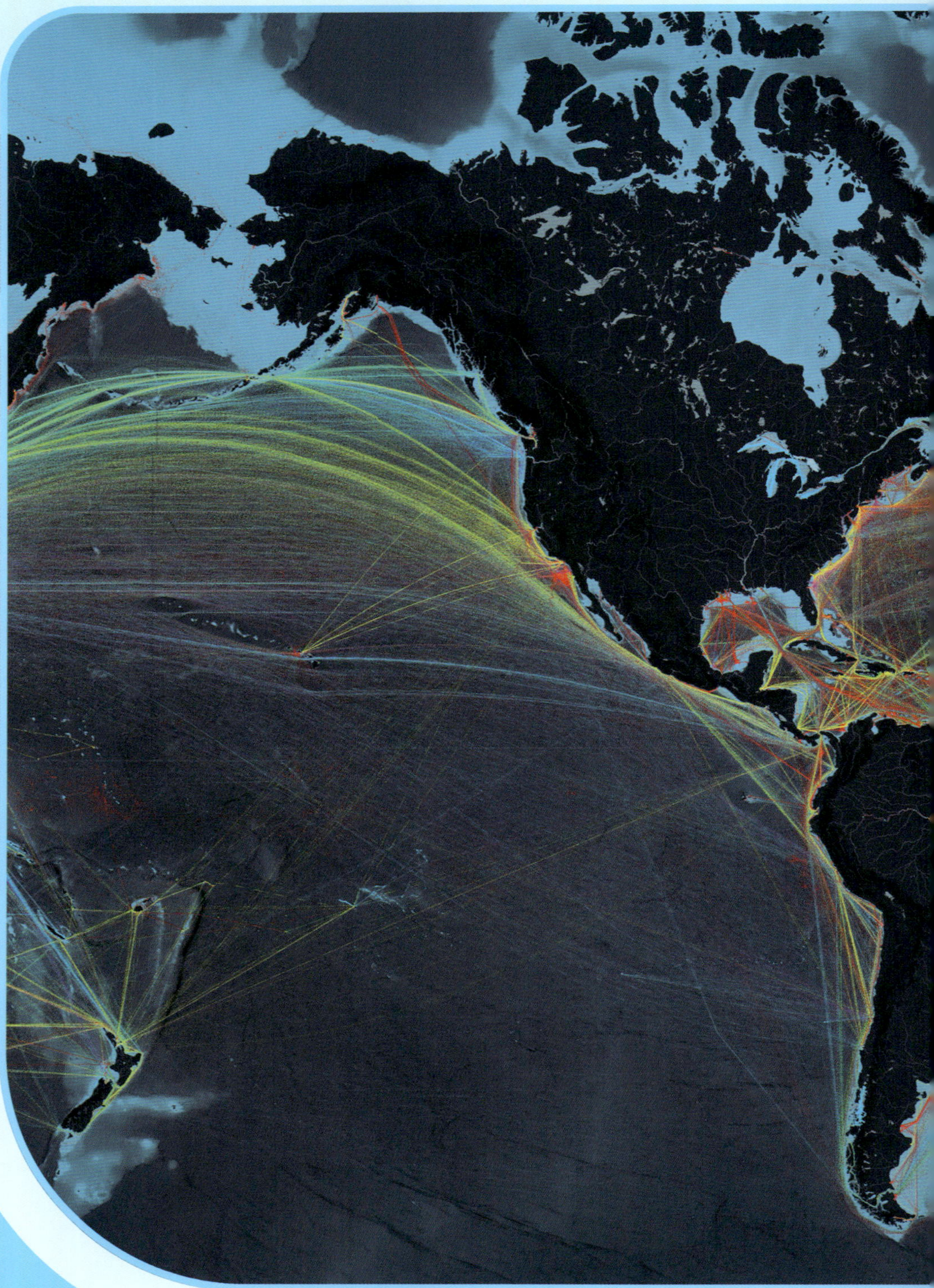

As you read this sentence, around 50,000 merchant ships are crisscrossing the world's oceans. These ships keep the world economy ticking over. They carry everything from cars and petrol to rubber ducks and bananas.

This map shows the shipping routes of all merchant vessels tracked by satellite on one day in 2012. It doesn't account for the thousands of other vessels, such as ferries, fishing boats, and superyachts. The tracked merchant ships include tankers and container vessels, which hold goods in huge steel shipping containers.

Ocean highways

MAPPING THE WORLD'S SHIPPING ROUTES

HUMAN WORLD

75

Piled high
Most manufactured goods are carried around the world in large metal boxes called containers. Lorries drive the containers to and from ports, but they cross the oceans aboard container ships. Each ship carries up to 15,000 containers, and there can be up to 20 million containers on the move around the world at any moment.

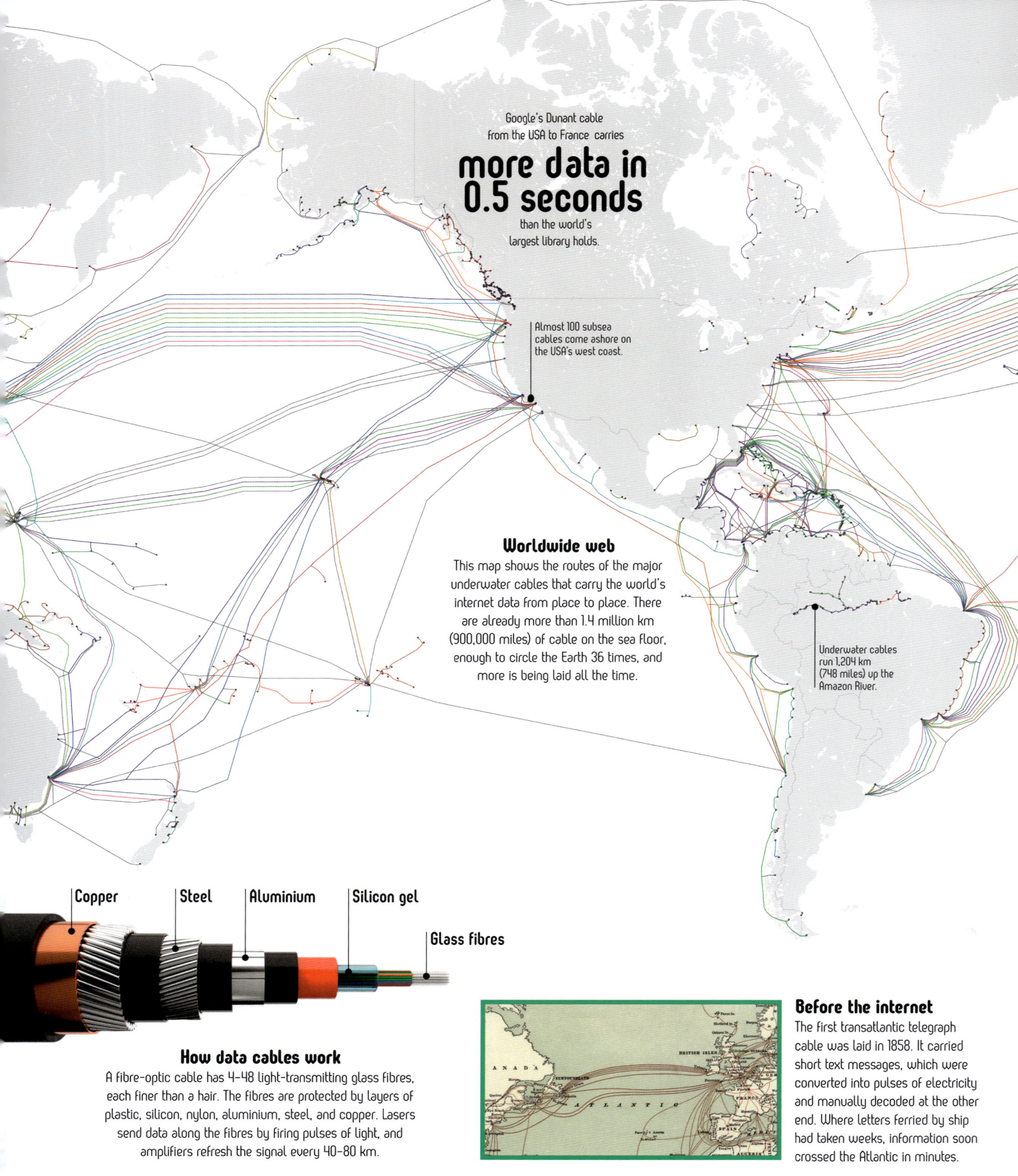

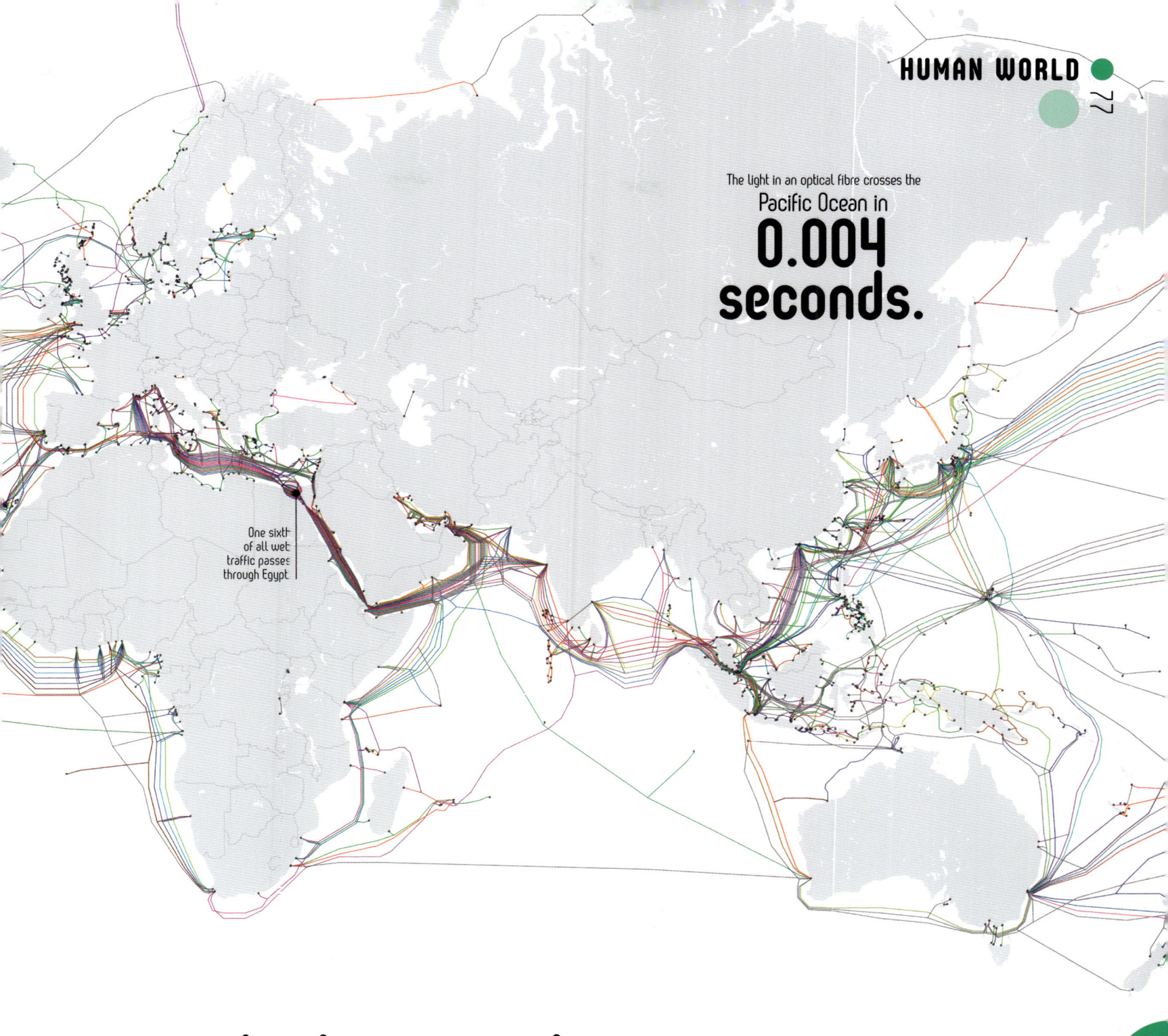

HUMAN WORLD

The light in an optical fibre crosses the Pacific Ocean in **0.004 seconds.**

One sixth of all wet traffic passes through Egypt

Internet highways

Faster and far cheaper than satellites, fibre-optic cables on the ocean floor form the backbone of the internet. Fewer than 600 of these submarine cables, each barely thicker than your thumb, carry around 99 per cent of all international data around the planet at lightning-fast speeds.

CHARTING SUBMARINE DATA CABLES

Round-the-world walk

The first person to make a verified round-the-world trip on foot was Dave Kunst of the USA, who set off from Minnesota in 1970. It took more than four years and he wore out 21 pairs of shoes. Sadly, his brother John, who accompanied him, was killed by bandits so Dave took a four-month break before resuming the trip with another brother.

The fastest round-the-world bike trip was **78.5 days,** completed by the UK's Mark Beaumont in 2017.

PRUDHOE BAY, ALASKA

KARAGINSKY

NEW YORK CITY

Longest boat trip
The furthest you can sail in a straight line is from Karaginsky in eastern Russia to Sonmiani in Pakistan – a distance of 32,090 km (19,940 miles).

The Pan-American Highway has a notorious break called the Darién Gap, where you have to hike through deadly swamps and jungle.

Longest flight
The longest nonstop scheduled flight is 15,332 km (9,527 miles) from New York City to Singapore and takes 18 hours 50 minutes.

While some people seek adventure by scaling mountains or riding waves, others love to travel. For most of us, long journeys are just a way of getting from A to B. For a few daring individuals, however, the challenge of a difficult journey matters more than the destination. To set a record, you need to go further or faster than anyone has gone before. This map shows some of the longest and most challenging journeys you can possibly do – whether by foot, boat, train, plane, or car.

USHUAIA

Longest journeys
RECORD-BREAKING ROUTES

Longest road
The world's longest motorable road is the Pan-American Highway (a network of different roads). It runs 30,600 km (19,000 miles) from northern Alaska to Ushuaia, Argentina.

Longest walk
According to Google Maps, the longest walk on Earth is 22,387 km (13,911 miles) from Cape Town in South Africa to Magadan in Russia. Nobody has done this yet.

HUMAN WORLD

The fastest route from New York to Singapore is over the North Pole.

MOSCOW

TALON — MAGADAN

SAGRES

Google Maps's longest walk includes ferries across the Black Sea and Suez Canal.

SONMIANI

PYONGYANG

SINGAPORE

The longest road in a single country is Australia's Highway 1, which is 14,500 km (9,010 miles) long.

CAPE TOWN

This sailing route looks curved on a rectangular world map but is a straight line on a globe.

Longest drive
The longest drive you can do without using ferries or hiking across gaps starts from Sagres in Portugal and ends at Talon in Russia, a distance of 15,141 km (9,408 miles).

Longest train trip
The furthest train trip without changing trains is 10,214 km (6,346 miles) from Moscow in Russia to Pyongyang in North Korea. Trains run once a week and the trip takes 8 days.

Record road trip
Swiss couple Emil and Liliana Schmid set the world record for the longest journey made in a single car. Their trip in a Toyota Landcruiser took them through 186 countries between 1984 and 2017 and totalled 741,065 km (460,476 miles).

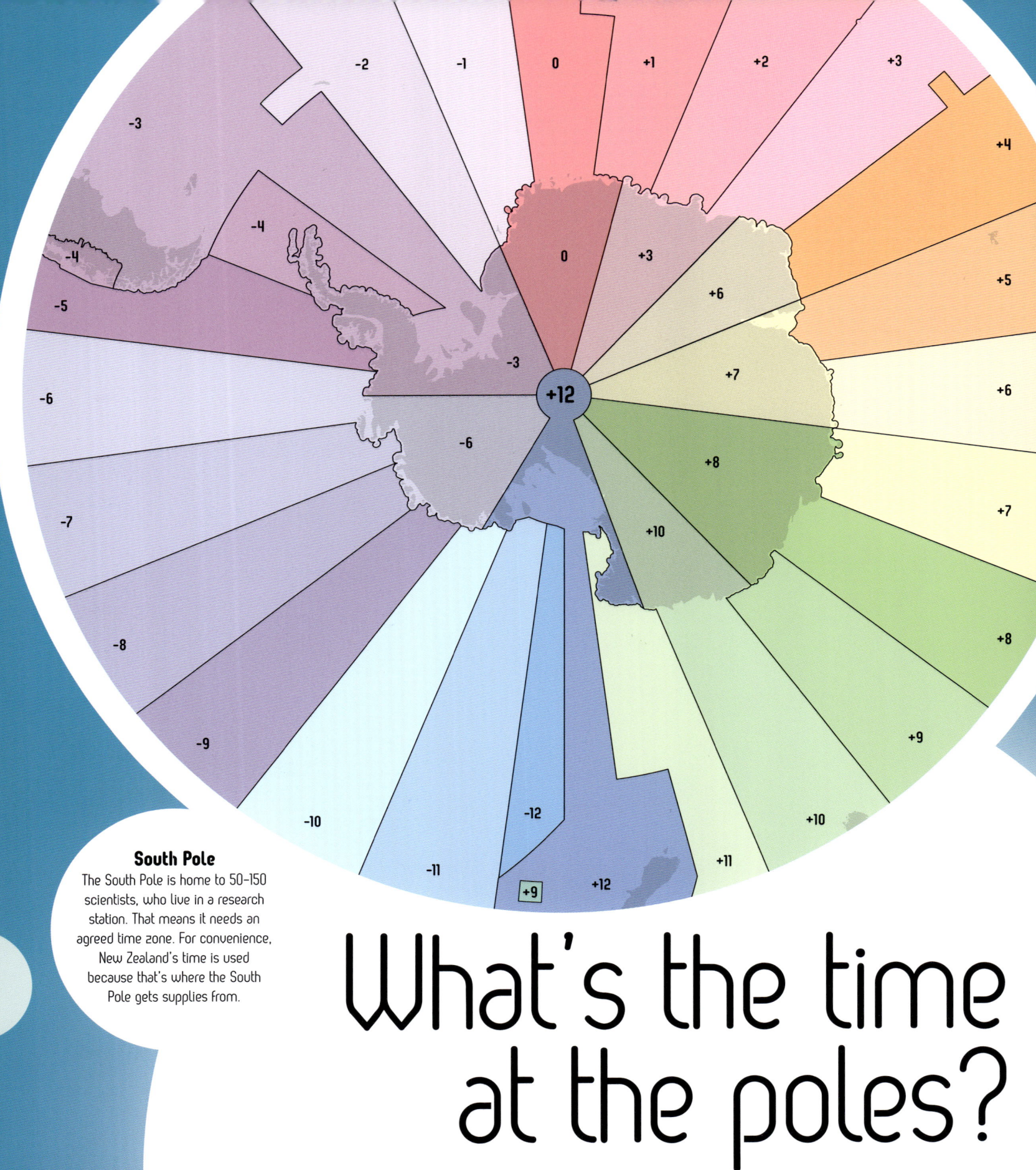

South Pole
The South Pole is home to 50–150 scientists, who live in a research station. That means it needs an agreed time zone. For convenience, New Zealand's time is used because that's where the South Pole gets supplies from.

What's the time at the poles?

MAPPING THE WORLD'S TIME ZONES

HUMAN WORLD

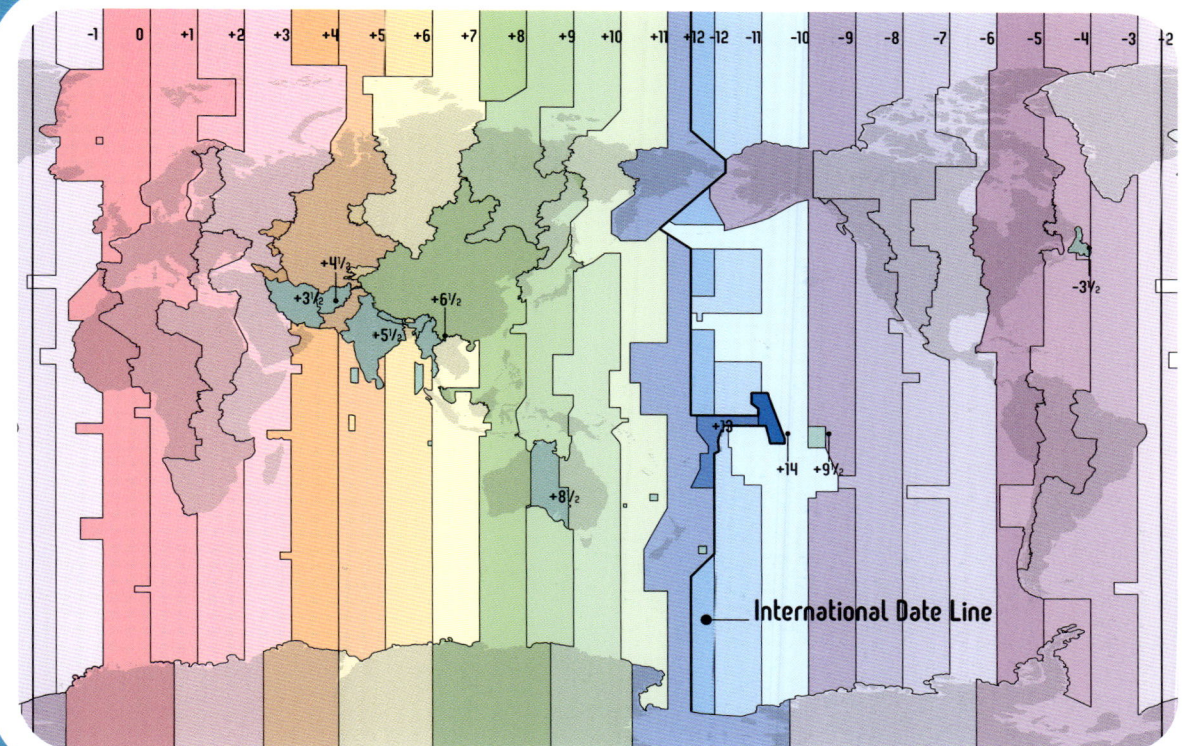

Time zones
The 24 vertical strips on this world map show the different time zones. The strips aren't perfectly vertical as time zones trace the borders of countries or states. The numbers show how time zones vary from "universal time coordinated" (UTC), which is the time in London, UK.

Date line
If you travel east across the International Date Line, the time stays the same but the date changes to yesterday. Cross from east to west and you jump into tomorrow.

North Pole
Nobody lives at the North Pole, which is in the middle of a icy sea. As a result, the North Pole has no agreed time zone – it's whatever time you want it to be. Explorers tend to use UK time or the time zone of the country they came from.

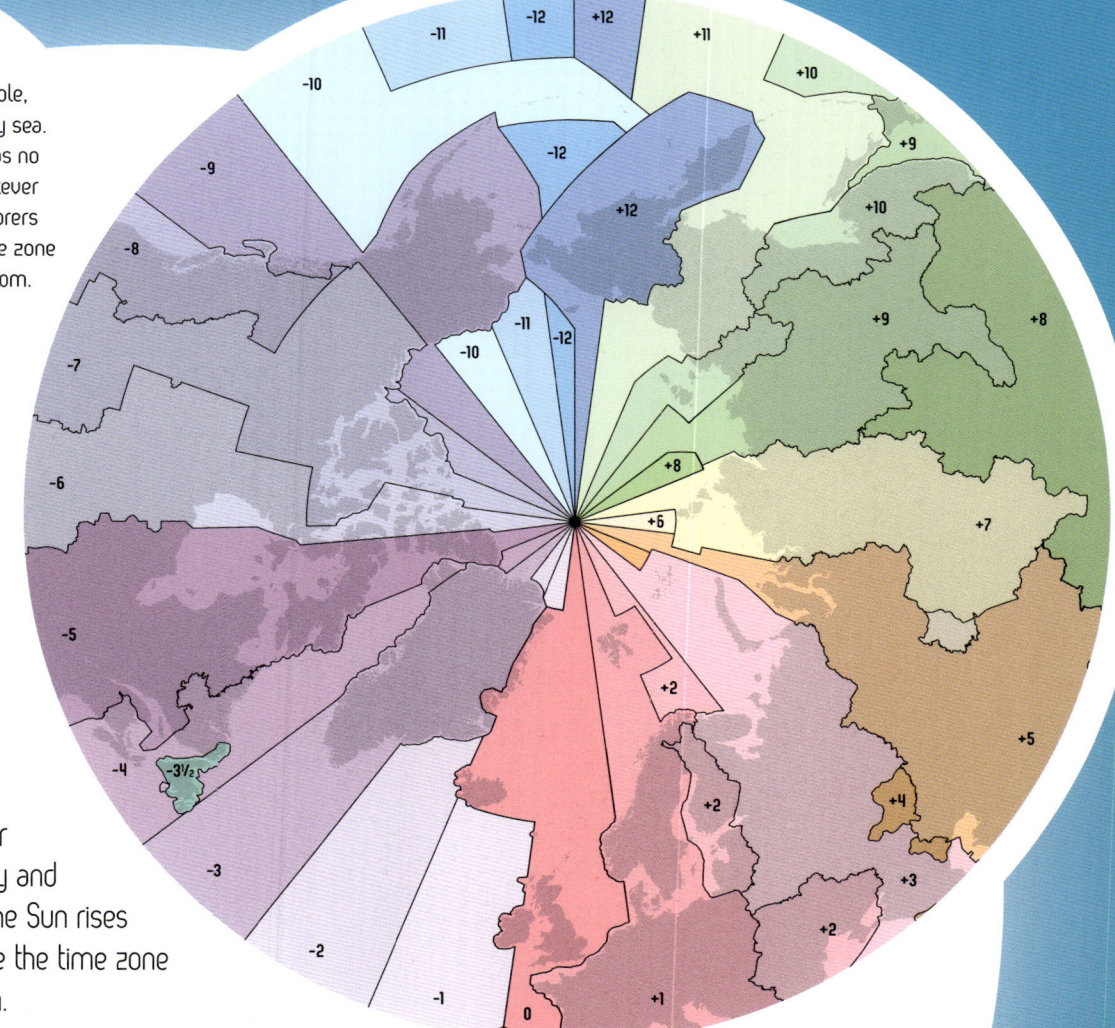

The world has 24 main time zones that meet at each pole. So what's the time there? There are different time zones to make sure that midday is about the brightest time of day and midnight the darkest time in every country. Travel east or west and you leave one time zone and enter another. This doesn't work at the poles, where it's impossible to go east or west. Even stranger, there's only one day and one night each year at the poles, since the Sun rises and sets there only once a year. To solve the time zone puzzle, each pole has a different solution.

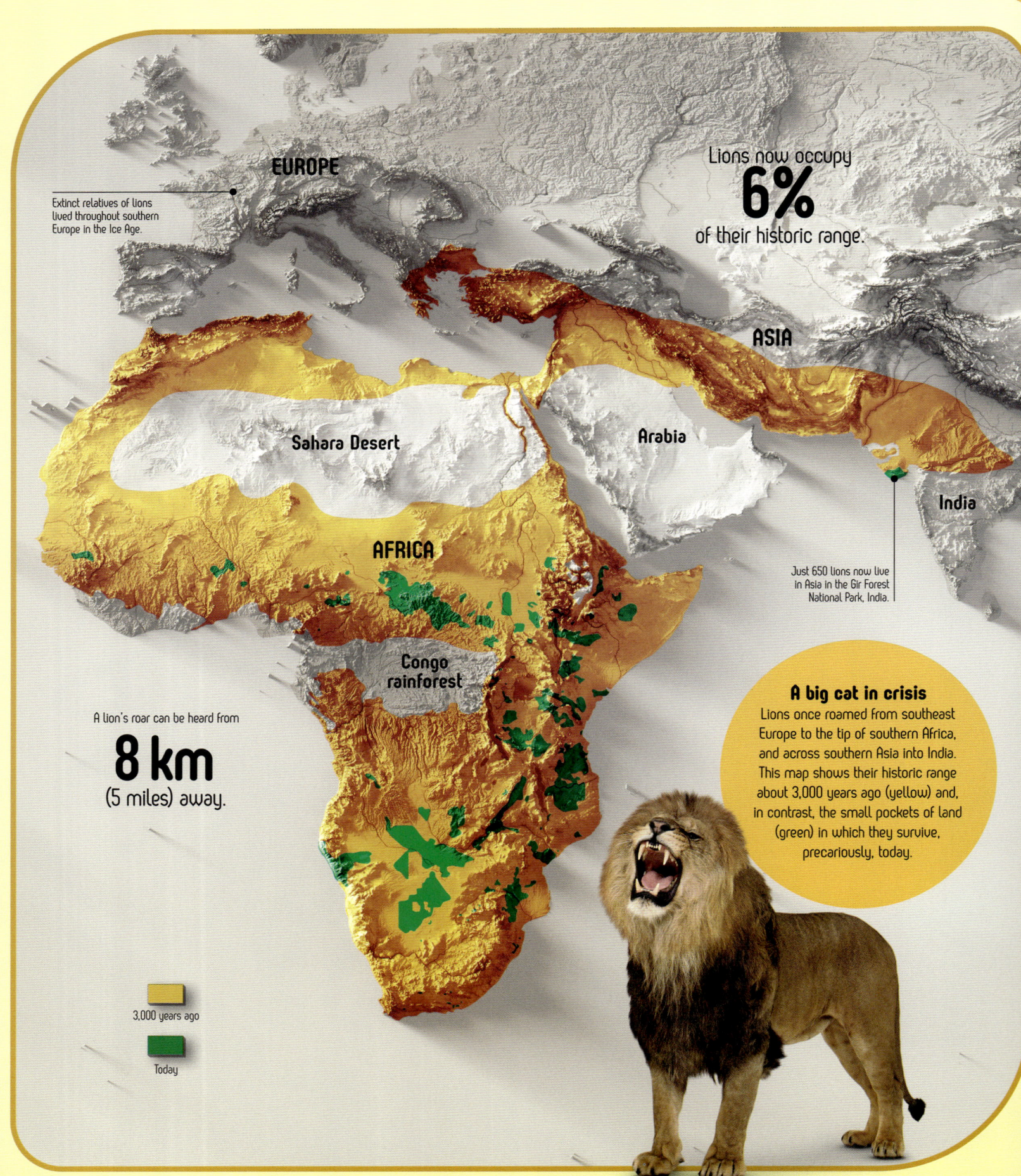

Where the wild things aren't

MAPPING OUR LOST ANIMALS

Wherever humans go, they affect the wildlife around them, most often by encroaching on their natural habitats for farming or settlement, or by hunting them for food, medicine, and even sport.

Lions are a prime example of an animal species that has been decimated by human activities. About 50 years ago, approximately 200,000 wild lions lived in Africa, but today there are only about 20,000. This reduction is due to loss of their natural open grassland habitat to human settlements and farming, or from direct conflict with humans. Lions are now considered vulnerable to extinction by the end of the 21st century, along with many other large wild animals.

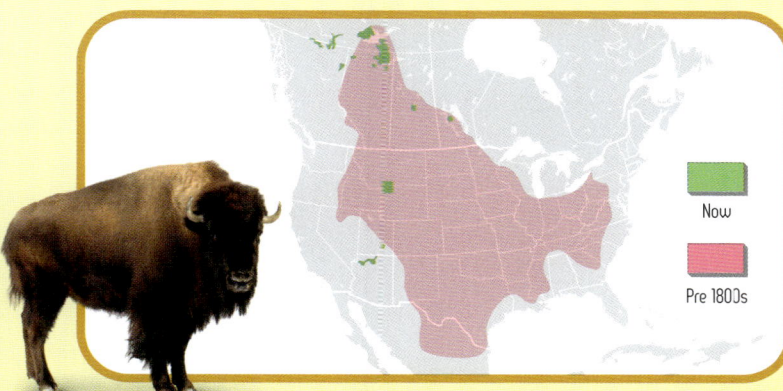

Where did all the bison go?
The American bison was brought to the edge of extinction by hunting. About 30-60 million ranged across North America before the arrival of Europeans in the 15th century. By 1889, only a few hundred were left. That number has now risen to 30,000 in wildlife reserves and over 400,000 in commercial herds.

Space invaders
While many wild animals fare abysmally due to human activities, some have prospered. Below are maps showing the present-day distribution of three animal species that have spread well outside their home territory and are now considered "invasive alien species".

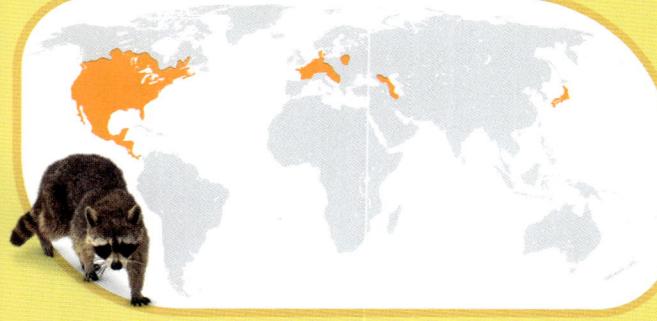

Common raccoons
These little critters once lived only between North America's east coast and the Rocky Mountains. Due to escaped pets and fur farms, common raccoons now exist all over the USA and in parts of Asia and Europe.

Brown rats
Despite sometimes being known as Norway rats, these furry pests originated in the forests of northern China, but have spread all over the world on trade ships. They now prefer living around humans in towns and cities.

Red foxes
The highly adaptable red fox has colonized cities throughout the northern hemisphere. Europeans took the species to Australia in the 19th century to hunt, but it spread like wildfire and has driven several marsupial species to extinction.

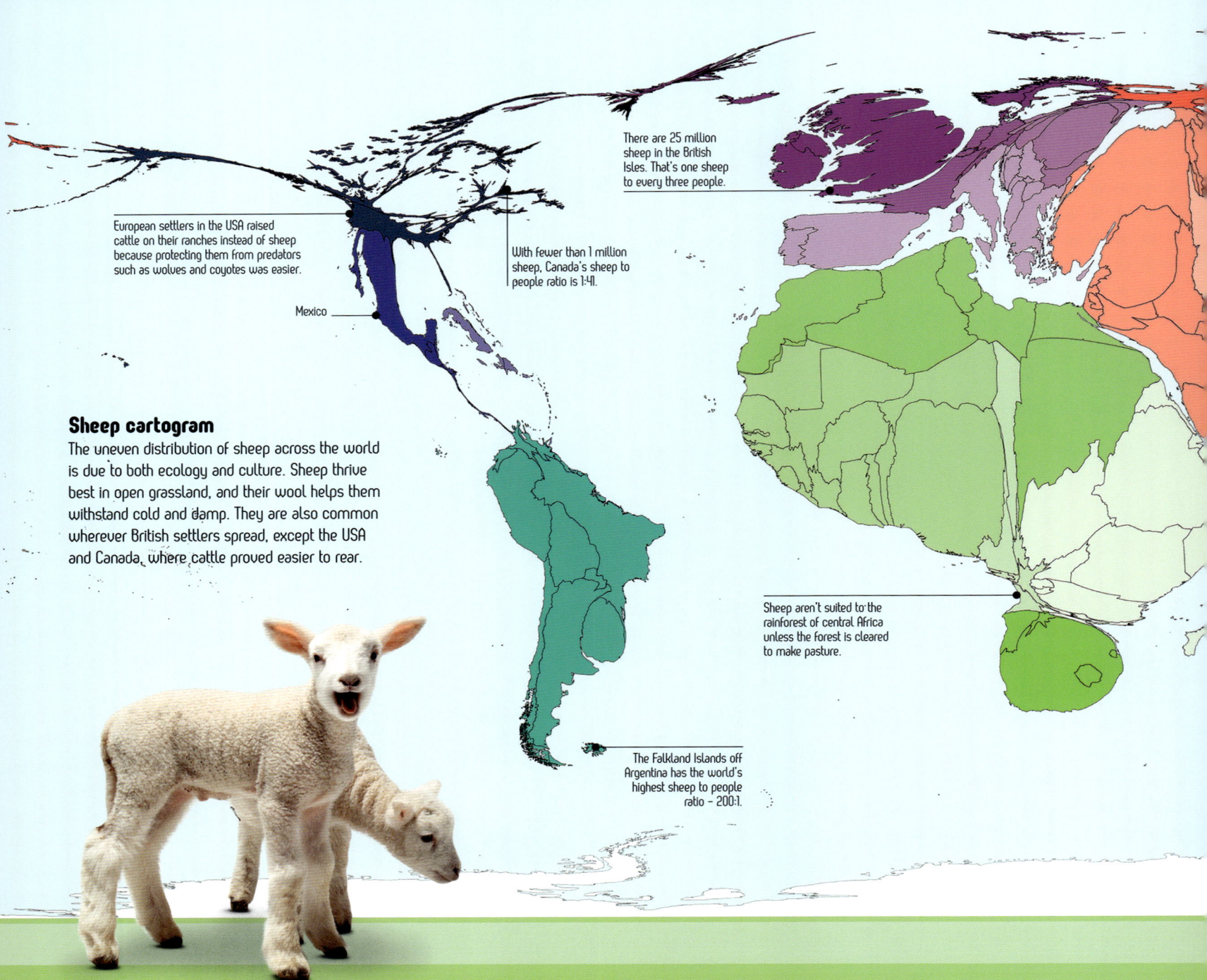

Sheep cartogram

The uneven distribution of sheep across the world is due to both ecology and culture. Sheep thrive best in open grassland, and their wool helps them withstand cold and damp. They are also common wherever British settlers spread, except the USA and Canada, where cattle proved easier to rear.

European settlers in the USA raised cattle on their ranches instead of sheep because protecting them from predators such as wolves and coyotes was easier.

Mexico

There are 25 million sheep in the British Isles. That's one sheep to every three people.

With fewer than 1 million sheep, Canada's sheep to people ratio is 1:41.

Sheep aren't suited to the rainforest of central Africa unless the forest is cleared to make pasture.

The Falkland Islands off Argentina has the world's highest sheep to people ratio – 200:1.

Where sheep live

HOW CARTOGRAMS WORK

Most maps focus on physical or human geography, but cartograms work in a different way. These balloon-like graphics shrink and stretch countries to make data easy to understand.

The cartogram above shows where all the world's sheep live by resizing each country in scale with the number of sheep. At a glance, we can see that about half of Europe's sheep are in the UK – a nation of lamb eaters – but there are very few sheep in the USA and Canada. Cartograms can display any kind of data from wealth and population size to what people eat, drink, read, or watch on TV. All the maps here feature livestock, revealing differences in farming and dietary habits around the world.

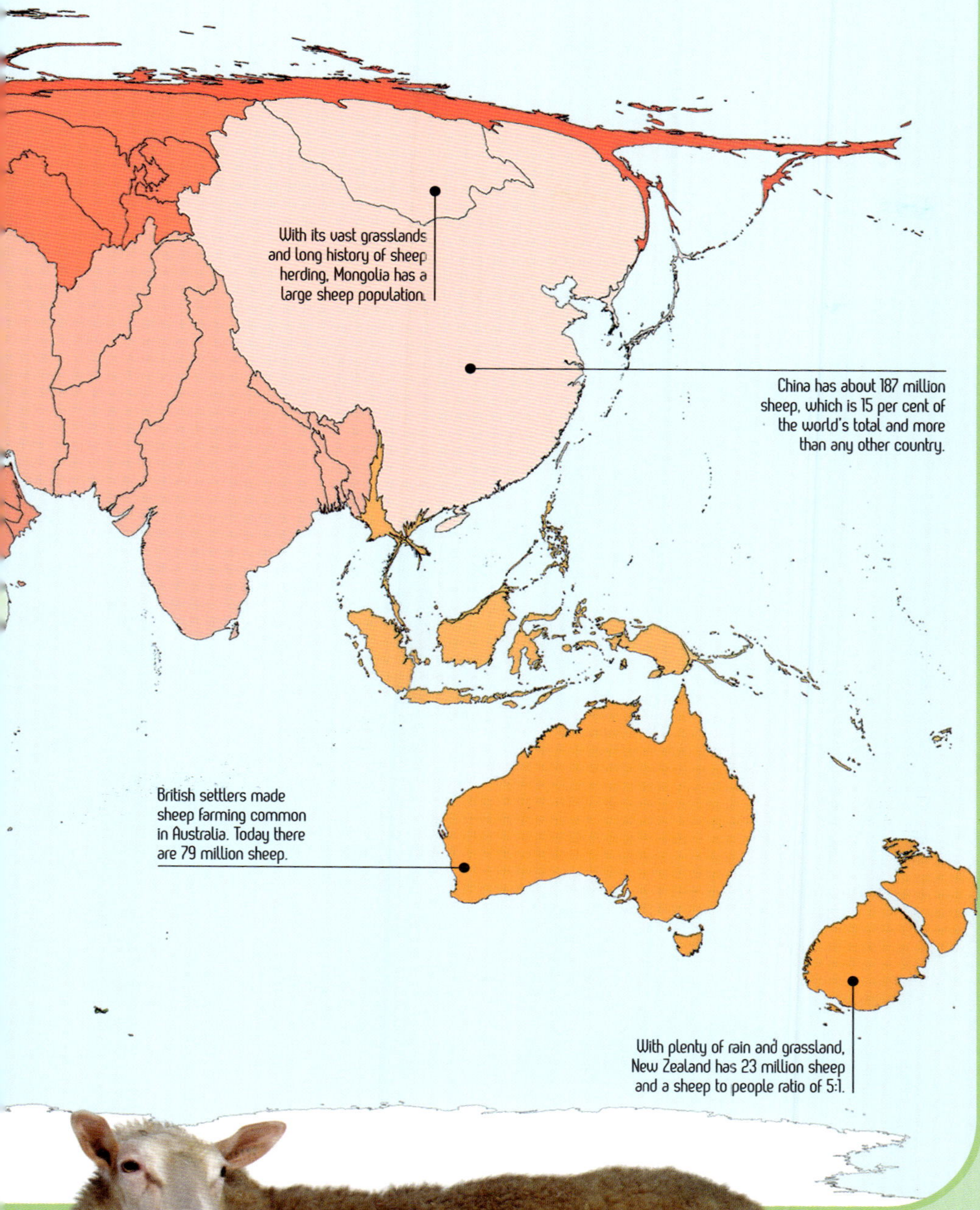

WORLD OF ANIMALS

With its vast grasslands and long history of sheep herding, Mongolia has a large sheep population.

China has about 187 million sheep, which is 15 per cent of the world's total and more than any other country.

British settlers made sheep farming common in Australia. Today there are 79 million sheep.

With plenty of rain and grassland, New Zealand has 23 million sheep and a sheep to people ratio of 5:1.

Cattle
Cattle farming is big business in South America, where the warm climate and expansive grasslands allow year-round grazing. Brazil has the most (234 million cows), but less than India (308 million). While South American farmers rear cattle for meat, Indian farmers rear them for dairy products, as killing a cow is illegal in many states.

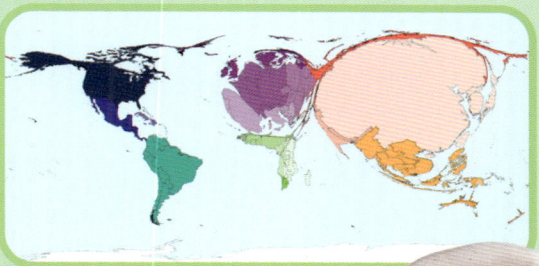

Pigs
It is forbidden to eat pork in the Muslim religion, which is why the Muslim countries of North Africa and Asia are tiny in this cartogram. In contrast, pork is a staple food in China, where there are more than 400 million pigs – more than half the world's total.

Llamas and alpacas
Nearly all the world's llamas and alpacas live in Peru and Bolivia in South America, which dominate this cartogram. These mountain animals are farmed for their wool, but they never caught on outside South America after the invention of synthetic fabrics made natural textiles less profitable.

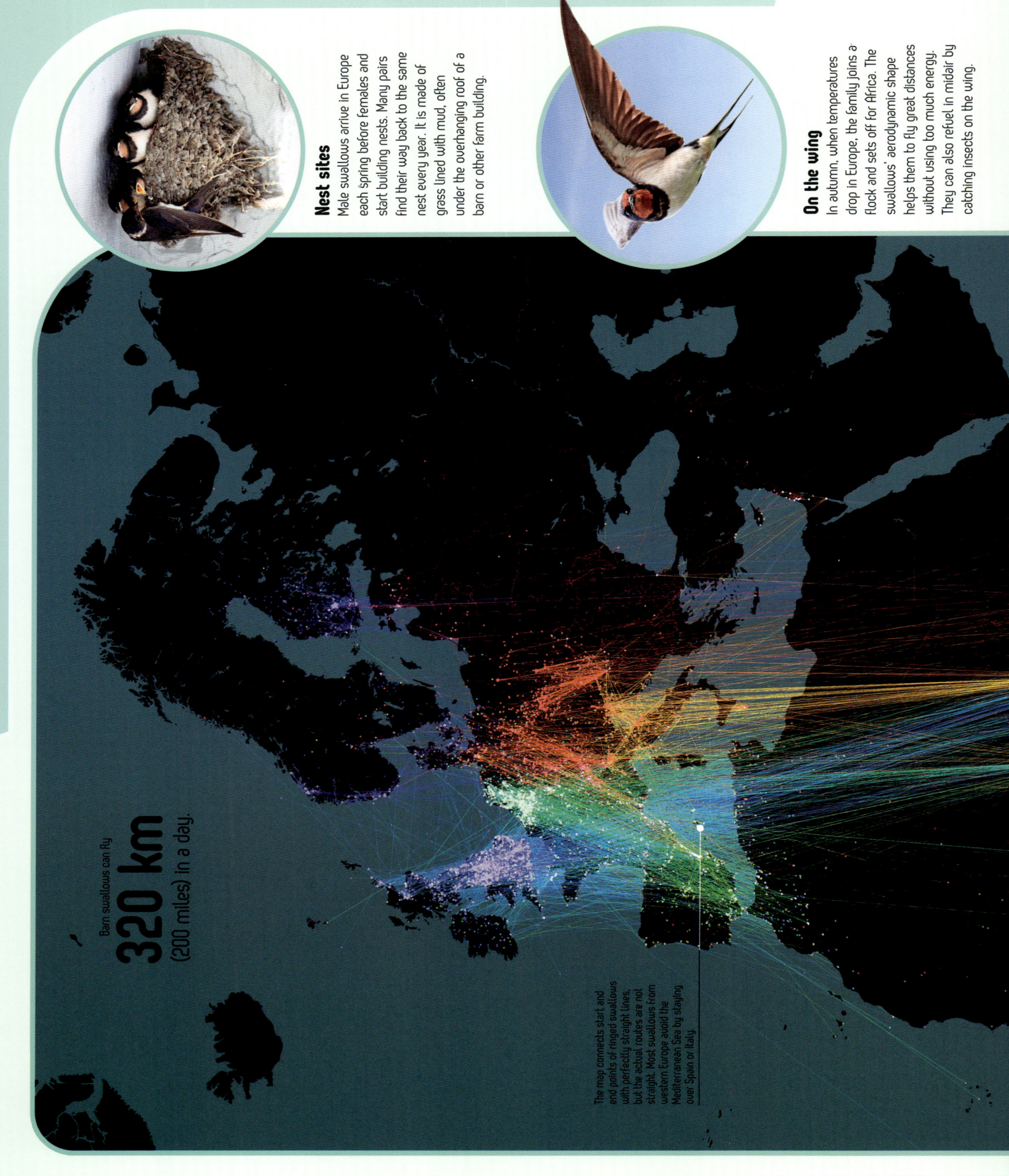

Nest sites
Male swallows arrive in Europe each spring before females and start building nests. Many pairs find their way back to the same nest every year. It is made of grass lined with mud, often under the overhanging roof of a barn or other farm building.

On the wing
In autumn, when temperatures drop in Europe, the family joins a flock and sets off for Africa. The swallows' aerodynamic shape helps them to fly great distances without using too much energy. They can also refuel in midair by catching insects on the wing.

Barn swallows can fly **320 km** (200 miles) in a day.

The map connects start and end points of ringed swallows with perfectly straight lines, but the actual routes are not straight. Most swallows from western Europe avoid the Mediterranean Sea by staying over Spain or Italy.

WORLD OF ANIMALS

Resting at night
Swallows can sleep with one half of the brain at a time while flying, but they also stop at night to rest. They form large communal roosts in reeds, bushes, and trees near water.

Earth's magnetic field

Finding the way
Until recently, how swallows and other migratory birds find the way was a mystery. Scientists now know that these birds navigate by looking for familiar landmarks and by following the Sun, stars, and Earth's magnetic field. Their eyes are thought to contain special proteins that react to blue light, making Earth's magnetic field visible as a shimmering pattern.

A swallow's migration can take **6 weeks.**

Swallows from Eastern Europe spend their winters in central Africa.

Swallows from the British Isles migrate to South Africa.

Where swallows fly

This map charts the vast distances flown by barn swallows each year as they migrate between their nesting sites in Europe and their wintering sites in Africa.

A barn swallow weighs little more than a walnut but can fly 10,000 km (6,200 miles) and back again on its annual migration. The reason swallows make such epic journeys is their need for food. Swallows prey on flying insects, which are abundant during summer in Europe but disappear in winter. In Africa, insects are available all year round, but swallows there face stiff competition from other fly-catching birds.

MAPPING BARN SWALLOW MIGRATION

Where eagles roam

TRACKING ANIMAL JOURNEYS

How far do eagles really roam? To find out, scientists attached GPS trackers to 19 young steppe eagles and tracked them for a year. The birds spent summer in Kazakhstan, Central Asia, before heading south and west for winter on their first annual migration. The GPS data revealed epic voyages of thousands of miles over deserts and mountains, taking the birds as far as Africa and India. They avoided flying over large bodies of water, preferring to hug the coastline or soar above mountains, where updraughts of warm air (thermals) helped them stay aloft without using precious energy to flap their wings.

The average lifespan of a steppe eagle is
25 years.

Happy hunting
In summer in Central Asia, steppe eagles feast on burrowing rodents called ground squirrels, but on migration they eat whatever they can find – foxes, voles, birds, lizards, locusts, and more. They hunt from the air, using their keen vision to spot prey hundreds of metres below.

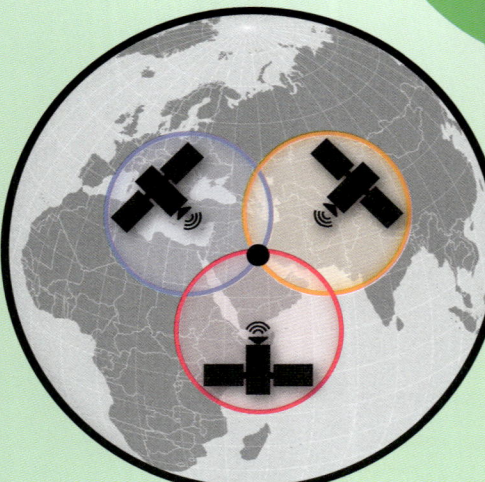

GPS tracking
Each bird had a tiny GPS receiver to track its location, but how do these work? GPS satellites send radio signals from space, and the receiver calculates its distance from the satellite. The bird's exact location can then be pinpointed at the intersection of each of the satellites' distance ranges.

Migrating steppe eagles fly up to
355 km
(220 miles) a day.

WHERE EAGLES ROAM

KAZAKHSTAN

IRAN

INDIA

SAUDI ARABIA

Flight tracker
On the map, the routes of 19 steppe eagles are shown in a different colours. The stars show places they lingered in. A few of the eagles surprised researchers by heading for unexpected countries – one ran up a large phone bill when its GPS tracker sent all its location data from Iran.

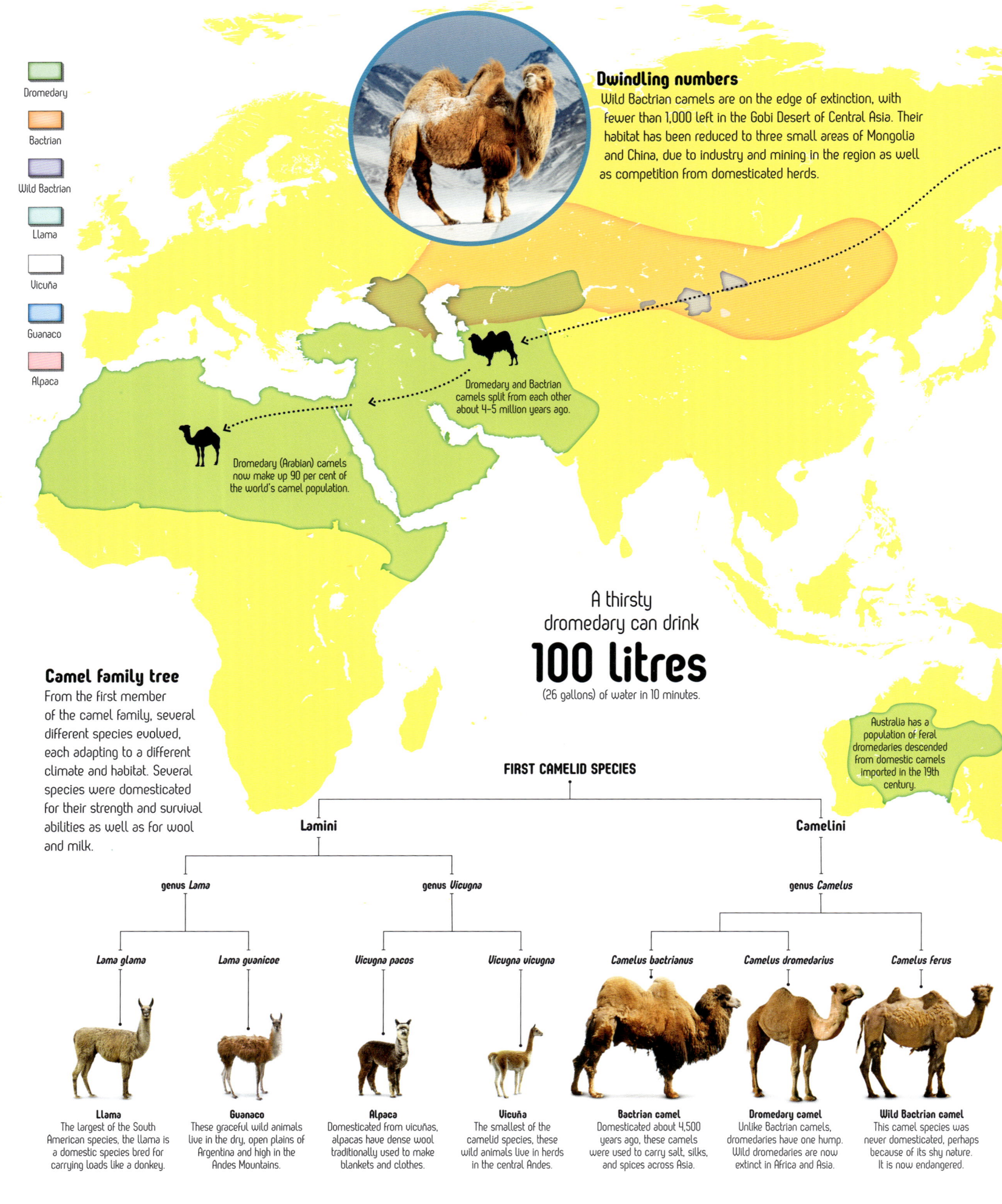

WORLD OF ANIMALS

Camels crossed the Bering Land Bridge that linked North America and Asia 16-12 million years ago.

Camelops, the last camel species in North America, became extinct about 10,000 years ago, which coincided with the arrival of human hunters to the continent.

The camel family split into two branches about 16 million years ago.

Camelids crossed into South America 3 million years ago.

Thick wool helped South American camelids survive high in the Andes Mountains.

Ships of the desert

MAPPING THE MIGRATION OF CAMELS

Camels started their evolutionary journey 40 million years ago in North America, before mysteriously vanishing from the continent altogether. Since then, their ability to survive in harsh climates and inhospitable terrain has allowed them to flourish across the globe.

The fossil record for camelids (members of the camel family) begins with a small, harelike creature that lived in dry grasslands in North America. Over time, the species divided into two family lines, with ancestors of llamas and alpacas migrating to South America while the ancestors of dromedaries and Bactrian camels spread to Asia and Africa. All these species share key features that help them survive in bitterly cold or dry places, such as wide hooves to walk on sand or snow, dense wool, super-dry droppings to conserve water, hard-wearing teeth to eat cacti, and the ability to endure long periods without food and water.

Windscreen wipers
All camelids have long, interlocking eyelashes to help keep sand, dust, or snow out of their eyes. They also have a third eyelid that sweeps across the eye like a windscreen wiper to wash away debris. These adaptations probably first developed to keep snow out of their eyes in blizzards.

Camels can store enough fat in their humps to last

15 days
without eating.

Deadly animals

HUMAN DEATHS FROM ANIMALS

The phrase "deadly animal" conjures up images of fierce predators such as lions or sharks. However, the creatures that cause most harm to humans rarely use size or strength. The deadliest animals are those that kill by spreading disease or by using toxins. Smaller creatures, including some of the most venomous snakes and spiders, don't kill humans for food – we're too big for that. They will only strike out with their fangs or stingers if they are accidentally disturbed or frightened.

Alaska yellowjacket
Dangerous for people with severe allergies – they can go into shock within 20 minutes of being stung.

Northern black widow spider
A small spider with big fangs. Bite symptoms include severe pain, fever, and vomiting.

Eastern diamondback rattlesnake
The largest rattlesnake in the USA, it can grow to 2.4 m (8 ft) long, with fangs 2.5 cm (1 in) in length.

Fer-de-lance
This fast-moving pit viper is the most dangerous snake in Central and South America, killing more people annually than any other species.

Brazilian wandering spider
Also known as the banana spider, its bite can cause pain, fever, vomiting, and even heart attacks.

Brazilian pit viper
This snake's bite causes internal bleeding and excruciating pain.

Africanized bees
These bees are highly aggressive. Deaths are caused by multiple stings.

South American rattlesnake
Its venom attacks the human nervous system more seriously than that of other rattlesnakes.

Adder
Britain's only venomous snake. Its bite is painful, but rarely fatal. It is still wise to seek medical attention.

Honey bees
Death from a single bee sting occurs only if a person has a severe allergic reaction.

Deathstalker scorpion
This scorpion's sting causes intense pain, paralysis, and sometimes death.

Scorpions inject venom from the sting in their tail.

Disease carriers
Animals that spread disease do so by passing on germs such as viruses or parasites. Blood-sucking insects such as mosquitoes and sandflies inject germs straight into a person's bloodstream.

Mosquito
Female mosquitoes feed on blood for their growing eggs, and they aren't fussy whether it's from a human or an animal. Unfortunately, as they feed, some species transmit the germs that cause malaria, yellow fever, or other deadly diseases.

Freshwater snail
Small, harmless-looking snails such as this one kill at least 10,000 people a year in tropical countries. The snails carry tiny, disease-causing worms that burrow into people's skin as they wade or swim in lakes, rivers, and rice paddies.

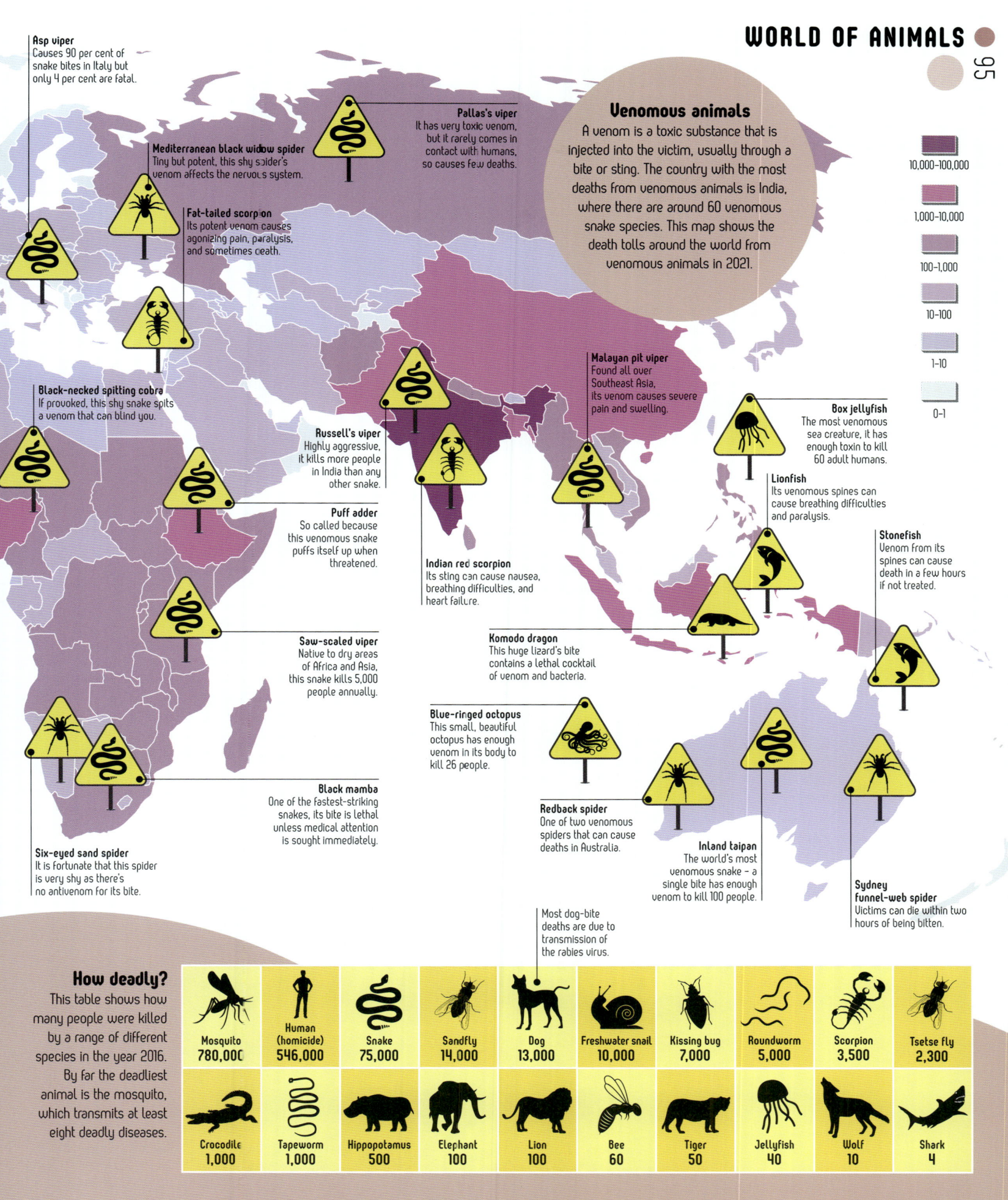

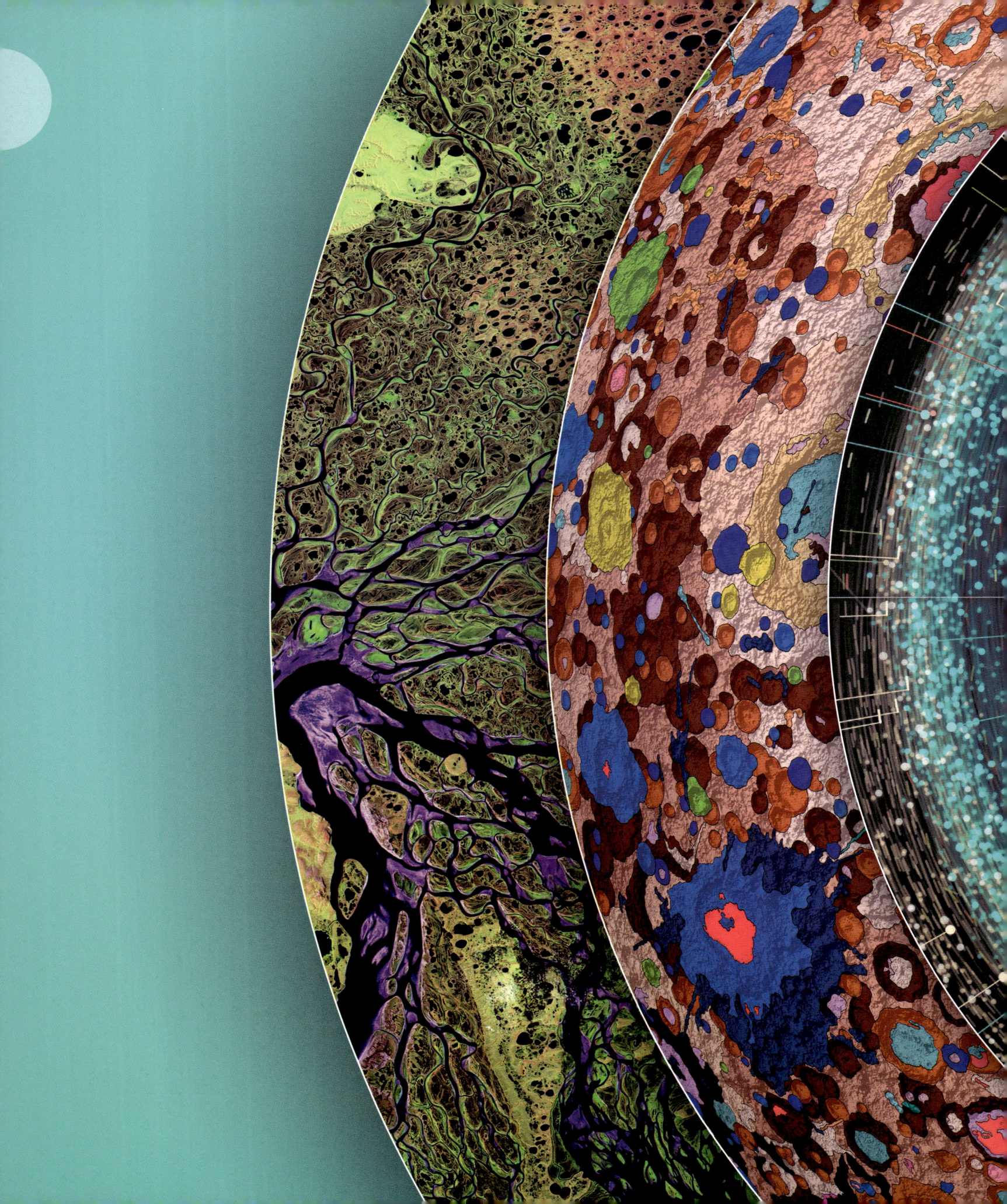

Earth at night

SATELLITE MAPS OF CITY LIGHTS

Seen from space, Earth comes alive with light at night. In some places, isolated towns twinkle like solitary stars. In others, megacities and urban sprawl light up great swathes of the planet's surface. Satellite images of our world in darkness show the patterns of human settlement. The brightest patches tend to be the most heavily built-up and densely populated areas. Deserts are almost blank, and dark seas are bordered by busy coastlines.

Aurora from space
Astronauts aboard the International Space Station (ISS) orbit about 400 km (250 miles) above us. This photo taken from the ISS shows the lights of Canadian cities under the green glow of the northern lights, known as the aurora borealis.

River of light
This computer-generated map merges Earth's physical terrain with satellite data to show city lights at night around the eastern Mediterranean. The resulting image reveals the River Nile and its delta brightly illuminated – more than 90 per cent of Egypt's 115 million people live in these areas.

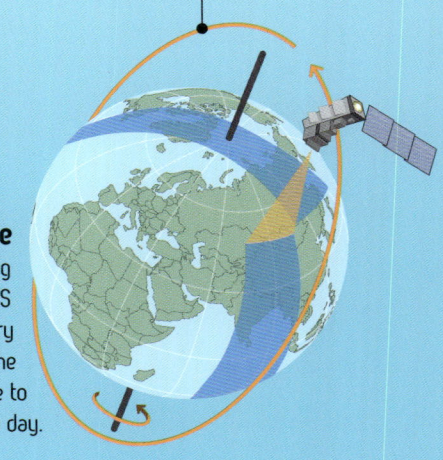

Orbit height 824 km (512 miles)

Suomi NPP satellite
The image on the facing page was made using data from the Suomi NPP satellite. This US observation satellite circles Earth once every 101 minutes. As it orbits from pole to pole, the planet turns beneath it, allowing the satellite to scan Earth's entire surface twice a day.

Lost in space

The Moon is not the only object orbiting Earth. Thousands of working satellites and the odd space station whizz around the planet along with vast quantities of space junk. Humans have littered near-space with the remains of previous missions – from old booster rockets to flecks of paint. As more missions are launched and collisions multiply, this cloud of debris becomes denser and more dangerous.

MAPPING SATELLITES AND SPACE DEBRIS

Satellite orbits
Satellites are placed in different kinds of orbit depending on their purpose. Low orbits are less costly and faster to communicate with, but high orbits command a broader view of Earth.

Trash cloud
This map shows the positions of 26,000 of the largest objects orbiting Earth on 3 January 2025. Only 4,000 of the dots are active satellites. The rest are junk. The true number of orbiting objects is far higher as there are millions of pieces of space debris too small to track.

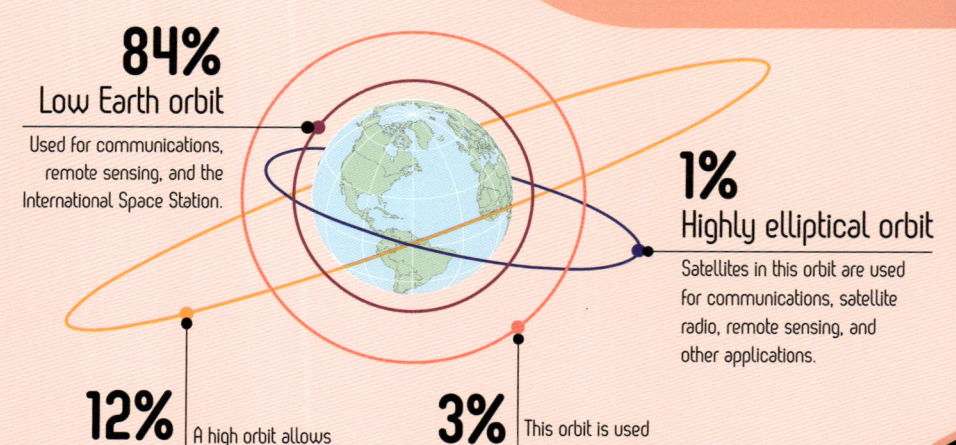

84% Low Earth orbit
Used for communications, remote sensing, and the International Space Station.

12% Geosynchronous and geostationary orbits
A high orbit allows communications and observation satellites to hover over a single location.

3% Medium Earth orbit
This orbit is used for navigation systems such as GPS.

1% Highly elliptical orbit
Satellites in this orbit are used for communications, satellite radio, remote sensing, and other applications.

By 2030 there will be an estimated **63,000** satellites in orbit.

Space collisions
Collisions between objects in orbit are rare but catastrophic. Orbital speeds are so high that even a penny-sized object can wreck a spacecraft. In 2009 the Iridium 33 communications satellite and a non-working Russian satellite crashed, generating more than 2,300 pieces of hazardous debris. Each collision makes the risk of more collisions higher.

SPACE 101

Earth is orbited by more than **100 million** particles of space debris.

Meteorite map

MAPPING METEORITE STRIKES

395 meteorites found on Earth originally came from Mars.

The Cape York meteorite (the world's second largest at 58 tonnes) landed near Meteorite Island by Meteor Bay in Greenland 10,000 years ago.

Meteorite obsevations are clustered in densely populated places.

Meteorites that land in rainforests are rarely found.

44 tonnes of space rocks collide with Earth every day.

Only one confirmed strike of a human has ever occurred. The grapefruit-sized Hodges meteorite hit Ann Hodges of Alabama, USA, in 1954 while she was napping on her couch. She was bruised but survived.

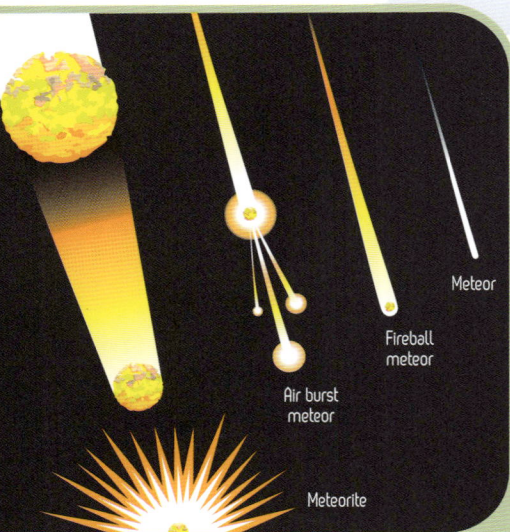

Space rocks

Space rocks are known as meteoroids before they hit Earth. Afterwards, their name depends on what happens. Meteors (shooting stars) burn up in the atmosphere, sometimes in a spectacular fireball or an airburst (explosion). Meteorites reach the ground.

Each day, around 25 million space rocks collide with our planet at supersonic speed.

Fortunately, the vast majority are tiny specks of grit that burn up in streaks of fire as they enter Earth's atmosphere. We call these meteors or shooting stars. A few dozen, however, are big enough to make it through the atmosphere and reach the ground, often disintegrating on the way. These fallen space rocks are meteorites and vary from the size of a pebble to the size of a house. This map shows every recorded landing of a meteorite larger than a gram in history, except for those in Antarctica. The true number of meteorite strikes is far greater – most land in oceans and are never seen or found.

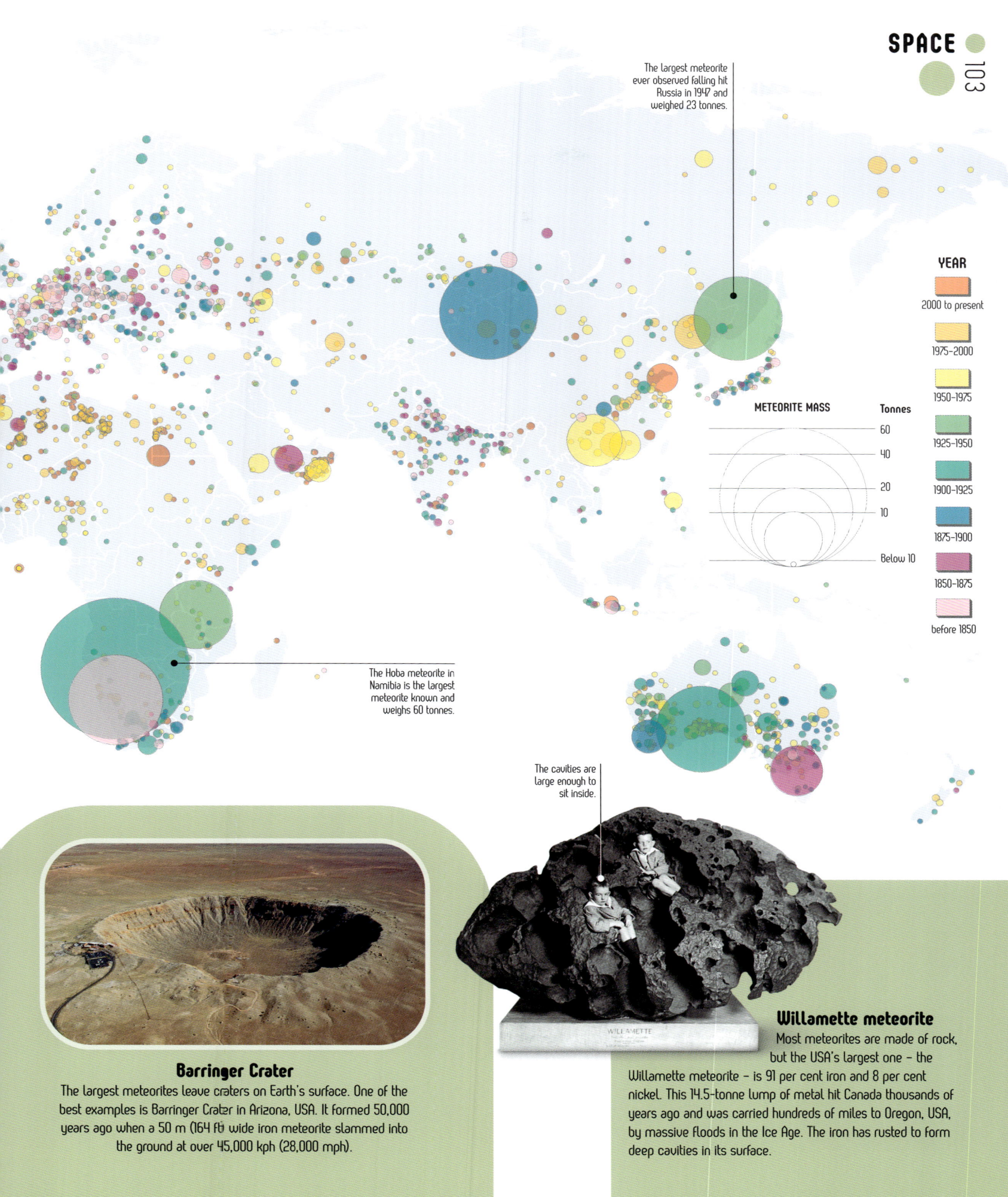

SPACE

103

The largest meteorite ever observed falling hit Russia in 1947 and weighed 23 tonnes.

YEAR
- 2000 to present
- 1975–2000
- 1950–1975
- 1925–1950
- 1900–1925
- 1875–1900
- 1850–1875
- before 1850

METEORITE MASS — Tonnes: 60, 40, 20, 10, Below 10

The Hoba meteorite in Namibia is the largest meteorite known and weighs 60 tonnes.

The cavities are large enough to sit inside.

Barringer Crater
The largest meteorites leave craters on Earth's surface. One of the best examples is Barringer Crater in Arizona, USA. It formed 50,000 years ago when a 50 m (164 ft) wide iron meteorite slammed into the ground at over 45,000 kph (28,000 mph).

Willamette meteorite
Most meteorites are made of rock, but the USA's largest one – the Willamette meteorite – is 91 per cent iron and 8 per cent nickel. This 14.5-tonne lump of metal hit Canada thousands of years ago and was carried hundreds of miles to Oregon, USA, by massive floods in the Ice Age. The iron has rusted to form deep cavities in its surface.

Destination Moon

MAPPING A PATH TO THE MOON

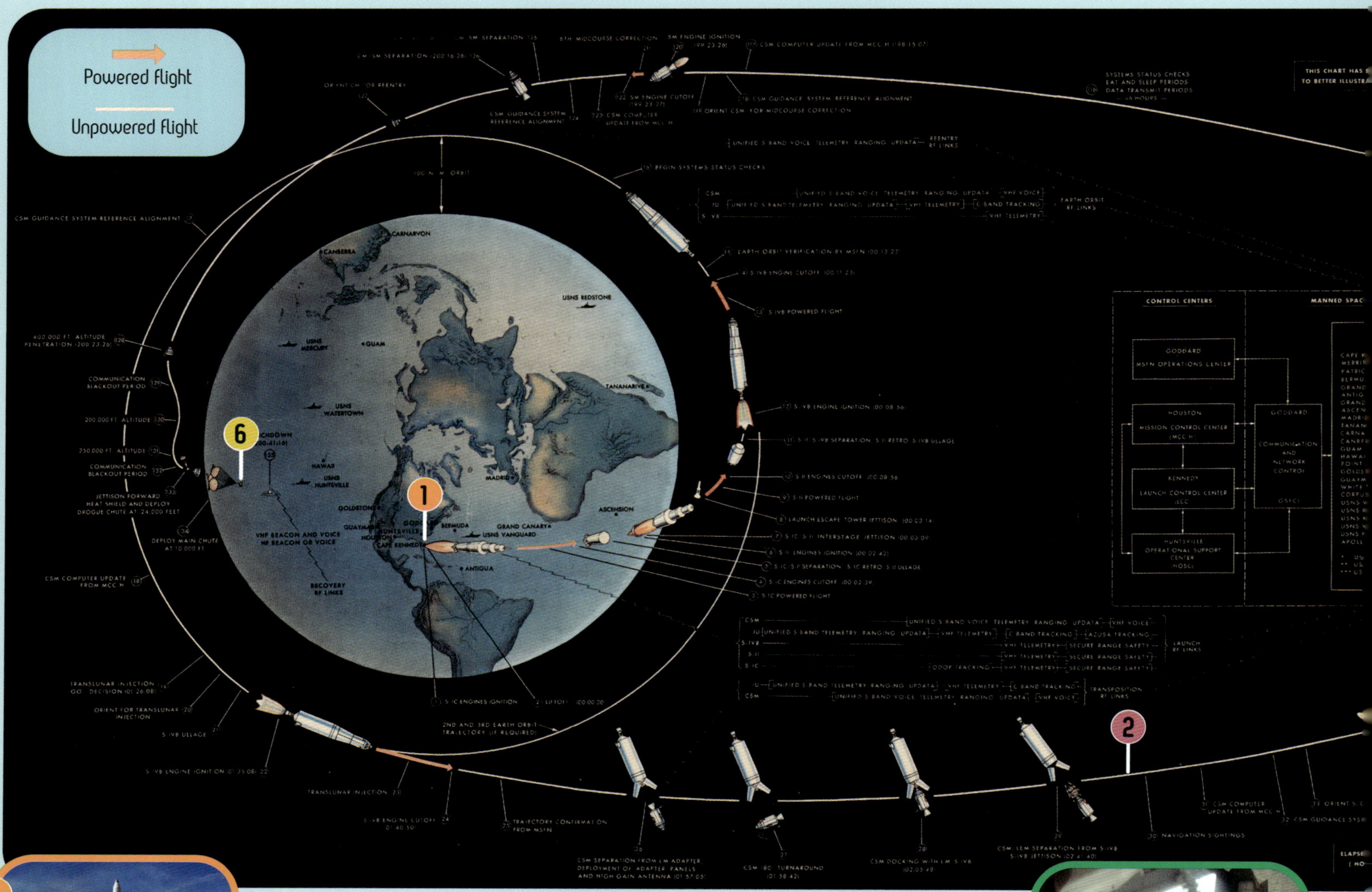

→ Powered flight
　 Unpowered flight

APOLLO MISSION MAP CREATED IN 1967

Lift-off
July 16 1969
The Saturn V rocket launches with the Apollo spacecraft at its tip. As tall as a 36-storey skyscraper, it is the most massive and powerful rocket ever to fly and generates more power than a million cars.

Goodbye Earth
July 16 1969
Apollo escapes Earth's gravity and hurtles towards the Moon. The crew watch Earth shrinking in the rear window and take photos.

Lunar Module
July 17 1969
Astronaut Buzz Aldrin carries out system checks inside the Lunar Module. It will later separate from the Command Module and land on the Moon's surface.

In 1961, US President John F. Kennedy made what seemed an impossible promise: to put people on the Moon before the 1960s were over. The Americans succeeded, and this map made by NASA two years before the first Moon landing shows exactly how. The Apollo spacecraft didn't simply fly in a straight line to the Moon. It followed a looping, figure-of-eight flightpath that allowed it to transfer from orbiting Earth to orbiting the Moon with as little fuel as possible. After circling Earth 1.5 times, it escaped our planet's gravity and used the Moon's gravity as a brake to enter lunar orbit. Among the map's 135 steps were many complex manoeuvres that put the astronauts' lives at great risk. The Moon is shown twice in the map to separate the perilous separation and descent to the surface (bottom) from the take-off 22 hours later (top).

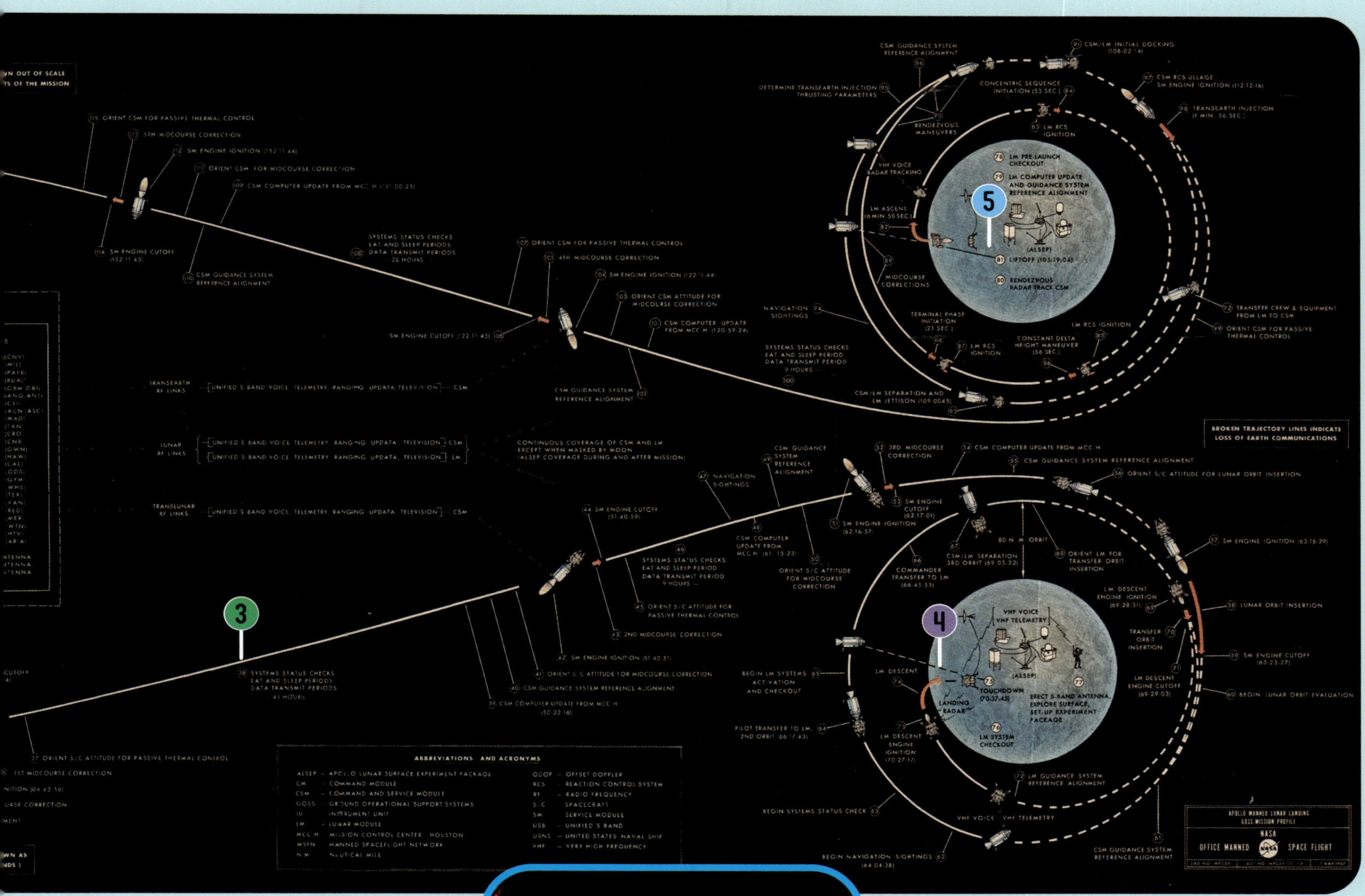

One small step
20 July 1969
A sixth of the world's people watch in awe as astronauts Neil Armstrong and Buzz Aldrin descend a ladder to set foot on the Moon.

On the Moon
21 July 1969
The men discover an eerie, dust-covered world under an inky black sky. In their 22 hours on the Moon, they plant a flag, collect rocks, set up experiments, and practise walking and jumping in gravity a sixth of Earth's.

Splashdown
July 24 1969
After returning to Earth, the Apollo spacecraft enters the atmosphere at 39,000 kph (24,000 mph). Friction with air slows the craft and turns its exterior into a blazing fireball. Parachutes then open to allow a safe splashdown in the Pacific Ocean. The three men receive a hero's welcome.

The far side
Locked by the pull of Earth's gravity, the Moon keeps the same side facing Earth all the time, so the far side wasn't revealed until spacecraft visited. They discovered even more craters than on the near side, with fewer maria.

FAR SIDE

Lunar rock

Four billion years ago, the Moon was bombarded by a blizzard of rocks from space.

Asteroids, comets, and meteorites pounded into it, punching holes in the lunar crust and throwing up clouds of debris. As the Moon has no atmosphere to weather its surface, most of the craters have stayed in place ever since – clues to a violent past. This colour-coded geological map shows everything we know about the Moon's ancient and scar-covered face.

THE MOST DETAILED MAP OF LUNAR ROCK EVER MADE

SPACE

Lava lands
Pinks and reds are different kinds of lava formation, including hills and domes formed from viscous lava and flat plains (maria) formed from runny lava. Early astronomers used the word maria (Latin for seas) because they thought these areas held water.

NEAR SIDE

- Crater rings — 4.4–3.9 billion years old
- Mixed features — 3.9–3.8 billion years old
- Impact basin — 3.8 billion years old
- Lunar maria — 3.8–3.2 billion years old
- Debris — 3.8–3.2 billion years old
- Craters — 3.2–1.1 billion years old
- Craters — 1.1 billion years old or younger

How lunar maria formed
The Moon's large, dark plains, or maria, formed when asteroids hit the crust with such force that it fractured, allowing lava from a once-molten interior to flood the surface. The lava floods erased signs of older craters, making the maria look relatively smooth and unscarred.

1. An asteroid or large meteorite hits the lunar surface and weakens the crust.
2. Lava erupts through cracks in the crust and floods the surface.
3. The lava cools and hardens to form a flat plain with no impact craters.

The near side
Seen through a telescope, the near side's maria appear dark. The brighter areas are craters or debris from craters. The largest craters are surrounded by radial streaks of pulverized rock, arranged like spokes around the hub of a wheel.

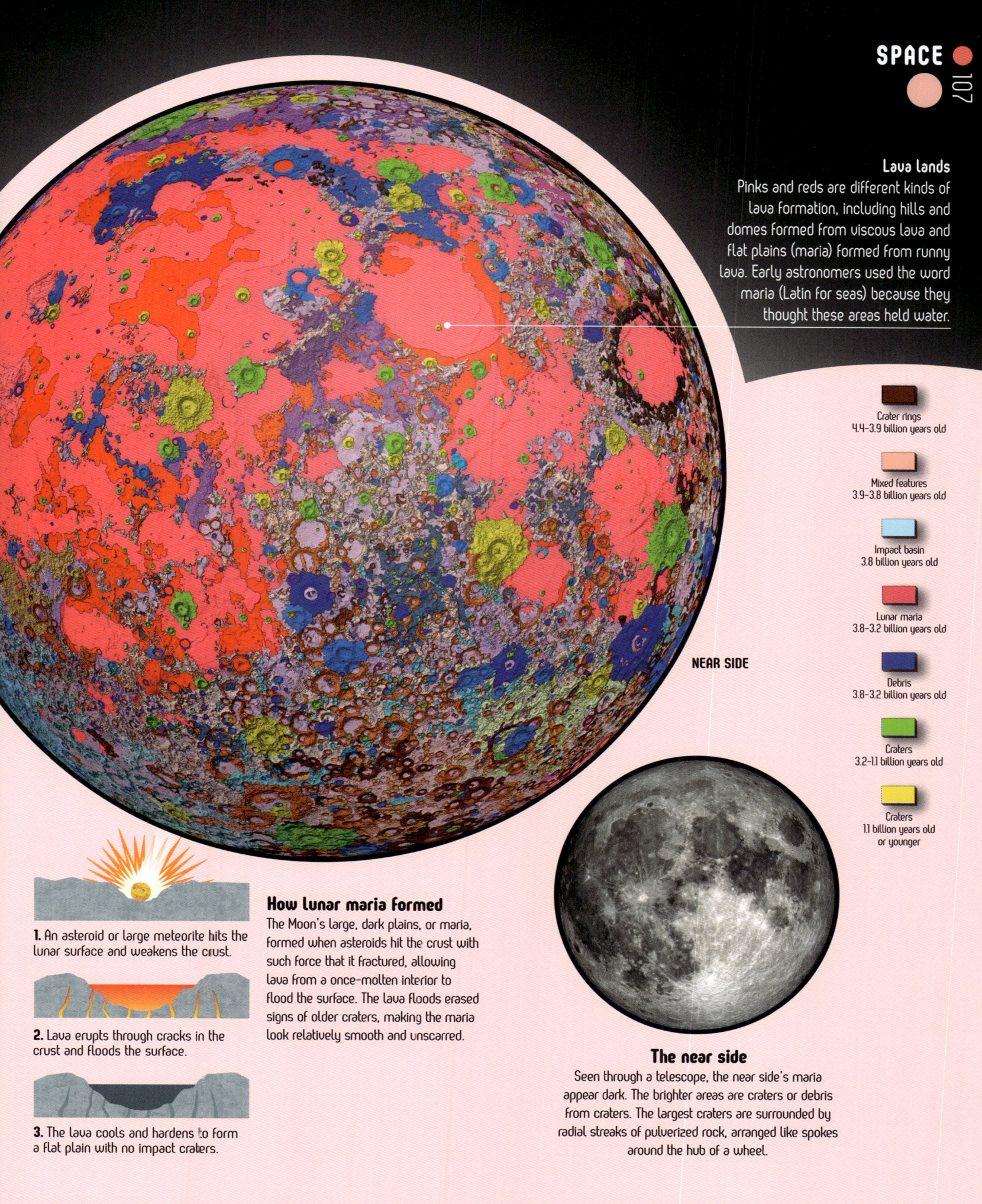

Hostile world

Mars may appear eerily similar to Earth, but looks can be deceiving. The red planet's atmosphere is too thin to support life, and without liquid water the desert is endless. The average surface temperature is a freezing -63°C (-81.5°F). No human would survive without a spacesuit.

Sixteen years in the making, this geological map of Mars pools data from four orbiting spacecraft. The colour-coded chart reveals a planet scarred by meteorite craters over 4 billion years. Unlike Earth, whose craters are worn away by weathering and erosion, Mars preserves a record of its violent past. The great swathes of red are plains formed by lava floods when Mars was volcanically active. Today, this desert world is disturbed by little but wind, though it still boasts the largest volcano known to science.

Martian rock

MAPPING THE GEOLOGY OF MARS

The surface of Mars is smaller than the **Pacific Ocean.**

SPACE

Volcanic plains
Extinct volcanoes
Impact craters
Lowlands
Highlands
Polar ice caps

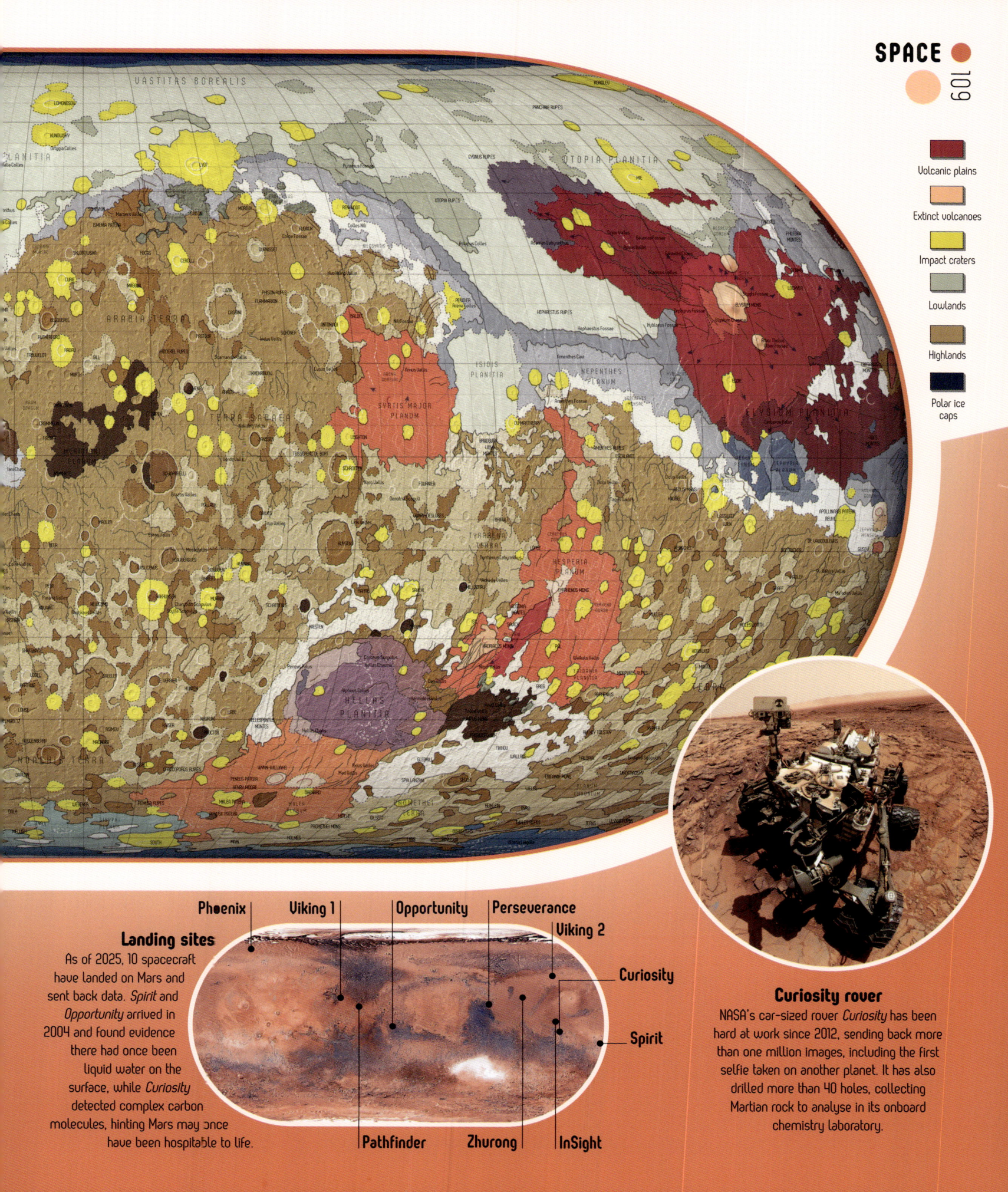

Landing sites
As of 2025, 10 spacecraft have landed on Mars and sent back data. *Spirit* and *Opportunity* arrived in 2004 and found evidence there had once been liquid water on the surface, while *Curiosity* detected complex carbon molecules, hinting Mars may once have been hospitable to life.

Landing sites labelled: Phoenix, Viking 1, Opportunity, Perseverance, Viking 2, Curiosity, Spirit, InSight, Zhurong, Pathfinder.

Curiosity rover
NASA's car-sized rover *Curiosity* has been hard at work since 2012, sending back more than one million images, including the first selfie taken on another planet. It has also drilled more than 40 holes, collecting Martian rock to analyse in its onboard chemistry laboratory.

The solar system

Earth is not alone. It's part of a star system that formed 4.6 billion years ago and includes seven other planets, 293 moons, and millions of asteroids and comets, all orbiting our Sun.

This unusual view of the solar system gives us a bird's eye view of the Sun, planets, and more than 18,000 asteroids. Most of the asteroids are confined to the "Main Belt" between the orbits of Mars and Jupiter. This ring of asteroids has distinct clusters, shown here in different colours. Further out are the mysterious, icy "trans-Neptunian" objects beyond the orbit of Neptune.

OUR NEIGHBOURHOOD IN SPACE

- Centaur asteroid
- Outer Main Belt asteroid
- Comet
- Trans-Neptunian object
- Greek asteroid
- Trojan asteroid
- Hyperbolic asteroid
- Unclassified asteroid
- Inner Main Belt asteroid
- Unknown diameter
- Main Belt asteroid
- 10 km (6 mile) diameter
- Mars-crossing asteroid
- 100 km (60 mile) diameter
- Near-Earth asteroid
- 1000 km (600 mile) diameter

The Sun's family
Shown to scale, the Sun dwarfs the solar system's eight planets. The Sun contains 99.86% of the solar system's matter. This colossal mass exerts a huge gravitational pull, keeping everything in the Sun's vicinity trapped in orbit around it.

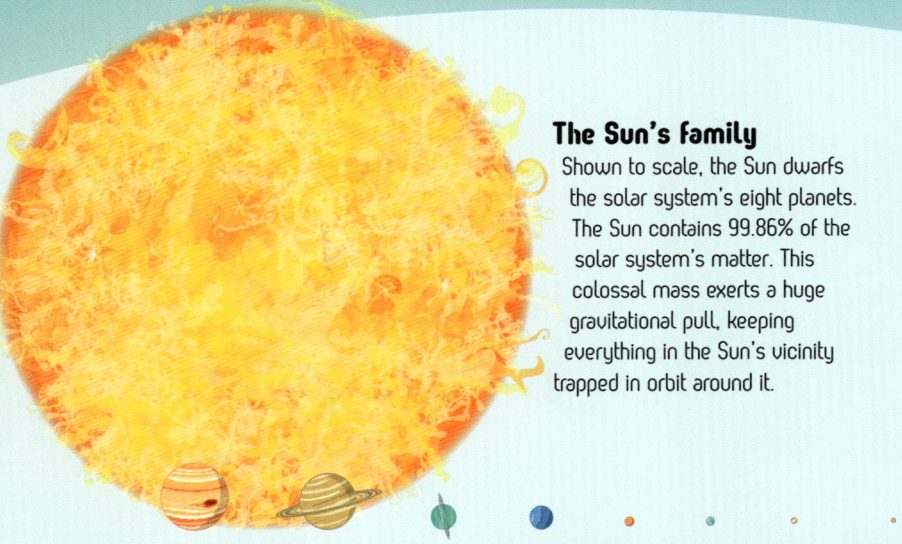

Jupiter   Saturn   Uranus   Neptune   Mars   Earth   Venus   Mercury

Orbital plane
The bodies of the solar system formed from a flat disc of dust and gas that once encircled the newborn Sun. As a result, they are confined to the same orbital plane and travel anticlockwise when viewed from above. Comets are an exception. They can hurtle into the inner solar system from any direction on wildly elliptical orbits.

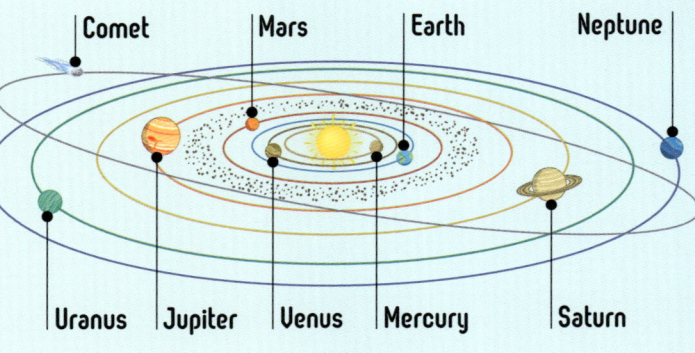

Comet   Mars   Earth   Neptune
Uranus   Jupiter   Venus   Mercury   Saturn

Asteroid impact
Asteroids are large space rocks too small to be classed as dwarf planets. In 2022 NASA made a daring attempt to change the path of an asteroid by crashing a spacecraft into it. The impact shortened the orbit of Dimorphos (above) around a larger asteroid by 33 minutes.

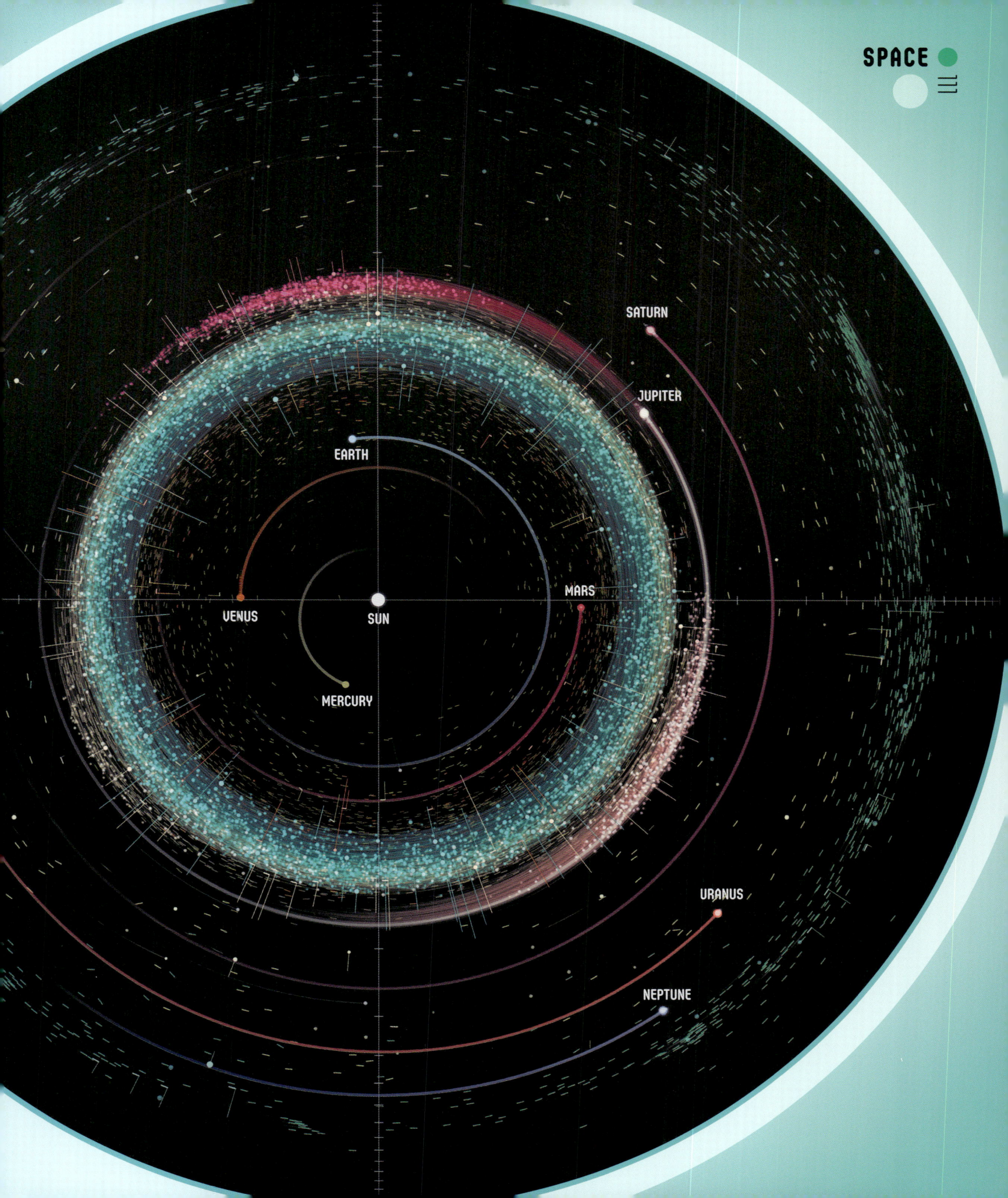

Cosmic eye

How do you map the entirety of existence? This incredible image condenses all of space and time into a single cosmic map centred on our solar system. From Earth we can see 46 billion light years in every direction, which means the spherical observable universe is a mind-boggling 92 billion light years across. Fitting all this into a single image involved a bit of mathematical wizardry known as a logarithmic scale.

MAPPING THE OBSERVABLE UNIVERSE

Across the universe
Starting from the centre, the Sun, planets, stars, and the dusty heart of our galaxy (the Milky Way), are shown in detail. The next ring out is our local region of the universe – the 60 million or so galaxies surrounding our Milky Way. Beyond that, more distant galaxies form clusters and superclusters. These join up in a vast "cosmic web" – the overall structure of the universe.

Looking back
The light arriving at our eyes from distant stars left their surface long ago. This means we see objects in space not as they are now, but as they once were. "Deep field" images like this one from the James Webb telescope peer back in time almost to the dawn of creation, capturing the first galaxies forming 13 billion years ago.

A light year
is the distance light travels in a year—about 9.5 trillion km (6 trillion miles).

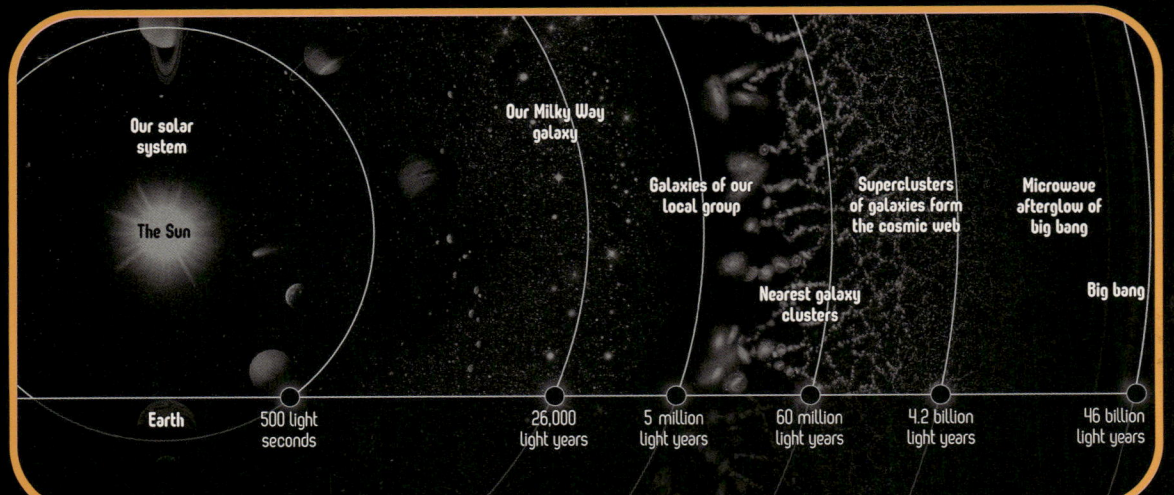

How the map works
To compress vast distances into a single image with recognizable parts, the circular map uses a logarithmic scale. This means that each equal step outward from the centre represents a distance many times greater than the last one. The outer edge marks the big bang 13.8 billion years ago, when the universe burst into existence from nothing. Light from the early universe appears further than 13.8 billion light years away because space has been expanding all that time

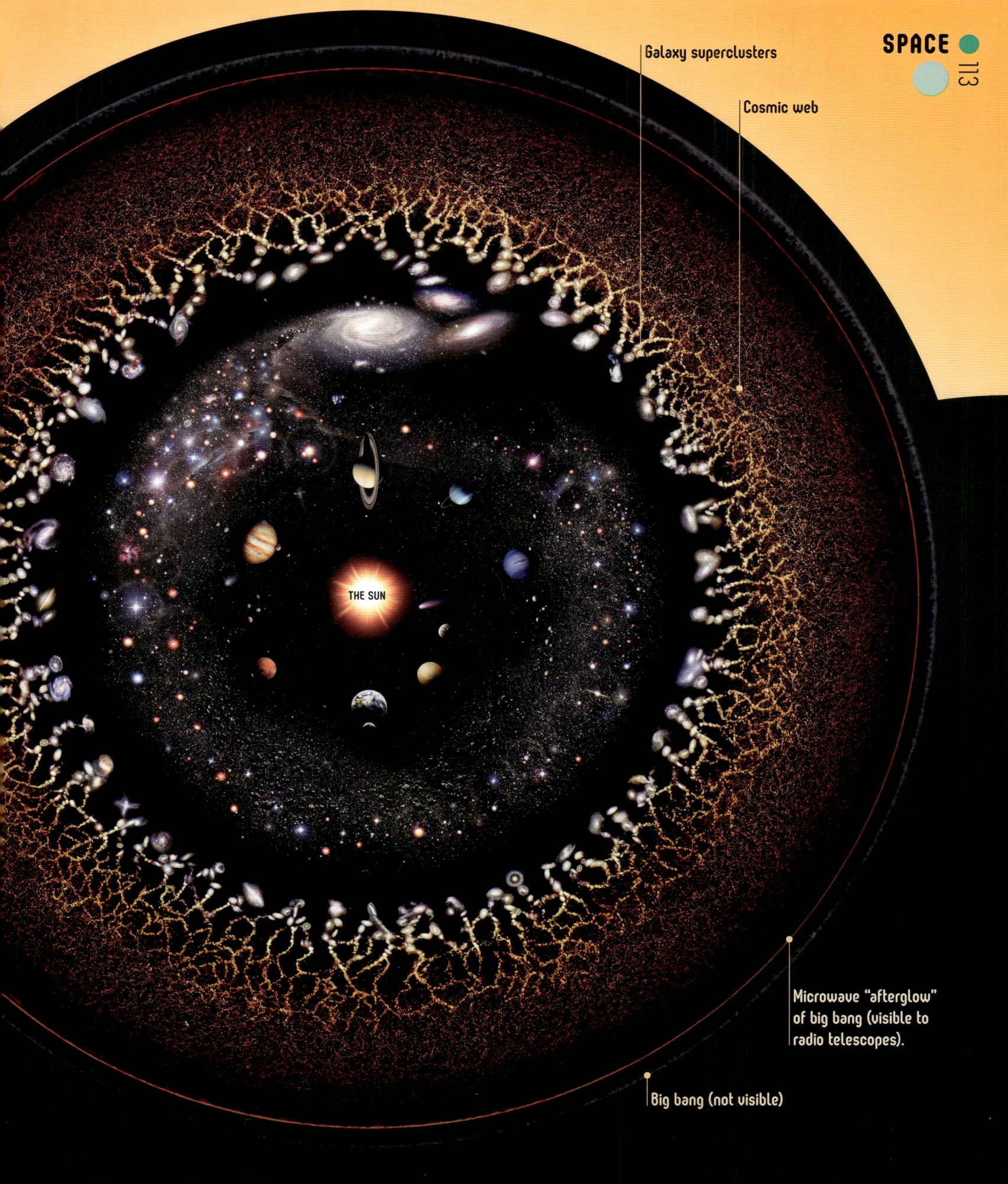

Earth from space
Before the era of satellites, map-making was a laborious process. Today, more than 1,000 Earth-observation satellites provide real-time views of every point on the planet. These false-colour images are from infrared satellites, which capture data regardless of cloud cover or time of day. Top left: centre-pivot irrigation fields in the Sahara (vegetation appears red). Lower left and upper right: river deltas in Siberia. Lower right: valleys folded by tectonic movements in the Moroccan desert.

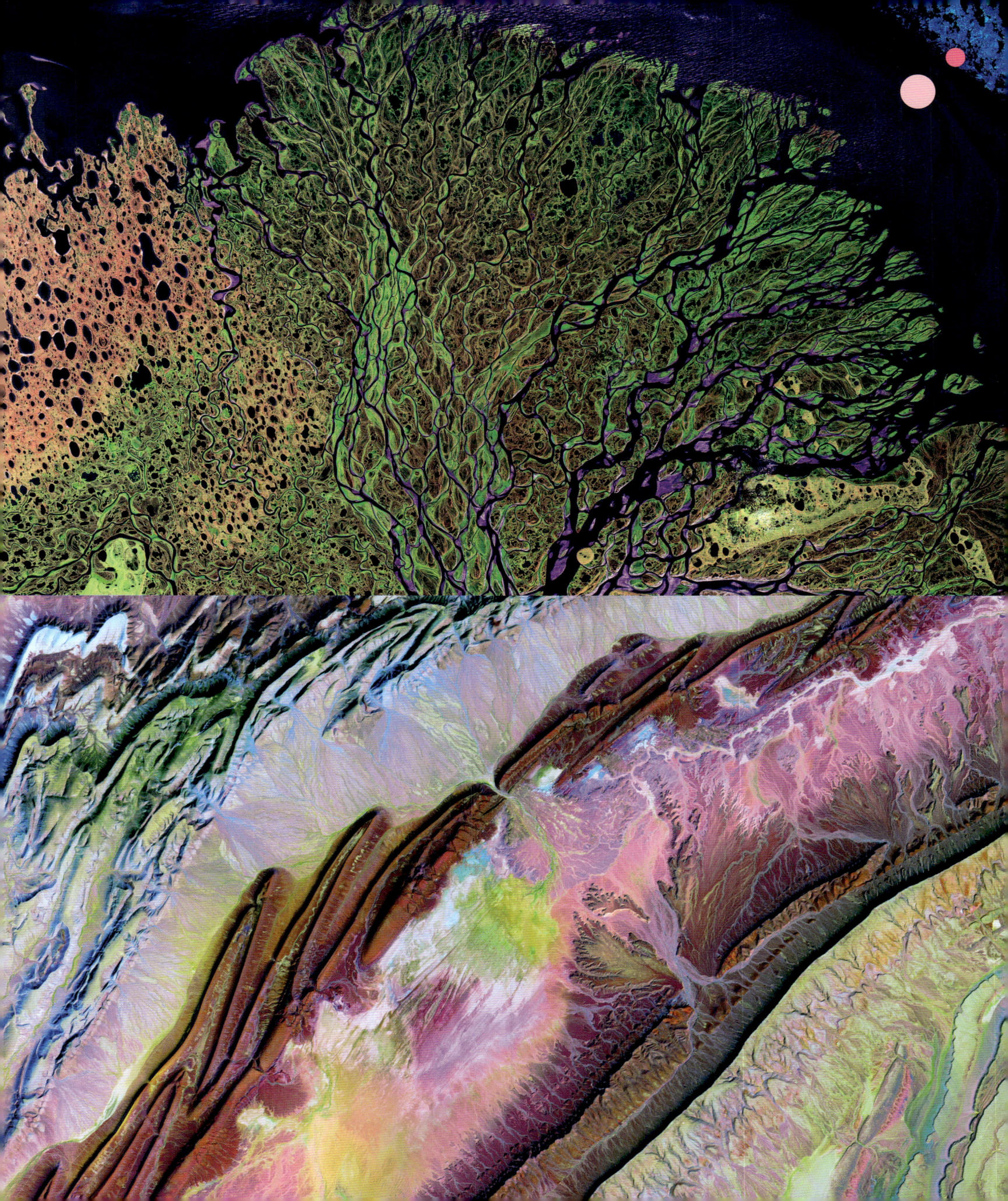

HISTORY

Searching for treasure with metal detectors is a popular hobby in the UK, which is why so many hoards have been found there.

Egypt was an important grain producer for the empire, especially along the fertile banks of the River Nile.

Israel has a large number of archaeological digs, which is why so many hoards have been found there.

100 million people lived under Roman rule at the height of the empire.

This modern reconstruction of a Greek warship is very similar to the ships the Romans used.

Paving the way
Even in far-flung parts of the Empire, such as Britain, the Romans built long, straight, paved roads to make travel for their troops and the transportation of goods easier.

Gold jewellery
One of the largest and most impressive hoards of Roman treasure was found in Norfolk, England. It includes exquisite gold jewellery, such as this ornate woman's armlet, and around 15,000 gold and silver coins.

Skilled seafarers
The Romans' military might and sailing skills played a key role in the spread of the empire. Their warships were long galleys powered by banks of oars on either side. Their trade ships were shorter and sail powered with deep hulls.

HISTORY

Where the treasure lies
Most of the gold dots indicating Roman hoards are within the same geographical area as the Empire. However, hoards have been found as far afield as eastern China thanks to trade networks.

There was high demand among wealthy Romans for silks from China. The silks were taken to India – Rome's eastern trade hub – to be sold, and Roman coins found their way back to China.

Empire at its peak
Starting in Italy, the Roman Empire spread to conquer vast swathes of Europe, North Africa, and the Mediterranean, reaching its greatest extent 117 C.E. The hostile deserts of Africa and Arabia and the dense forests of northern Europe remained unconquered.

Precious metals
Roman ships sailed to India to buy spices, silk, and other goods. Indian merchants insisted on being paid in gold and silver. They often made deep cuts in the coins to check they were solid gold or silver and not forgeries.

Ancient Rome was one of the largest and long-lived empires in history. And wherever the Romans went, they left a lasting legacy – from running water and paved roads to buried treasure. The Romans buried hoards of coins to protect them from theft or taxes and to make offerings to the gods. This map shows the location of every hoard found in modern times – a total of 13,800 hoards in 72 countries. It reveals that the reach of Rome extended far beyond the empire's border.

Roman treasure

MAPPING ROMAN HOARDS

- Indian Ocean
- Persian Gulf
- East Asia has few cities because knowledge of the region was limited.
- Lakes and rivers are green.
- Mountain ranges are orange and purple.
- Each city is marked by a circle and Arabic name.
- Caspian Sea

The Book of Roger

King Roger II of Sicily (1095–1154) yearned to know what the world was really like. In 1138, he asked Muhammad al-Idrisi, an Arab traveller and scholar, to make him the ultimate map of the world. Completed in 1154, the *Kitab Rujar* (Book of Roger) covered Europe, Asia, and northern Africa – at that time, Europeans had no knowledge of southern Africa, the Americas, or Australia. Al-Idrisi studied existing maps and interviewed travellers about places they had visited. His careful research resulted in the most detailed world map that anyone had ever seen.

THE WORLD KNOWN TO EUROPEANS IN 1154

HISTORY

Red Sea | Egypt | Mediterranean Sea | The south of Africa appears landlocked, suggesting the mapmakers did not know it was possible to sail all around it.

A non-existent river is shown flowing west across the Sahara desert.

The island of Sicily is oversized because of its importance to King Roger.

Turkey | Greece

Assembling a masterpiece
Al-Idrisi's book contained 70 separate maps that could be joined together to make a single map of the known world, as above. The maps followed Islamic mapmaking tradition, with south at the top.

Wonder of the world
On the coast of Egypt, where the River Nile's many branches flow into the Mediterranean Sea, al-Idrisi included the Lighthouse of Alexandria. This tower stood more than 100 m (300 ft) tall, and was one of the Seven Wonders of the Ancient World.

Lighthouse of Alexandria

The island of Britain
Al-Idrisi's text describes Britain as being shaped like an ostrich's head. The long pointed beak represents Cornwall, while the oval sticking out at the bottom is Scotland. Al-Idrisi writes of flourishing towns and fertile land, but notes that, "all is in the grip of perpetual winter".

The world in 1375

THE MOST ACCURATE WORLD MAP OF THE MEDIEVAL ERA

In the Atlantic Ocean is a compass rose – the first one known on a sailing chart. Shaped like a star, it shows which way is north, south, east, and west.

England is shown with the king's coat of arms: three gold lions on a red banner.

Sweden

The coastlines and ports of Europe, by then well known to sailors, are accurately drawn.

A Turkish bey, or chieftain, is shown in traditional dress.

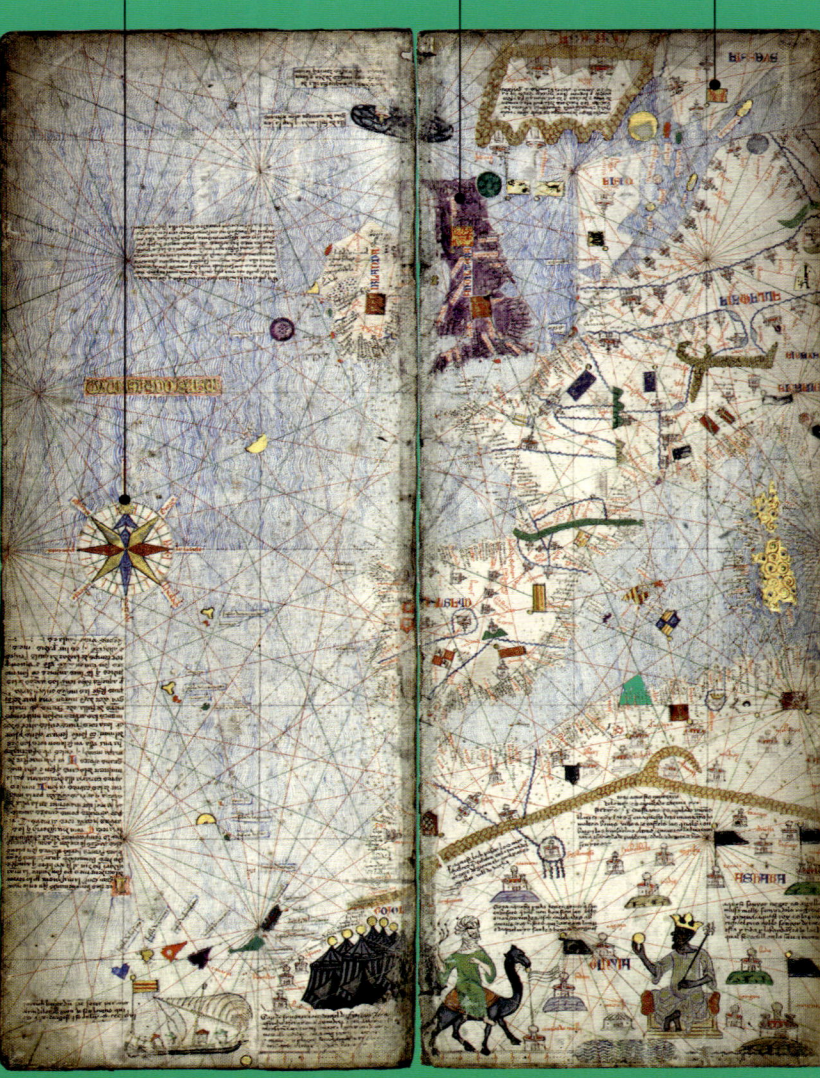

Sicily and other territories ruled by the King of Aragon, who commissioned the map, are highlighted with gold.

The richest man in the world
In the 14th century, the Mali empire in West Africa grew immensely rich by mining and trading gold and salt. Tales of Mali's wealth reached Europe, and its ruler, Musa I, was said to be the richest man in the world. On the map, Mansa (emperor) Musa is shown holding a large piece of gold.

The map is **3 metres** (10 ft) long and painted on animal skin, which was stretched and treated to use as paper.

HISTORY

123

Two centuries after the Book of Roger, a Spanish mapmaker from Mallorca, Abraham Cresques, created an even more extraordinary map of the world. Cresques drew on the latest sailing charts, which meant distances were more accurate than the travellers' accounts of journey times used previously. Also known as The Catalan Atlas, Cresques's map reveals an impressive knowledge and understanding of other peoples and lands.

Cresques populated the map with foreign leaders, such as the Mongol ruler of the time, Jani Beg.

The map was designed to be laid flat and viewed from different angles, so some text and figures appear upside down.

The devil is shown as a batlike creature with wings.

India is correctly drawn as a large triangular peninsula for the first time.

In places where Cresques had little information about place names, rulers, or geographical features, he filled the space with illustrations of biblical stories or mythical creatures, such as this mermaid in the Indian Ocean.

The Travels of Marco Polo

The map shows Marco Polo, a famous explorer who went on an epic journey from Venice to China and back again 100 years before the map was drawn. Cresques drew on Polo's stories about Asian places, people, and animals.

Evil king Gog

The map features the mythical evil king Gog riding a horse. According to European myths, Gog was in league with the devil and was prophesied to bring death and destruction to the world.

Turning iron into gold
Fra Mauro includes some fantastical-sounding places, such as a lake on one Indian Ocean island that was said to turn iron into gold. His description next to the island says he is merely reporting what he was told, which suggests he didn't believe it himself.

Egyptian pyramids
Among the many monuments shown on the map are some familiar ones, such as the pyramids of Egypt beside the River Nile. Fra Mauro adds a note beside them saying, "It is said that the pharaohs stored their grain inside them".

Palace of the emperor
Until the 19th century, China was called Cathay by Europeans. The domes of the emperor's palace are embellished with gold leaf. Fra Mauro writes beside it that when the emperor travels, he sits in a gold and ivory carriage decorated with priceless gemstones and drawn by a white elephant.

Small islands around the circumference of the map symbolize the edge of the known world. Beyond them, Fra Mauro says, no one can survive.

A world of wonders

This beautiful map was created by a Venetian monk named Fra Mauro around 1450 for the Republic of Venice. It was the first medieval map to show the whole of the African continent. Glinting with gold, the map measures more than 2 m (6 ft) across and shows a wonderful world of fine cities, palaces, exotic islands, and trade opportunities – one that was just opening up to European explorers.

The world in 1450
Fra Mauro interviewed travellers who visited him in his small monastery room on an island in the Venetian lagoon, northern Italy. The map represents the world described to him, including Africa, Asia, and Europe (but not yet the Americas). South is at the top, as in Islamic maps.

FRA MAURO'S MAP OF THE WORLD

HISTORY

125

Fra Mauro wrote about 3,000 inscriptions in red and blue describing the places he included on the map.

Morocco

Spain

Italy

British Isles

Scandinavia

Russia

A crater on the Moon

is named after Fra Mauro, in honour of his contribution to world cartography.

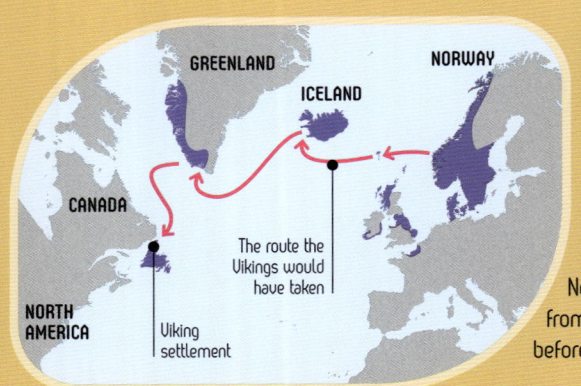

Did the Vikings get there first?

Columbus became famous for being the first European to discover the Americas, but archaeological evidence suggests the Vikings beat him to it. In 1960, Norwegian explorers found remains of a Viking settlement on the coast of Newfoundland, Canada, dating from 1000 CE, which is 500 years before Columbus.

Mistaken identity

Between 1492 and 1504, Columbus made four voyages to the Americas, looking for a westward sea route to Asia, where he hoped to find precious gold and spices. He landed on several Caribbean islands, as well as Central and South America (not North America), but was always convinced he had reached the Indies.

It's thought the Americas are painted green because Europeans were impressed by lush forests they saw there.

Red and white flags mark the islands Columbus claimed for King Ferdinand and Queen Isabella of Spain.

The Caribbean islands that Columbus explored are mapped in detail, compared to the American mainland, which was still unfamiliar.

This illustration shows St Christopher, the patron saint of travellers, carrying the baby Christ safely over water.

The equator is marked in red.

Columbus called indigenous Americans

Indians

because he thought he'd reached "the Indies" (South and East Asia).

Columbus mistook the island of Cuba for China.

The compass rose contains an image of the Virgin and Child, a symbol of Catholic faith.

In 1492, Christopher Columbus made a voyage that would change history. Although he never realized it, he had discovered the Americas, paving the way for Europeans to colonize the "New World".

This famous map was created in 1500 by Spanish navigator Juan de la Cosa, who sailed in the same fleet as Columbus. It was the first to show the Americas – but not in their entirety. De la Cosa deliberately placed the new land on the left edge of his map because only the eastern seaboard was explored. What lay further west – and whether the land was part of Asia or a whole new continent – was unknown.

A New World

THE FIRST MAP OF AMERICA

Uncharted territory

On the chart, the Americas stand out as a vast green landmass yet to be explored. By contrast, the "Old World" of Europe, Africa, and Asia, which de la Cosa knew more about, is packed with place names and illustrations.

HISTORY

127

West Africa's coast and interior are highly detailed, as by now the Portuguese had explored it in detail.

British Isles

Each port is labelled, including Genoa, where Columbus came from.

As in earlier maps such as the Catalan Atlas (page 122), the map depicts mythical rulers, including the Queen of Sheba.

The area of the map showing Asia is vague, suggesting de la Cosa had limited sources for this part of the world.

Three wise men
As in other medieval maps that were commissioned by Christian rulers, de la Cosa's map features scenes from the Bible. Here, the three wise men are shown on their way to Bethlehem bringing gifts of gold, frankincense, and myrrh to the new Christ child.

Taste of the Americas
European, Asian, and African diets would be quite different if it weren't for Columbus. Potatoes, peppers, corn, tomatoes, chillies, pineapple, and cacao (used to make chocolate) were all shipped from the Americas. Many grew well in European soil and provided people with exciting new foods and flavours.

POTATO    BELL PEPPER

CACAO

America's birth certificate

THE MAP THAT NAMED A CONTINENT

In 1507, the German mapmaker Martin Waldseemüller drew the very first world map to show the Americas as separate from Asia. He also gave it the name we use today. Waldseemüller chose the name "America" in honour of Italian explorer Amerigo Vespucci, who claimed that the lands lying to the west of Europe were an entirely different continent, not part of Asia as was previously thought.

The mountains on the west coast of the very strange-looking North America are probably a lucky guess. They do exist, but no Europeans had been there at the time.

The map shows Ptolemy, a scholar of ancient Greece, whose world map influenced European mapmakers for more than 1,000 years.

Lost and found
Hundreds of copies of Waldseemüller's map were printed in 1507 along with an accompanying booklet describing it. The booklets survived, but the maps disappeared and nobody saw one for centuries – until 1901, when this single surviving copy was found in the library of a German castle.

Cuba
Waldseemüller named the island of Cuba "Isabella" after the Spanish queen Isabella I of Castile.

South America
Portuguese and Spanish sailors had explored areas of South America, so this continent is more detailed than North America, although it also has a very strange shape. The name "America" appears in what is now Argentina.

South Africa pokes out of the frame at the bottom. European sailors had by now sailed all around it and discovered it to extend further south than in early world maps by the Greek philosopher Ptolemy.

HISTORY

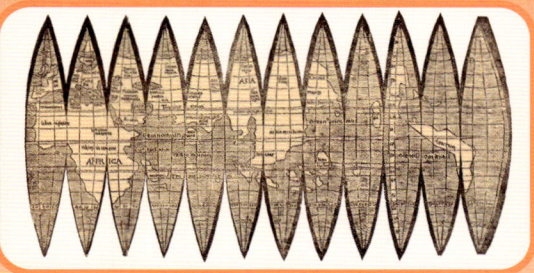

Do-it-yourself globe
As well as creating the detailed world map shown below, Waldseemüller made a much simpler version designed to be cut out and made into a globe.

Oddly, this small map of the Americas does not have a gap between the two continents, as on the main map.

Italian explorer and author Amerigo Vespucci went on at least two voyages (possibly four) to the Americas between 1497 and 1504. His accounts were published and became a smash hit in Europe at the time.

One curious mystery about this map is that it includes the Pacific Ocean, which wasn't discovered by Europeans until 1513 – six years after Waldseemüller's map.

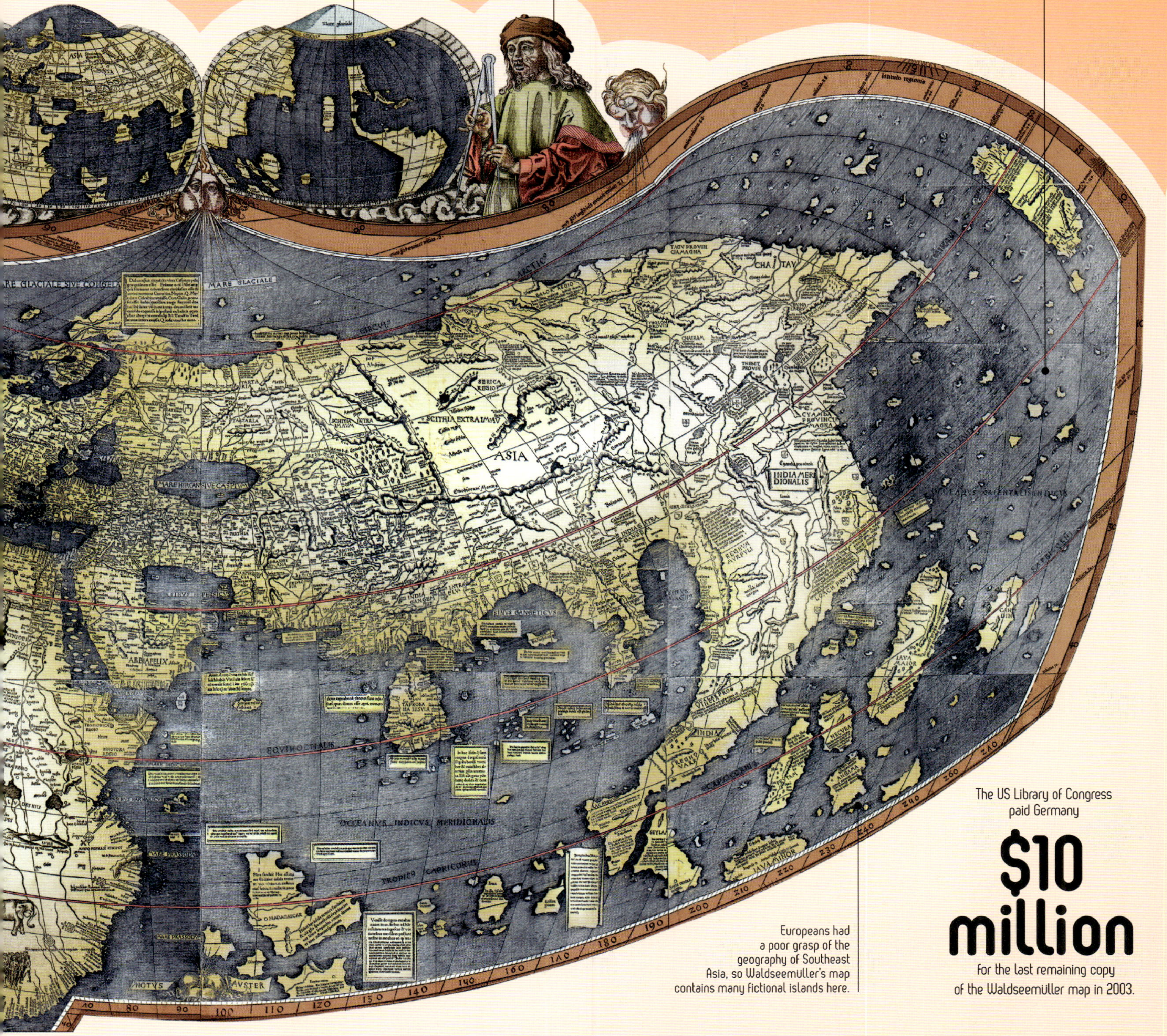

Europeans had a poor grasp of the geography of Southeast Asia, so Waldseemüller's map contains many fictional islands here.

The US Library of Congress paid Germany **$10 million** for the last remaining copy of the Waldseemüller map in 2003.

Attack on Vienna

A MAP OF A CITY AT WAR

This map is an unusual 360-degree aerial view of the walled city of Vienna and and its surroundings during a brutal battle in the year 1529. The Turkish army led by sultan Suleiman the Magnificent surrounded the city during a war between the Turkish and Austrian empires. Against the odds, the Viennese successfully defended their city, forcing the Turks to retreat. The map takes a view of the battle from on high, capturing key moments from the three-week attack in a single image.

The many tents in the enemy encampments indicate the size of the Turkish army.

Austrians and Turks fought on horseback. The Turks are shown wearing turbans and the Austrian soldiers are in suits of armour.

21,000
Austrian soldiers defended Vienna against more than 100,000 Turks.

Sacking and burning
The Turks ransacked the land and burned villages outside the city walls. It is said that they also kidnapped and then enslaved any surviving women and children.

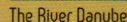
The River Danube

The circular shape conveys the sense of a city surrounded and attacked on all sides.

Mystery artist
German printer Nikolaus Meldemann, who published the map in 1530, visited Vienna after the battle and bought the original map from an artist who had watched the battle from the top of St Stephen's Cathedral, which still stands today. The artist – whose name remains a mystery – sketched events as they happened.

16,000
Turkish soldiers lost their lives during the siege.

HISTORY

131

At one point, Suleiman's army succeeded in breaching the wall with an explosion, but the rubble blocked their way into the city.

Camel trains

Suleiman's army arrived by horse and camel, neither of which was much use against a fortified city. The camels were particularly unsuited to the rain-soaked terrain. The Turkish Empire was a huge global power at the time, and Suleiman's ambition was to conquer the whole of Europe.

St Stephen's Cathedral, at the heart of the city, was used as a watchtower.

The brutality of war

It seems the Turks weren't the only ones to commit atrocious acts during the battle. This grisly scene in the city appears to show two Turkish prisoners being tortured or executed while a crowd of Austrians look on.

A wall of fortifications surrounded the city.

The Austrians defended the city with guns and pikes (long poles tipped with spears).

The Turks set fire to buildings outside the city.

Whirling beast
Beside Norway is a whirlpool swallowing a ship. Magnus describes this as a beast called "the horrible charybdis". It is thought this represents a dangerous tidal current off Norway's coast.

Hungry serpent
A huge sea serpent is shown wrapping itself around a ship. Magnus describes it as 60 m (200 ft) long, with sharp scales and flaming eyes, "plucking sailors from their ships to devour them".

Under attack
In several places, the sea creatures are shown attacking each other. Here some sort of baleen whale and its calf are being hunted by an orca (killer whale).

Iceland is filled with volcanoes described as having peaks "glistening with eternal snow" and bases "flaming with eternal fire".

Sailors try to scare off two whales by blowing trumpets and throwing barrels overboard to distract them.

On the Faroe Islands, men climb on a beached whale and chop it up for meat.

Two men light a fire on the back of a whale, perhaps having mistaken it for an island.

Scotland

Orkney Islands

Shetland Islands

HISTORY

133

Norwegian soldiers with bows and arrows are shown travelling on skis.

Baltic Sea

A giant man standing over a lion represents Starchaterus, a Swedish fighter who, Magnus says, was famous throughout Europe.

Wind roses show the direction of the winds for sailors and navigators.

The fearsome kraken
A famous sea monster in Nordic legend is the kraken, which crushes ships with its many arms. Magnus writes that it had "sharp horns round about, like a tree rooted up by the roots".

It took Olaus Magnus **12 years** to research and make the map.

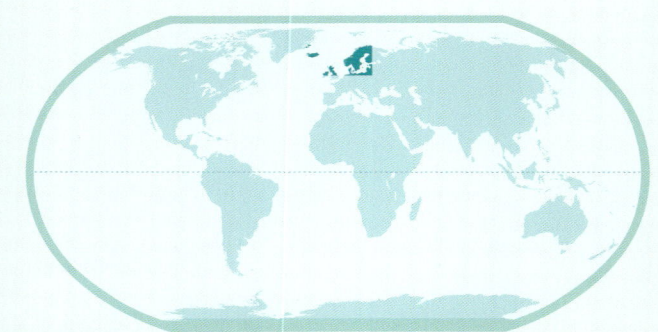

Here be dragons!

This map, known as the Carta Marina, was the first to show the far north of Europe in such detail, but what makes it so famous is the host of fiendish monsters that fill the seas. It was published in 1539 by Olaus Magnus, a Swedish Catholic priest. The map features lively illustrations of daily life on land and at sea, where many of the sailors are fighting for their lives against foul sea beasts.

SEA MONSTERS OF NORTHERN EUROPE

World War II wrecks
This map shows the locations of 14,500 ships that were attacked and sunk by battleships, submarines, and aircraft during World War II (1939–45). Most were non-combat merchant ships (blue dots) carrying equipment, food, fuel, and raw materials needed for the war effort.

Stealth attacks
Over 3,000 ships were sunk by torpedoes from German submarines during the war. However, the submarines weren't immune to detection. U-352 (right) was one of 785 to be sunk.

RMS *Lancastria*
This British cruise liner carrying troops was hit by a German plane in 1940. A bomb went down a chimney and exploded in the engine room. The ship sank 20 minutes later.

Admiral Graf Spee
This German battleship, built to outrun and outgun most enemy ships, was sunk by her own crew off the coast of Uruguay following a battle with three British warships.

SS *Thistlegorm*
The steamship SS *Thistlegorm* sank in the Red Sea in 1940. Its cargo of motorcycles and other military kit has since become covered in sponges and corals to form an artificial reef that is now home to hundreds of fish and other creatures.

Deep down on the seabed lie sunken ships, lost treasure, and other relics – some hundreds, or even thousands, of years old. Ever since humankind set sail, many voyages have ended in disaster with the accidental or deliberate sinking of vessels and their precious cargoes. Shipwrecks were more common near coastlines, with their treacherous currents and rocks, and many occured at times of war. The world's seas are littered with thousands of wrecks of boats, ships, planes, submarines, and even spacecraft, only some of which have been found and recovered. Untold numbers still lie hidden on the sea floor, awaiting discovery.

Shipwrecks
MAPPING THE SEA'S SECRETS

HISTORY 135

The Spanish galleon *San José* sank off Colombia in 1708 carrying treasure now believed to be worth

$17 billion.

Fire power
This tank was on board one of a fleet of ships sunk in a massive air attack by US forces on a Japanese naval base in 1944 and 1945. More than 100 ships and aircraft form a giant deep-sea wreck site.

- Warship
- Non-combatant ship
- ∘ Smaller ship
- ○ Larger ship

Space graveyard
Craft of another type lie on the seabed in the middle of the South Pacific. Point Nemo is further from land than any other point on the planet and is where rockets, satellites, and spacecraft are directed to crash, out of harm's way.

RMS *Titanic*
It was nature, not war, that sank RMS *Titanic* in 1912. Just four days into her maiden (first) voyage, the luxury liner struck an iceberg that sent her tumbling 3,800 m (12,500 ft) to the floor of the North Atlantic Ocean.

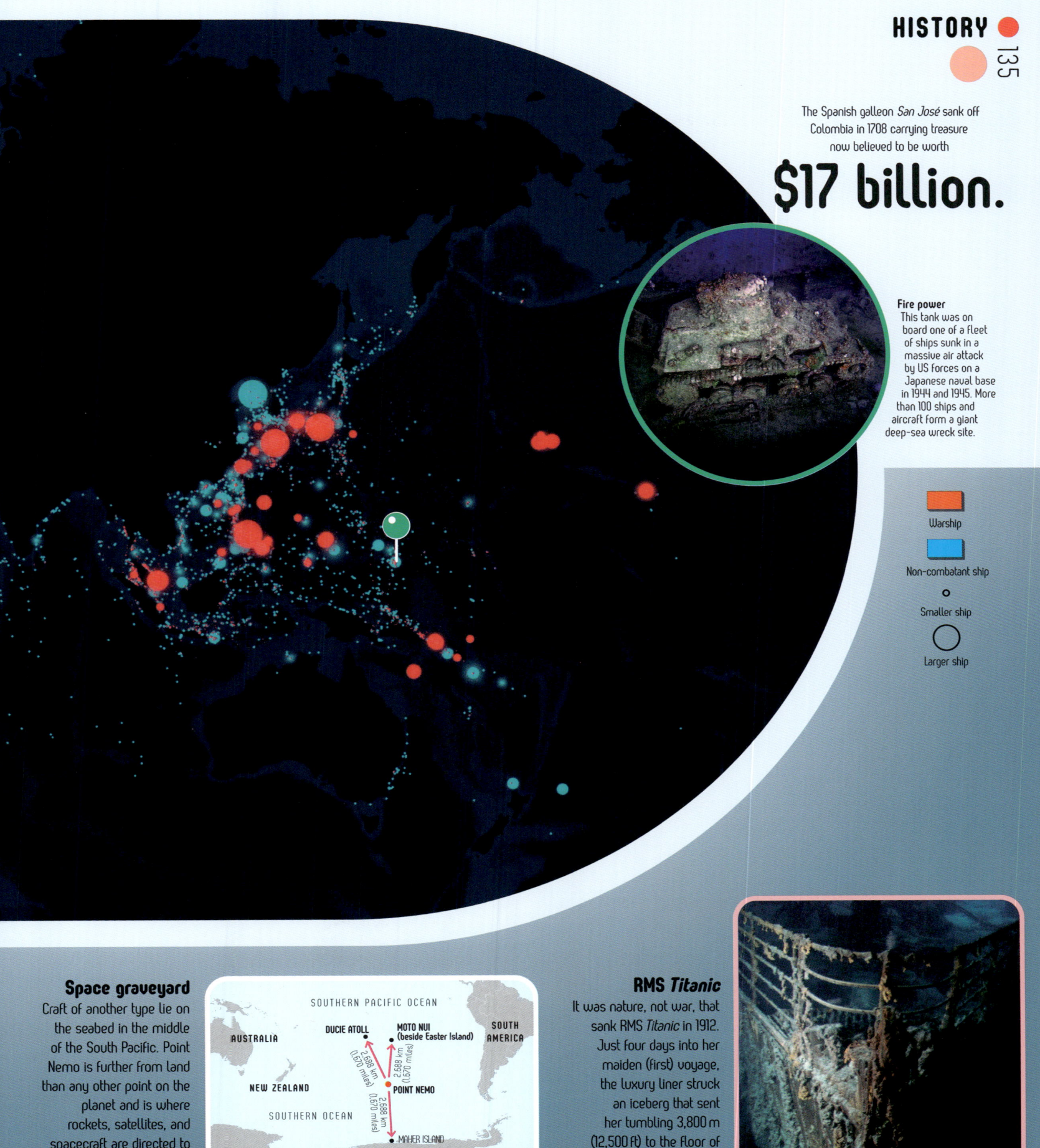

Rock solid North America

MAPPING NORTH AMERICA'S GEOLOGY

Earth's third-largest continent is a jigsaw of landscapes. Its underlying rocks are just as varied as its surface and include some of the oldest rocks on the planet.

Geologists use maps like this one to reconstruct the past. The colours show the age of the rock, from ancient to newly formed. Studying the bands of colour lets us see where mountains and uplands have been raised by the collision of plates, and then eroded away by water and ice.

Scoured by ice
The pink zone on the the map is the Canadian Shield – the ancient geological core of North America. During the ice ages, it was covered with glaciers up to 3.2 km (2 miles) thick. They crept across the continent, gouging out the Great Lakes and creating hundreds of thousands of smaller lakes.

Western mountains
While most of central and eastern North America is flat, the west is covered with mountains. Earth's crust crumpled and rose here because of a collision between two tectonic plates: the Pacific Plate and the North American Plate.

This computer-generated map makes higher ground look 3D. The colours come from a 1965 geological map, each colour representing a different age or type of rock.

Most of Greenland is covered by a vast ice sheet, which is the world's second-largest body of ice.

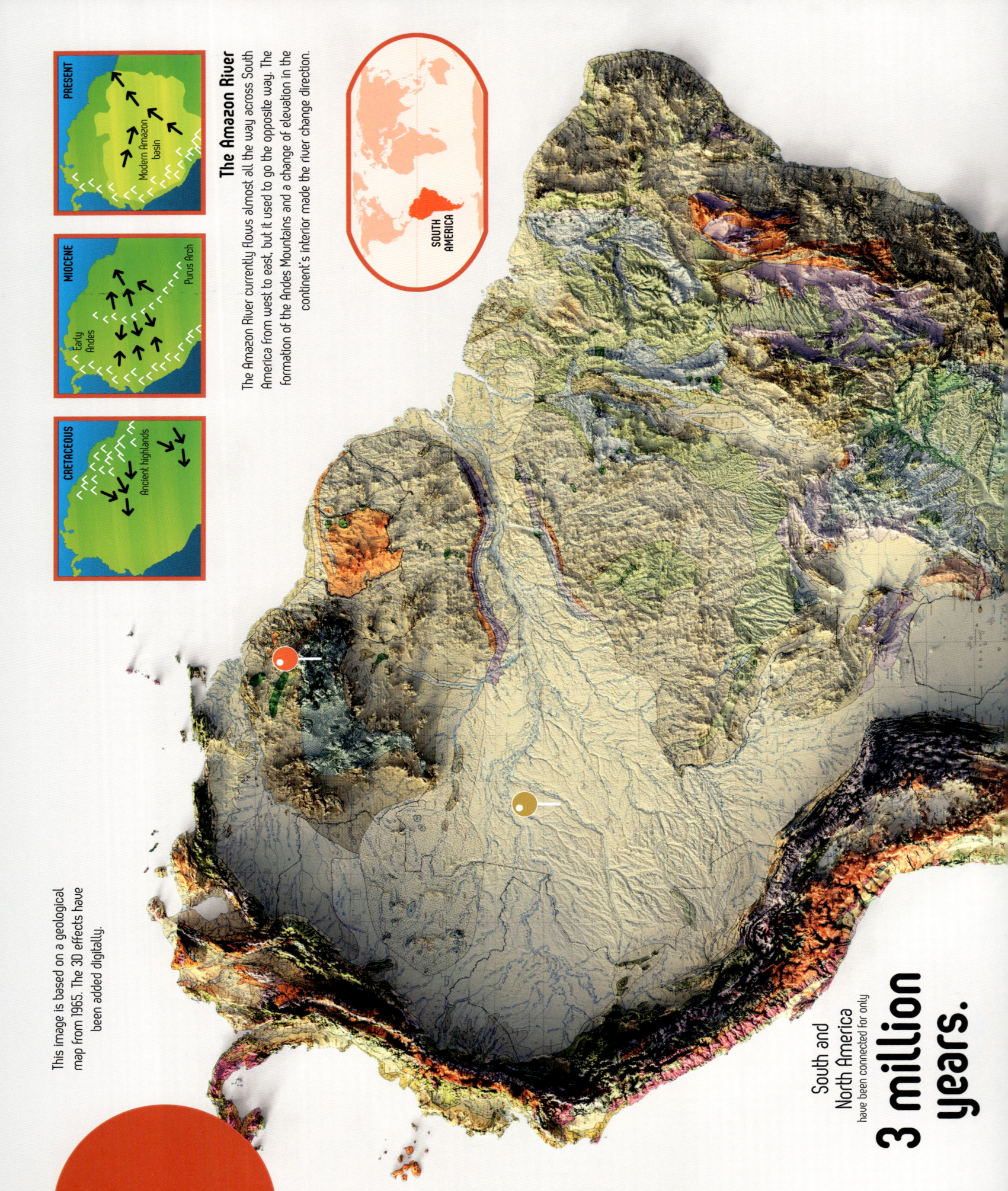

Rock solid South America

MAPPING SOUTH AMERICA'S GEOLOGY

REFERENCE

Rock age MYA = million years ago
- Quaternary sand 2.6 MYA to now
- Quaternary basalt 2.6 MYA to now
- Pliocene-Miocene 23–2.6 MYA
- Cretaceous sand 146–66 MYA
- Cretaceous volcanic 146–66 MYA
- Jurassic sand 200–146 MYA
- Jurassic volcanic 200–146 MYA
- Triassic sand 251–200 MYA
- Carboniferous 359–299 MYA
- Silurian 444–419 MYA
- Cambrian 539–486 MYA
- Precambrian sand 4,600–539 MYA
- Precambrian volcanic 4,600–539 MYA

The continent of South America is made up of three huge geological building blocks: two of high ground and one of low. In the north and the east are highlands – huge expanses of mountains and high plateaus. Along the west coast are the Andes Mountains. They are much younger than the highlands, and rose up as tectonic plates collided with each other. Between these two formidable barriers lie the vast, flat basins of the interior. Some of these basins are covered in such deep layers of sand and clay that they appear to be pancake flat.

The Andes

This 8,900 km (5,530 mile) long mountain chain formed 50 million years ago, when the Pacific sea floor and the South American continent collided. The two plates are still colliding today, causing frequent earthquakes and volcanic eruptions.

Guiana Highlands

The Guiana Highlands contain South America's most ancient rocks, which formed at least 1.7 billion years ago. Erosion has worn away at hard igneous and metamorphic rock, creating flat-topped mountains that tower dramatically over lower areas.

The Amazon basin

This enormous, low-lying area is covered with deep layers of sediment, dropped off by water on its long journey from the highlands to the ocean. The well-watered sandy soil supports the world's largest area of tropical forest.

This image is based on a geological map from 1958. The 3D effects have been added using computer animation.

Rock solid Africa

MAPPING AFRICA'S GEOLOGY

The world's second-largest continent is built from five vast slabs of ancient crust, which finished coming together 300 million years ago. Since then, thick layers of sedimentary rock have built up across Africa and then been heavily eroded by ice, water, and wind. The pink areas of this map reveal where ancient igneous and metamorphic rock has been exposed to the surface once again. Much of the continent is made up of huge plateaus – flat areas that are high above sea level. Lower-lying land is mainly found around Africa's coast.

REFERENCE 143

Rock ages
MYA = million years ago

 Quaternary 2.6 MYA to now

 Tertiary marine 66–2.6 MYA

 Triassic-Cretaceous 251–66 MYA

 Palaeozoic sandstone 539–251 MYA

 Precambrian 1,000–600 MYA

 Precambrian 2,000–1,000 MYA

 Precambrian 4,000–2,000 MYA

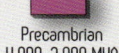 Precambrian more than 3,000 MYA

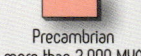 Basalt

 Volcanic rock other than basalt

The Congo basin
This vast depression covers an area of 3.4 million square kilometres (1.3 million square miles). It is criss-crossed by hundreds of rivers and streams, which support the world's second-largest rainforest. The basin sits on top of layers of sedimentary rock that formed when the area was underwater millions of years ago.

The Hoggar Mountains
The Sahara is the world's largest hot desert and covers almost a third of Africa. In the heart of this desert is an ancient mountain range: the Hoggar Mountains. Its peaks of metamorphic rock tower above the surrounding sandy desert.

Kilimanjaro is the world's
tallest
freestanding mountain.

Mount Kilimanjaro
Volcanic activity along the Great Rift Valley has created Africa's highest peaks, including the highest of them all: Mount Kilimanjaro. The peak of this dormant volcano is 5,895 m (19,341 ft) above sea level – so high that it is covered with snow all year round despite being just a few kilometres away from the tropical rainforest on its lower slopes.

Rock solid Europe

MAPPING EUROPE'S GEOLOGY

Europe is part of the larger continent of Eurasia, with the long chain of the Ural Mountains marking the boundary between Europe and Asia. The Ural Mountains are just one of Europe's mountain chains. There are others in the northeast, northwest, and along much of the northern coast of the Mediterranean Sea. Europe's southern mountains formed in a collision between its tectonic plate and the African plate. The continent also has two landlocked seas: the Black Sea and the Caspian Sea.

Iceland is the most volcanically active place in Europe as it sits on the rift between two tectonic plates.

The Scandinavian mountains are part of an ancient chain that was once joined to the Appalachian Mountains in the USA.

Italy has **9** active volcanoes.

Mediterranean Sea

Active volcanoes
The ongoing collision between the tectonic plates carrying Europe and Africa created the Alps and Pyrenees mountain ranges and the active volcanoes of southern Italy. Mount Etna in Sicily (above) is Europe's most active volcano, erupting several times every year.

Mediterranean Sea
Six million years ago, the Mediterranean Sea was cut off from the Atlantic Ocean. It dried out, leaving behind a layer of salt over a kilometre thick. Around 5.5 million years ago, the Mediterranean refilled when the Atlantic flooded through the Strait of Gibraltar in what may have been the most spectacular waterfall in Earth's history.

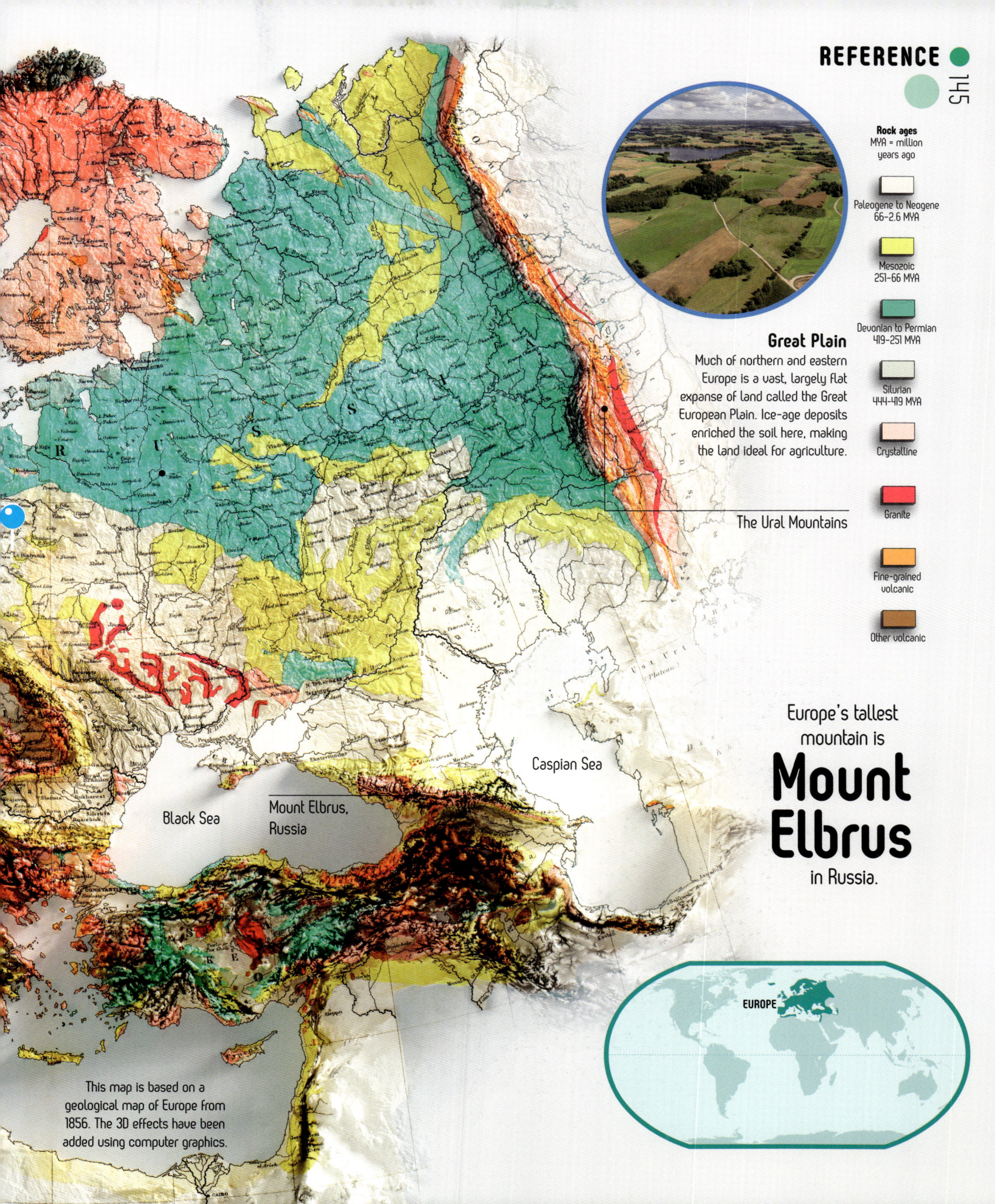

REFERENCE 145

Rock ages
MYA = million years ago

- Paleogene to Neogene 66–2.6 MYA
- Mesozoic 251–66 MYA
- Devonian to Permian 419–251 MYA
- Silurian 444–419 MYA
- Crystalline
- Granite
- Fine-grained volcanic
- Other volcanic

Great Plain
Much of northern and eastern Europe is a vast, largely flat expanse of land called the Great European Plain. Ice-age deposits enriched the soil here, making the land ideal for agriculture.

The Ural Mountains

Europe's tallest mountain is **Mount Elbrus** in Russia.

Mount Elbrus, Russia

Black Sea

Caspian Sea

EUROPE

This map is based on a geological map of Europe from 1856. The 3D effects have been added using computer graphics.

Rock solid Australia

MAPPING AUSTRALIA'S GEOLOGY

Australia is the world's smallest and flattest continent and contains some of the oldest geological wonders. Much of Western Australia is made up of two ancient blocks of rock that formed more than 3 billion years ago. Until around 30 million years ago, the Australian continent was joined to Antarctica and much nearer the South Pole. Over time, it separated and drifted north, its climate turning hot and dry. The arid climate reduced erosion by rain and rivers, preserving ancient landscapes. Today, Australia has a huge, dry, low-lying interior surrounded by an outer rim of hills and mountains.

This image is based on a geological map from around 1873. The 3D effects have been added digitally.

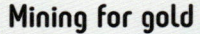
The Yilgarn craton

Mining for gold
Much of Western Australia is made up of the Yilgarn craton. This is one of the most ancient parts of Earth's crust and includes mineral grains that are 4.4 billion years old. The rock here is rich in gold, iron, and nickel, which makes it an important area for mining.

AUSTRALIA

The Jack Hills

Ancient rocks
The oldest grains of rock discovered on Earth so far are from the Jack Hills in Western Australia. The rocks here contain crystals of a tough mineral called zircon. Zircon contains atoms of uranium that turn to lead over millions of years. By measuring the ratio of uranium to lead, scientists worked out that the grains are 4.4 billion years old.

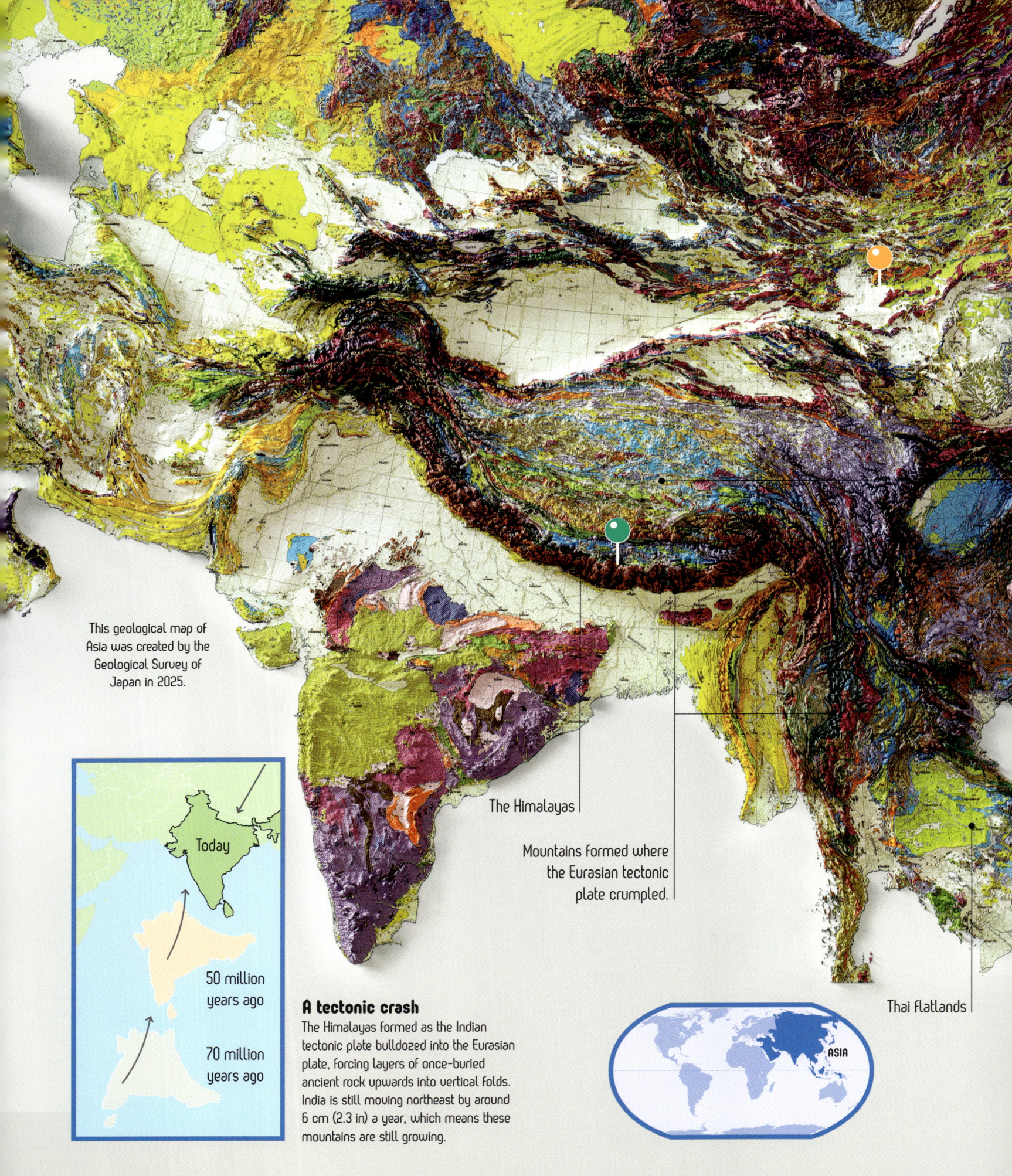

Shadowed by mountains
The Gobi Desert is dry because it is in the rain shadow of the Himalayas. All the water carried by winds from the south falls as rain or snow over the mountains. Therefore, little or no water reaches the land on the other side.

The Chinese Plain (lowlands)

The Tibetan Plateau

Rock solid Asia

MAPPING ASIA'S GEOLOGY

Earth's largest and highest continent is crowned by the Himalayas, a giant crescent of mountain ranges that formed over the last 50 million years.

This geological map reveals the colourful chaos created as the Indian subcontinent, which was once connected to Africa, collided with the mighty Eurasian tectonic plate. Mountains and high plateaus cover three-quarters of Asia, but the continent also has vast flatlands. The plateaus are high and dry, and the low-lying flatlands include some of the world's biggest floodplains and swamps.

Mountain goddess
Mount Everest in Asia has the highest peak on the planet, at 8,849 m (29,032 ft) above sea level. The mountain's Tibetan name is Chomolungma, after a local Tibetan goddess. Thousands of people have tried to climb Everest, but not all survive. Every year, several people die due to altitude sickness, falls, or cold.

REFERENCE

Rock age
MYA = million years ago

 Quaternary 2.6 MYA to now

 Neogene 23–2.6 MYA

 Paleogene 66–23 MYA

 Cretaceous 145–66 MYA

 Jurassic 200–146 MYA

 Triassic sandstone 251–200 MYA

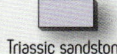 Triassic volcanic 251–200 MYA

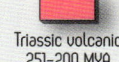 Permian 299–251 MYA

 Devonian–Silurian 444–359 MYA

 Ordovician 486–444 MYA

 Proterozoic 2,500–542 MYA

 Archaean 4,000–2,500 MYA

Types of map

There are many different types of map, each designed to give a particular view of a place of interest. General-purpose maps combine several kinds of information, while specialist maps focus on one or two subjects. As this book demonstrates, a map may represent the whole world, a tiny fraction of it, or even another planet or the universe. What nearly all maps have in common is that they try to represent a three-dimensional space on a two-dimensional page or screen while telling us something useful about it.

Political maps
These show the boundaries between countries or administrative regions and usually include major cities. This example shows the countries and states of North and Central America.

No two neighbouring countries are the same colour, making them easy to tell apart.

States or regions within the same country are the same colour but different shades.

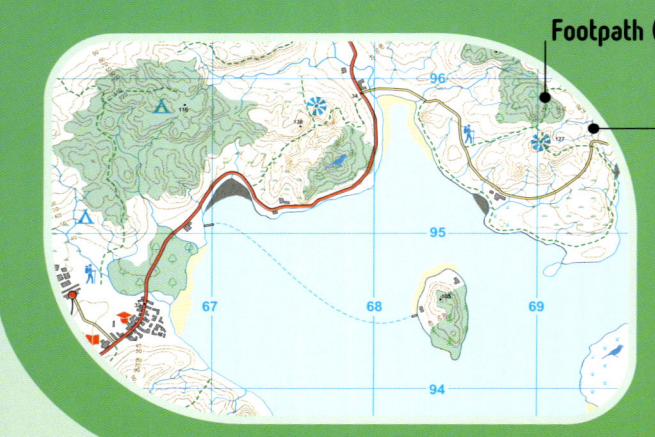

Footpath (green dashes)

River (blue line)

Topographic maps
Often used for hiking or walking, topographic maps show features of the landscape in great detail, such as the shape and height of hills.

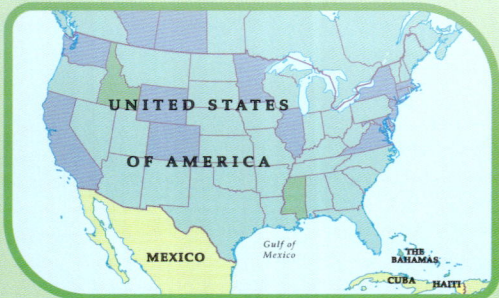

Choropleth maps
These maps use a set of distinct colours to represent data. This example shows how average income varies across different US states.

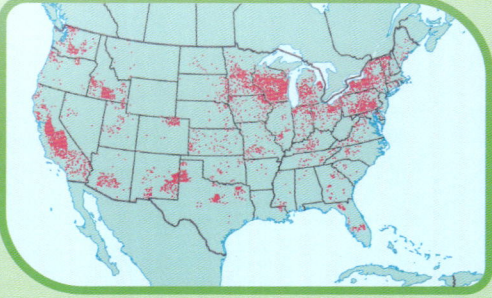

Dot maps
The dots mark events or objects – in this case one dot stands for 1,500 cows. Where many dots appear close together, we know there are thousands of cows.

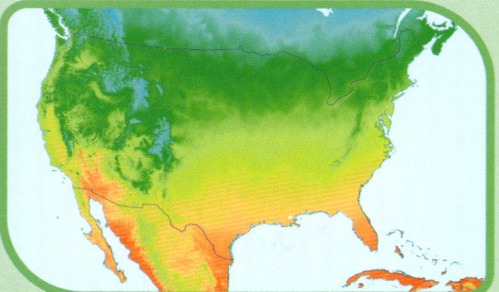

Heat maps
Heat maps use a spectrum of colour variation to show variations in data. This one shows temperature, but it works for rainfall or other kinds of data, too.

REFERENCE

151

Physical maps
Natural features such as mountains, valleys, lakes, and rivers are represented by different colours on physical maps, with the larger features named.

Lowlands are varying shades of green.

Mountains are coloured brown and grey.

The key helps us to decode the map by explaining the colours.

ELEVATION
- 2,000–4,000 m
- 1,000–2,000 m
- 500–1,000 m
- 250–500 m
- 100–250 m
- 0–100 m

Land use maps
As the name suggests, these maps show how humans exploit the land, using colours and symbols.

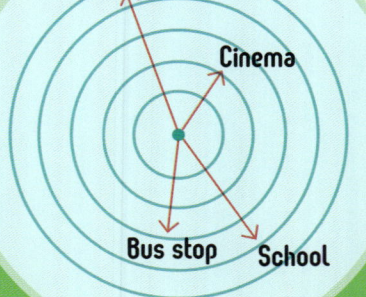

Desire-line maps
Desire-line maps show direction and movement from a location. This one maps how far away local amenities are from a person's home.

Google Maps provides more than **20 billion km** (12 billion miles) of directions every day.

Mercator and Peters projections
The Mercator projection was designed to maintain the correct shapes of continents, but their sizes are not in proportion. The Peters projection keeps the size of continents in proportion but their shapes are distorted.

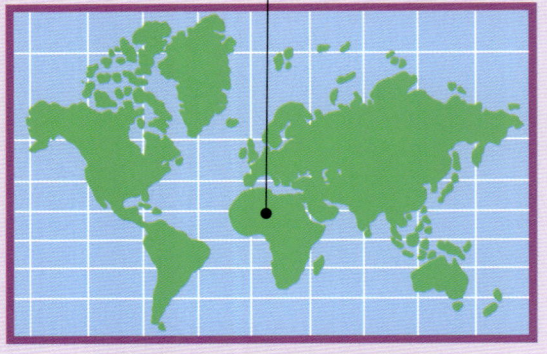

Africa is the correct shape but looks much smaller than it really is.

MERCATOR PROJECTION

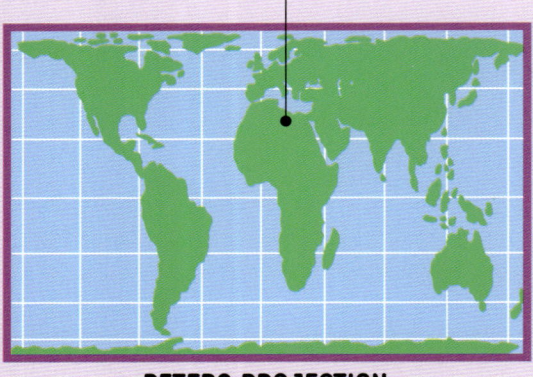

Africa covers the correct area here but looks taller and thinner than it really is.

PETERS PROJECTION

Cylindrical projections
To turn a sphere into a rectangle, the traditional method is to project points on the sphere onto a cylinder, which is then "unrolled" to make a rectangle. Cylindrical projections stretch polar regions, making them appear larger than reality.

In reality, Greenland would fit 13.5 times into Africa.

Antarctica looks bigger than any other continent but is in fact only the fifth largest.

Goode's homolosine
This projection avoids oversized polar regions by cutting "interruptions" out of ocean areas near the poles. The result looks like an orange peel and keeps the country sizes relatively accurate.

Antarctica is the correct size but broken up into four parts in this projection.

Map projections

Accurately mapping the curved surface of the globe onto a flat surface without any distortion is an impossible task – but an essential one. Mapmakers call the process projection because it works a bit like shining light through an old-fashioned film reel to cast an image on a wall. There are many different projections, some designed for a particular purpose, others more stylish than practical.

REFERENCE

Azimuthal projection

The far north and south are heavily distorted in most projections, but the azimuthal method takes one pole as the centre and maps that hemisphere (north or south) onto a disc around it. This unusual view is helpful for polar explorers.

Projecting half a sphere onto a circle gives a better map of the pole.

Conic projections

These fan-shaped maps are made by projecting part of the globe onto a cone, which is then unrolled. Two examples are shown here. Conic projections balance shape and area well and are especially useful for regional or national maps.

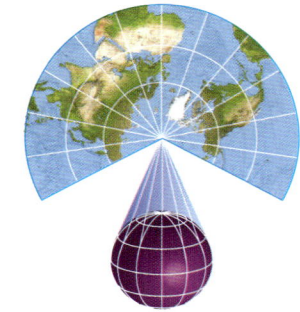

Shapes and areas are less distorted, but grid lines are angled or curved.

With its wavy grid lines, this map is not designed for plotting a course.

The Winkel tripel

German mapmaker Oswald Winkel designed his "tripel" (triple) as a compromise – it isn't a perfect representation of area, direction, or distance, but it balances all three. The curved grid lines give this two-dimensional map a bulging waistline, like Earth itself.

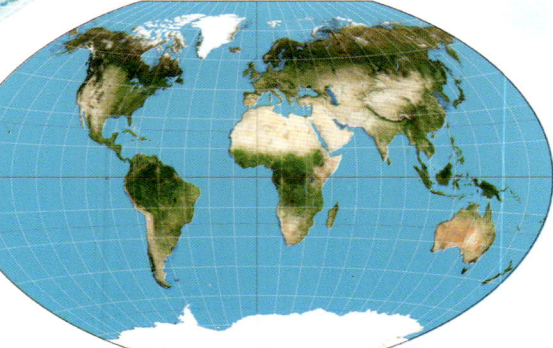

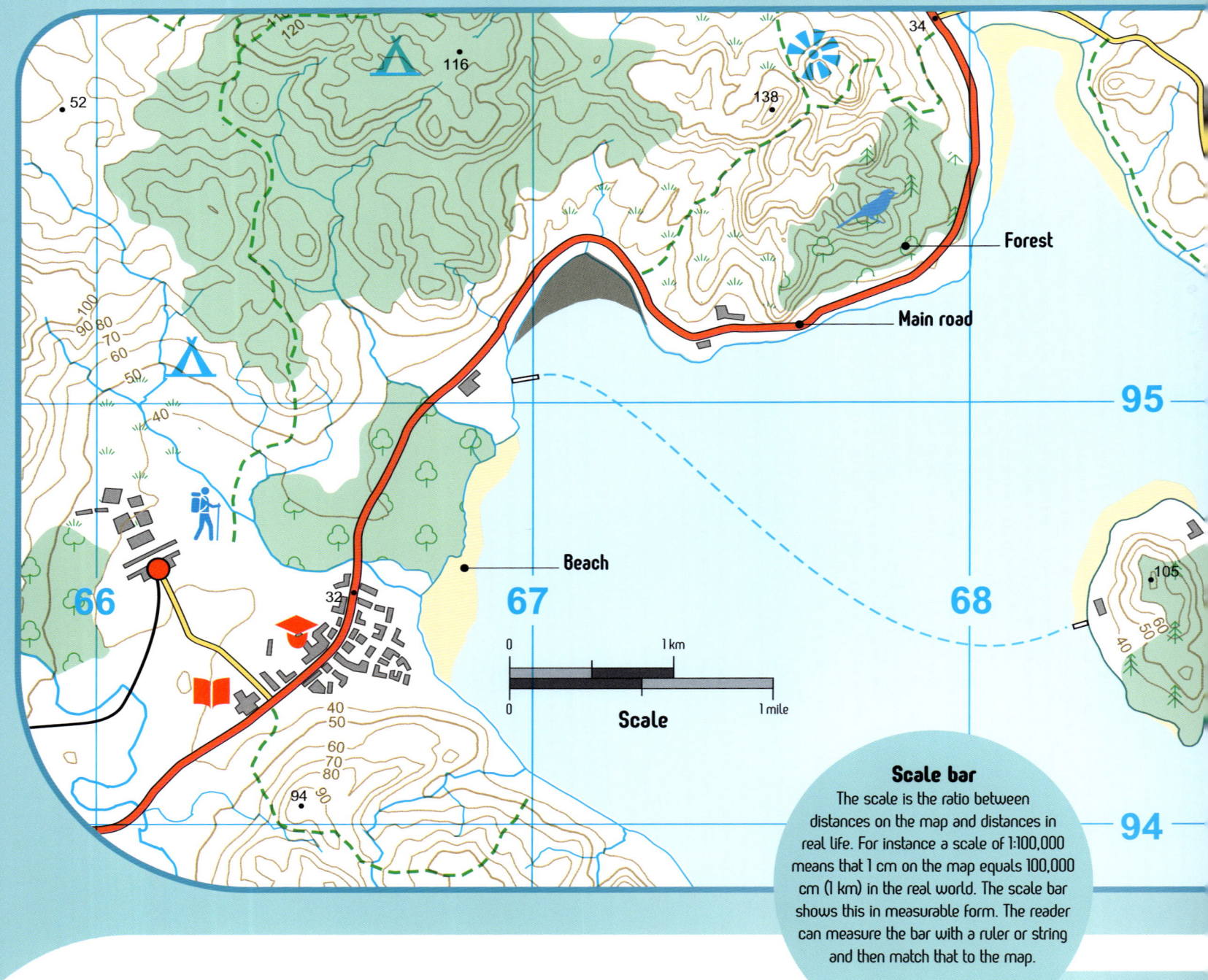

Scale bar
The scale is the ratio between distances on the map and distances in real life. For instance a scale of 1:100,000 means that 1 cm on the map equals 100,000 cm (1 km) in the real world. The scale bar shows this in measurable form. The reader can measure the bar with a ruler or string and then match that to the map.

For those who enjoy off-road adventures like hiking and camping, knowing how to read maps can be a vital, even life-saving skill.
Topographic maps are the best choice for exploring the great outdoors. They offer detailed, accurate information about a small area of land at a large scale, making them perfect for planning and finding the way. Topography refers to the vertical shape of the land – like hills and valleys – but topographic maps also show footpaths, roads, rivers, forests, marshes, and more. For those who understand the symbols, these maps are a treasure trove of information.

Reading maps

Orienteering
is a sport that combines endurance running with reading maps.

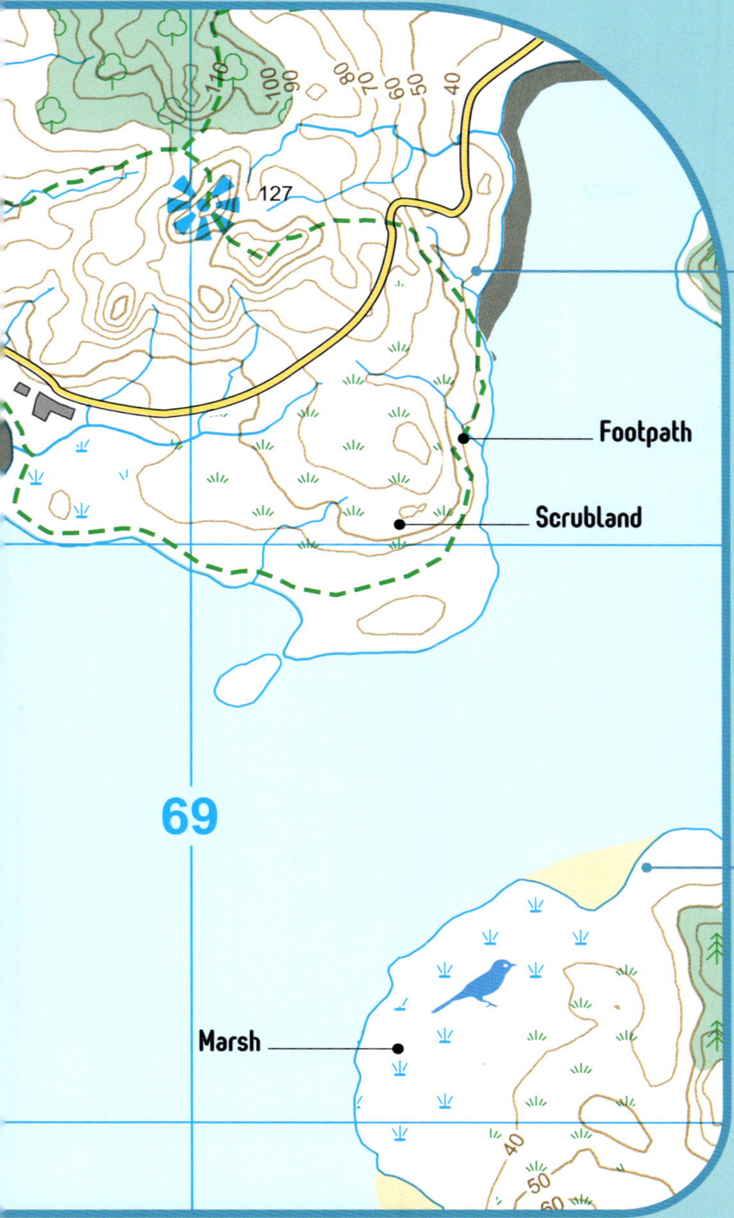

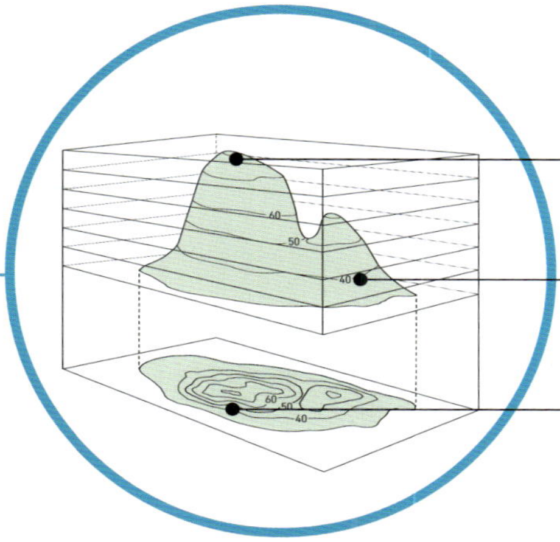

REFERENCE

155

The smallest circle represents the top of the hill.

The numbers show metres (or feet) above sea level.

Contour lines that are close together indicate a steep slope.

Contour lines
Contour lines link places of equal height above sea level. Skilled users can read these to spot slopes too steep for walking.

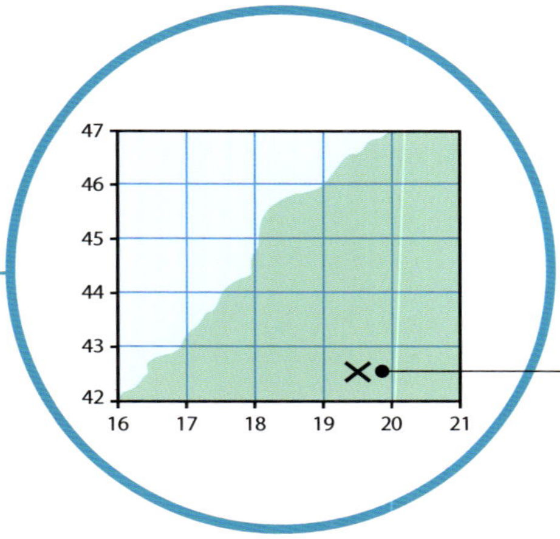

X is 19.5 squares east and 42.5 squares north, so its grid reference is 195425.

Grid references
Numbered lines form a grid of equal-sized squares on a topographic map. You can specify any point precisely with a grid reference. The "easting" (position in an east-west direction) is given first, then the "northing".

Map keys
The key explains the symbols featured on the map. Many of these are universal, so an experienced map reader will soon learn the most common symbols and rarely need to consult the key.

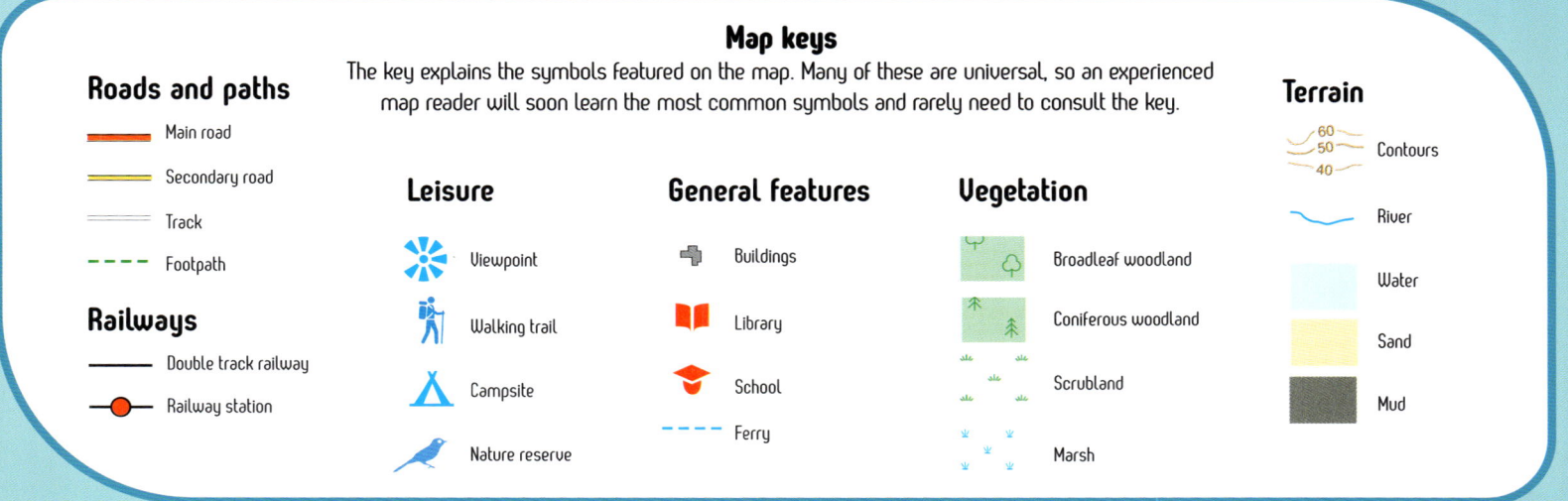

Roads and paths
- Main road
- Secondary road
- Track
- Footpath

Railways
- Double track railway
- Railway station

Leisure
- Viewpoint
- Walking trail
- Campsite
- Nature reserve

General features
- Buildings
- Library
- School
- Ferry

Vegetation
- Broadleaf woodland
- Coniferous woodland
- Scrubland
- Marsh

Terrain
- Contours
- River
- Water
- Sand
- Mud

Index

A
Africa
  camels 92, 93
  geology 142-3
  size 67
Agulhas rings 25
air 26
air pressure 26
airports, busiest 73
al-Idrisi, Muhammad 120, 121, 123
Aldrin, Buzz 105
alpacas 87, 92, 93
Alvarenga, José Salvador 11
Amazon River/basin 28-9, 140, 141
Americas
  discovery of 126
  first world map including 128-9
  food 127
Amsterdam (Netherlands) 69
Andes (South America) 140, 141
animals
  Arctic 15
  deadly 94-5
  livestock 86-7
  mapping 84-5, 90-1
  marsupials 12
  migrations 88-9, 92-3
  tracking 90-1
Antarctic Peninsula 18
Antarctica 16-19, 52, 54, 146, 152
antipodes 62-3
Antipodes Islands 63
Apollo missions 104-5
Appalachians 139, 144
Arabian Peninsula 28
Arctic Ocean 14-15
Armstrong, Neil 105
Asia
  camels 92, 93
  geology 148-9
asteroids 110
astronauts 104-5
Atlanta airport 73
Atlantic Ocean
  Amazon Delta 28
  transatlantic telegraph cable 76
atmosphere
  climate change 18
  Mars 108
  seen from space 26
  space rocks 102
aurora borealis 99
Australia
  climate 13
  GDP 65
  geology 146-7
  livestock 87, 92
  place names 54, 55
  population 50, 51
  size 12-13, 67
azimuthal projections 153

B
Bactrian camels 92, 93
Barringer Crater (Arizona, USA) 103
Batman (Turkey) 56
bees 94, 95
Beijing (China) 69
Bering Land Bridge 93
Big Bang 112
billionaires 64
birds
  migration 88-9
  tracking 90-1
bison 85
Black Sea 144
Bland (Australia) 57
boat trips, longest 78
Boca Raton (Florida, USA) 70-1
Bolivia 87
borders 52
Boring (Oregon, USA) 57
Bratislava (Slovakia) 68
Brazil
  GDP 64
  livestock 87
  size 66-7
Britain
  al-Idrisi's map 121
  Carta Marina 133

C
California (USA) 64
camel trains 131
camelids 92-3
Canada
  city lights 99
  GDP 64
  livestock 86
  tornadoes 42
Canadian Shield 138
canyons
  Grand Canyon 32-3
  under ice sheets 18
  underwater 20, 32
Cape York meteorite 102
Caribbean islands 126
Carta Marina 132-3
cartograms 86-7
Caspian Sea 144
Catalan Atlas 122-3, 127
Cathay, Emperor of 124
cattle 86, 87
  ranches 13
Central American volcanic arc 139
centre-pivot irrigation fields 114
Charybdis 132
Chicago (USA) 69
Chile, length 67
China
  GDP/wealth 64, 65
  historic maps 123, 124
  livestock 87, 92
  Roman trade with 129
choropleth maps 150
cities
  built to design 70-1
  road networks 68-9
  seen from space 98-9
climate
  latitude twins 60
  Mars 108
climate change 18, 30
coins, Roman 129
Colorado River (USA) 32, 33
Columbus, Christopher 126-7, 128
comets 110
commercial flights 72

Congo Basin 143
conic projections 153
continents 12
  changing shape and position 21
  map projections 152
contour lines 155
countries
  meaning of names 55
  number of 52-3
  real names 58-9
  sizes 66-7
  Texas 67
craters
  lunar 106, 107, 125
  Mars 108
  meteorite 103
Cresques, Abraham 123
crocodiles 30, 95
cruise ships 134, 135
crust
  Earth's 12, 15, 20, 21, 138, 139, 142
  Moon's 107
Cuba 128
Curiosity rover 109
currents, ocean 22-5, 134
cyclones 40
cylindrical projections 152

D
data cables 76-7
Date Line, International 81
de la Cosa, Juan 126-7
deep ocean currents 22
Denali, Mount (Alaska, USA) 139
Denmark 52, 53, 133
deserts
  at night 99
  Australian 13
  driest 19
  rivers 30-1
desire-line maps 151
diamond 27
dingo fence 12
dinosaurs 18, 141
disease 94, 95
dogs 95
dot maps 150
drainage basins 28-9

INDEX 157

drives, longest 79
dromedary camels 92, 93
drumlins 36
dry valleys 30
Dull (Scotland) 57
Dunant cable 76
Dymaxion map 8–9

E
eagles 90–1
Earth
   and Solar System 110
   at night 98–9
   from space 27, 114–15
   gravity 104
   magnetic field 89
   rotation 15, 22, 40
earthquakes 44–5, 144
economy 64–5
Egypt
   ancient 124
   borders 52
   human settlement 98
   web traffic 77
Elbrus, Mount (Russia) 145
endonyms 58–9
England 67
Enhanced Fujita scale 42, 43
equator 61
Erebus, Mount (Antarctica) 19
erosion 33, 108, 138, 141, 142
Eurasia 144
Europe
   compared to Australia 13
   geology 144–5
   known world in Middle Ages 120–5
   swallow migration 88–9
   voyages of exploration 123, 124, 126–9
Everest, Mount (China/Nepal) 59, 14–9
evolution, camelid 92–3
exonyms 58–9
extinctions 84, 85, 92

F
Falkland Islands 86
far side of the Moon 106
farming 86–7, 145
Faroe Islands 132, 133
ferries 74
fibre optic cables 76, 77
Finland 57, 133
fishing boats 74
Fisk, Harold 34, 35
flags 52–3
flight routes
   aviation 72–3
   birds 90, 91
   longest 78–9
floodplains 149
food
   and migration 88–9
   from New World 127
forests 38
fossils 32, 93, 141
foxes, red 85
Fra Mauro 124–5
Fuller, Richard Buckminster 9

G
galaxies 112, 113
Galton, Francis 69
Gamburtsev Range (Antarctica) 19
garbage patch, Pacific 22
GDP (gross domestic product) 65
geological maps
   Africa 142–3
   Asia 148–9
   Australia 146–7
   Europe 144–5
   Grand Canyon 32–3
   lunar 106–7
   Mars 108–9
   North America 138–9
   North Pole 14–15
   South America 140–1
geosynchronous/geostationary orbits 100
Germany
   GDP/wealth 64
   name 59
   size 67
geysers 139
glaciers 16, 27, 36, 138
global conveyor belt 22, 23
globes 129

Gobi Desert (China/Mongolia) 92, 149
gold mining 146
Goode's homolosine 152
Google 76
Google Maps 151
GPS 90, 100
Grand Canyon (USA) 32–3, 106
gravity 110
Great Divide (North America) 139
Great Dividing Range (Australia) 147
Great European Plain 145
Great Lakes (Canada/USA) 138
Great Rift Valley (Africa) 143
Greece 58
Greenland 9, 12, 15, 52, 53, 55, 138, 152
grid references 155
groundwater 27
guanacos 92
Guiana Highlands 141
Gulf Stream 22, 23
gyres 22

H
habitat loss 85
heat maps 150
Heezen, Bruce 20, 21
hemispheres, opposite 62–3
hiking 154
Himalayas (Asia) 73, 148, 149
historical maps 120–33
Hoba meteorite 103
Hodges, Ann 102
Hoggar Mountains (Algeria) 143
homicides 95
Horn of Africa 74
hot springs 139
hotspots 147
human settlements 50
   night images from space 98–9
hunting 85
hurricanes 40–1

I
ice caps 27
ice flows 16–17
ice sheets 15, 16, 18–19, 138, 145
   depth of 18
ice shelves 17
icebergs 16, 17, 135
Iceland 133, 144
icosahedron 8
igneous rock 142
India
   cattle 87
   economy 64, 65
   geology 149
   real name 58, 59
   Roman trade with 118, 119
   size 67
Indigenous Americans 126
Indonesia 67
inequality 65
infrared satellites 114
International Date Line 81
International Space Station 99, 100
internet highways 76–7
invasive alien species 85
Islamic mapmaking 120–1
islands 12, 21, 53
Italy 67, 144

J, K
Jack Hills (Western Australia) 146
James Webb Telescope 112
Japan
   GDP 65
   real name 58, 59
   size 67
Jeju to Seoul flights 72
jewellery, gold 118
journeys, longest 78–9
Jupiter 110
Kazakhstan 90
keys 155
Kilimanjaro, Mount (Tanzania) 143
Kirkpatrick, Mount (Antarctica) 19
Kitab Rujar 120–1
Kraken 133
Kuiper Belt 110
Kunst, Dave 78

L
lakes
   lava 107
   North America 138

under ice sheets 18, 19
water in 27
Lancastria, RMS 134
land use maps 151
landslides 36, 38
language zones 59
lasers 34, 35, 36-7, 76
latitude 60-1
lava 36, 107, 108, 139
flows 39
LiDAR (light detection and ranging) 36-9
life on Earth 26, 27
light years 112
Lighthouse of Alexandria 121
lights, city 98-9
lions 84, 85, 95
llamas 87, 92, 93
logarithmic scales 112
London (UK) 60, 61, 69, 81
longitude 61, 152
lost cities 36
Low Earth orbit 100
lunar orbit 104
lunar rock 106-7
lunar seas 107
Luxembourg 65

M

magnetic field, Earth's 89
Magnus, Olaus 132-3
Mali Empire 122
Manila (Philippines) 51
mantle, Earth's 27, 44
maps
2D of 3D world 8-9
projections 152-3
reading 154-5
types of 150-1
Mars 110
geology 108-9
marsupials 12
Maya 36
meanders 35
medieval era 120-5
Mediterranean Sea 144
night image of 98
Roman control 118, 120

swallow migration 88
megabergs 17
Meldermann, Nikolaus 130
Mercator projections 152
merchant shipping 74-5
Mercury 110
metamorphic rock 142
meteorites 102-3, 106, 107, 108
meteoroids 102
meteors 102
mid-ocean ridges 21
midday 81
midnight 81
migrations 88-9, 90
Milky Way 112
Mississippi River (USA) 28, 34-5
Monaco 50
money 64-5
Mongolia 87, 92
monoliths 147
monsters 132-3
Moon
flightpath 104
landings 104-5
lunar rock 106-7
width of 10, 12
mosquitoes 94, 95
mountains
Africa 143
Asia 148-9
longest range 20-1
North America 138, 139
real names 59
South America 140, 141
under ice sheet 18, 19
underwater 20-1
Musa I of Mali 122
myths and legends 133

N

NASA 25, 109
national parks 46
navigation, birds 89
near side of the Moon 107
Neptune 110
New World 126-7
New Zealand 57, 87
Niger, River (Africa) 30

Nile, River (Africa) 30, 31, 98, 121
No Name (Colorado, USA) 56
no-fly zones 73
North America
camelids 93
geology 138-9
North Pole 14-15
geographic and magnetic 15
lunar 107
time zone 81
Norway 57, 132, 133
numbers, as place names 56

O

oases 31
observable universe 112, 113
observation satellites 99
oceans 27
biggest 10
currents 22-5
depth 20
mapping 20-1
night images 99
ocean floor 15
shipping routes 74-5
shipwrecks 134-5
submarine data cables 76-7
Opportunity rover 109
orbits
moon missions 104
satellites 100
Solar System 110
Orkney Islands (UK) 132
Ottoman Empire 130-1
Outback 13
oxbow lakes 35

P

Pacific Ocean
garbage patch 22
pirate attacks 74
Ring of Fire 44-5
size of 10-11
space graveyard 135
submarine data cables 77
Pan-American Highway 78
per capita income 65
Peru 67, 87

Peters projections 152
physical maps 151
pigs 87
pirate attacks 74
place names
curious 56-7
longest/shortest 57
meaning of 54-5
real names 58-9
planets 110
plastic pollution 22
plateaus 141, 142, 149
Pluto 110
Point Nemo 135
poles 25
map projections 152, 153
time zones 80-1
political maps 52-3, 150
pollution 22
Polo, Marco 123
Popocatepetl (Mexico) 44
population 50-1
Portugal, voyages of discovery 128
predators 94
projections, map 8, 152-3
Ptolemy 128
pyramids 36, 124

R

raccoons, common 85
radar surveys 18, 19, 30
railways 155
rain shadows 149
rainfall 30, 31
rainforests 18, 28, 141, 143
rats, brown 85
Red Sea 74, 134
Ring of Fire 44-5
river basins 28-9, 141, 143
rivers
Australia 147
changing paths 34-5
deltas 28, 29, 114
in the desert 30-1
water in 27
roads 154, 155
longest 78, 79
longest trips 79

INDEX

networks 68-9
Roman 118, 119
robots 109
rockets 104, 135
rocks
age of 15, 146
lunar 105, 106-7
Martian 108-9
North American 138-9
Roger II of Sicily 120-1
Romans
Empire 129
gold hoards 118-19
shipwrecks 135
Ross Ice Shelf (Antarctica) 19
round-the-world trips 78
Russia
size 12
wealth 64

S

Saffir-Simpson scale 41
Sahara Desert (Africa) 30-1, 67, 114, 143
sailing charts 123
salt water 27
San José 135
Sandwich (England) 56
satellites 25, 35, 74, 90, 98-9, 135
mapping 100-1, 114-15
Saturn 110
Saturn V rockets 104
scale/scale bar 154
Scandinavia 132-3, 144, 145
Schmid, Emil and Liliane 79
Scotland 52
sea levels, rising 16
sea monsters 132, 133
seas, lunar 107
sedimentary rock 32, 142, 143, 145
settlement patterns 13
Seven Wonders of Ancient World 121
sheep 86-7
shipping routes 74-5
ships, Roman 118
shipwrecks 134-5
shooting stars 102
Singapore 67
snails 94, 95

Solar System 110-11, 112
sonar 20
South Africa 57
South America
camelids 93
cattle 87
geology 140-1
New World 126, 128
South Korea 72
South Pole 9, 16, 18, 146
lunar 106, 107
time zone 80
space
debris 100-1
mapping 112-13
rocks 102-3, 110
space shuttle 30
space stations 100
spacecraft
Mars 109
Moon 104-5
space graveyard 135
Spain, voyages of discovery 126-7, 128
Spirit rover 109
splashdown 105
St Stephen's cathedral (Vienna) 130
strata, rock 33
submarine data cables 76-7
submarines 134
Sudan 52
Suleiman the Magnificent, Sultan 130, 131
Sun 25, 110, 112
sunlight 26, 27
Suomi NPP satellite 99
supercells 43
superclusters, galaxy 112
surface currents 22
swallows, barn 88-9
Sweden 53, 57, 133
Switzerland, size 66, 67

T

Taiwan 52
tankers 74
Taranaki, Mount (New Zealand) 46-7

tectonic plates 12, 15, 20, 21, 44-5, 115, 138, 141, 144, 148, 149
telegraph cables 76
temperatures
Mars 108
oceans 25
Terra Australis 54
terrain 154, 155
Texas 64
Tharp, Marie 20, 21
Thistlegorm, SS 134
Tibetan plateau 73
time
mapping the universe 112
time zones 63, 80-1
travelling 69
Titanic, RMS 135
Titicaca, Lake (Bolivia/Peru) 141
Tokyo (Japan) 68-9
topographic maps 150, 154-5
tornadoes 42-3
towns, names 55
trade, Roman 118, 119
trade winds 40
trains, longest journey 79
Transantarctic Mountains 19
transport
flight routes 72-3
longest journeys 78-9
road networks 68-9
shipping routes 74-5
treasure
Roman 118-19
shipwrecks 134, 135
tributaries 28, 33
tropics 25
Truth or Consequences (USA) 56
turtles 99
typhoons 40

U

Uluru (Australia) 147
United Kingdom 52
sheep 86
United Nations 52, 58
United States
flights 73
GDP/wealth 64, 65

hurricanes 41
livestock 86
size 67
submarine data cables 76
Tornado Alley 42-3
universe, mapping 112-13
Ural Mountains 144
Uranus 110
UTC (universal time coordinated) 81

V

vegetation 154, 155
removing 36-9
Venice 124
venom 94, 95
Venus 110
Vespucci, Amerigo 128, 129
vicuñas 92
Vienna, siege of 130-1
Vikings 126
volcanoes
Africa 143
Antarctica 19
Australia 147
Europe 144
lava flows 39
Mars 108
Ring of Fire 44-5
Vostok, Lake (Antarctica) 19

W

wadis 30
Waldseemüller, Martin 128-9
Wales 57
walks, longest 78, 79
war zones 73, 130-1, 134
water 10, 26-7
erosion 138, 142
on Mars 108, 109
running 129
temperatures 25
water cycle 16
wealth 64-5
Willamette meteorite 103
Winkel tripel 153
wolves 95
World War II, shipwrecks 134, 135

Acknowledgments

The publisher would like to thank the following people for their assistance in the creation of this book. Igor Karyakin for help with the steppe eagles map; Trent Schindler for help with the Ice Flows Antarctica map; Helen Peters for the index; Katie John for proofreading; Jennette ElNaggar for editing the US edition; Steve Hoffman for fact-checking; Jolyon Goddard and Zaina Budaly for addtional editorial help.

The publisher would like to thank the following for their kind permission to reproduce their photographs. Key: a-above; b-below/bottom; c-centre; f-far; l-left; r-right; t-top.

1 Eleanor Lutz: NASA / USGS (Mars). **Earth Resources Observation and Science (EROS) Center** (2020). Landsat 8-9 Operational Land Imager / Thermal Infrared Sensor Level-1, Collection 2 [dataset]. U.S. Geological Survey. https://doi.org/10.5066/P975CC9B (tc/& bc). **USGS Astrogeology Science Center:** Fortezzo, C.M., Spudis, P. D. and Harrel, S. L. (2020). Release of the Digital Unified Global Geologic Map of the Moon at 1:5,000,000-scale. Paper presented at the 51st Lunar and Planetary Science Conference, Lunar and Planetary Institute, Houston, TX (corners). **2 American Geographical Society Library, University of Wisconsin-Milwaukee Libraries:** (fr). **HydroSHEDS:** https://www.hydrosheds.org / Lehner, B., Grill G. (2013). Global river hydrography and network routing: baseline data and new approaches to study the world's large river systems. Hydrological Processes, 27(15): 2171-2186. https://doi.org/10.1002/hyp.9740 (fcl/data). **U.S. Geological Survey:** NASA (r). **Wien Museum:** Inv.-Nr. 48068, CC0 (https://sammlung.wienmuseum.at/en/object/125187/) (l). **3 Shaded Relief by Sean Conway for Muir Way. 5 American Geographical Society Library, University of Wisconsin-Milwaukee Libraries:** (crb). **Shaded Relief by Sean Conway for Muir Way:** (br, fbr). **6 Science Photo Library:** Library of Congress, Geography and Map Division (r); Karsten Schneider (c). **7 Shaded Relief by Sean Conway for Muir Way. NASA:** image created by Jesse Allen, using SRTM data provided courtesy of the University of Maryland's Global Land Cover Facility, and river data provided courtesy of the World Wildlife Fund HydroSHEDS Project (c). **8-9 Shaded Relief by Sean Conway for Muir Way. 10 Alamy Stock Photo:** Oleksiy Maksymenko Photography (tl). **12-13 GEBCO:** GEBCO Compilation Group (2024) GEBCO 2024 Grid (doi:10.5285/1c44ce99-0a0d-5f4f-e063-7086abc0ea0f) (bathymetry data). **Made with Natural Earth:** (land textures data). **12 ESO:** NASA's Scientific Visualization Studio (bl/moon). **14 Shaded Relief by Sean Conway for Muir Way. 15 Shaded Relief by Sean Conway for Muir Way:** (tr). **Shutterstock.com:** Steve Allen (ca). **16 NASA:** Kate Ramsayer (cl). **Made with Natural Earth:** (tl/land textures). **16-17 NASA:** Goddard Space Flight Center Scientific Visualization, Studio. **17 NASA:** GSFC / OIB (tr). **18 Science Photo Library:** Roger Harris (bl). **18-19 BAS:** Fretwell, P., Pritchard, H., Vaughan, D., Bamber, J., Barrand, N., Bell, R., Bianchi, C., Bingham, R., Blankenship, D., Casassa, G., Catania, G., Callens, D., Conway, H., Cook, A., Corr, H., Damaske, D., Damn, V., Ferraccioli, F., Forsberg, R., Zirizzotti, A. (2022). BEDMAP2 - Ice thickness, bed and surface elevation for Antarctica - gridding products (Version 1.0) [Data set]. NERC EDS UK Polar Data Centre. https://doi.org/10.5285/fa5d606c-dc95-47ee-9016-7a82e446f2f2. **19 Alamy Stock Photo:** Dan Leeth (tr). **Oceans at MIT:** LIMA / NASA (br/adapted from). **20 Lamont-Doherty Earth Observatory and the estate of Marie Tharp:** (br). **20-21 Science Photo Library:** Library of Congress, Geography and Map Division. **22 Science Photo Library:** Sinclair Stammers (bl). **23 Science Photo Library:** Karsten Schneider. **24-25 NASA:** Goddard Space Flight Center Scientific Visualization Studio. **26-27 Science Photo Library:** Adam Nieman. **26 NASA:** JPL / UCSD / JSC (bl). **Science Photo Library:** Wladimir Bulgar (tr). **28 River basin map of the United States by Robert Szucs / www.grasshoppergeography.com** (cl). **29 NASA:** image created by Jesse Allen, using SRTM data provided courtesy of the University of Maryland's Global Land Cover Facility, and river data provided courtesy of the World Wildlife Fund HydroSHEDS Project. **30 Alamy Stock Photo:** Jesse Kraft (tc). **Getty Images:** Frans Lemmens / Corbis (tl). **30-31 HydroSHEDS:** https://www.hydrosheds.org / Lehner, B., Grill G (2013). Global river hydrography and network routing: baseline data and new approaches to study the world's large river systems. Hydrological Processes, 27(15): 2171-2186. https://doi.org/10.1002/hyp.9740. **31 Alamy Stock Photo:** Delphotos (tr). **Shutterstock.com:** Patrick Poendl (tl). **32-33 Shaded Relief by Sean Conway for Muir Way. 33 Shutterstock.com:** Amanda Mohler (tc). **34 American Geographical Society Library, University of Wisconsin-Milwaukee Libraries:** (l). **Meander & Flow Design:** (r). **35 Earth Resources Observation and Science (EROS) Center** (2020). Landsat 8-9 Operational Land Imager / Thermal Infrared Sensor Level-1, Collection 2 [dataset]. U.S. Geological Survey. https://doi.org/10.5066/P975CC9B (bl). **36 Cambridge University Press:** Hansen, R.D. et al. (2023) 'LiDAR analyses in the contiguous Mirador-Calakmul Karst Basin, Guatemala: an introduction to new perspectives on regional early Maya socioeconomic and political organization', Ancient Mesoamerica, 34(3), pp. 587-626. doi:10.1017/S0956536122000244 (fig.16) (bc). **Dreamstime.com:** Mcloud (cb). **Earth Resources Observation and Science (EROS) Center** (2020). Landsat 8-9 Operational Land Imager / Thermal Infrared Sensor Level-1, Collection 2 [dataset]. U.S. Geological Survey. https://doi.org/10.5066/P975CC9B (r). **37 Image from the Washington Geological Survey (Washington State DNR):** (r). **38 Earth Resources Observation and Science (EROS) Center** (2020). Landsat 8-9 Operational Land Imager / Thermal Infrared Sensor Level-1, Collection 2 [dataset]. U.S. Geological Survey. https://doi.org/10.5066/P975CC9B (b). **Image from the Washington Geological Survey (Washington State DNR):** (t). **39 Earth Resources Observation and Science (EROS) Center** (2020). Landsat 8-9 Operational Land Imager / Thermal Infrared Sensor Level-1, Collection 2 [dataset]. U.S. Geological Survey. https://doi.org/10.5066/P975CC9B (t). **Image from the Washington Geological Survey (Washington State DNR):** (b). **40-41 NOAA:** NASA (base map) / NOAA's International Best Track Archive for Climate Stewardship (IBTrACS) data, accessed on 1 December 2024 / National Hurricane Center / Nilfanion (processing, via Wikipedia) (b). **41 Shutterstock.com:** aappp (cra). **42 European Severe Weather Database, ESWD:** (tl/European map data). **42-43 NOAA:** National Weather Service, Storm Prediction Center. https://spc.noaa.gov/wcm/#data / Tornado Archive. **43 Alamy Stock Photo:** Jeff Roberson / Associated Press (bc). **Getty Images / iStock:** Francis Lavigne-Theriault (br). **Shutterstock.com:** trgrowth (tl). **44 Alamy Stock Photo:** Marc Lester / Anchorage Daily News / AP (clb). **Getty Images:** Erik Gomez Tochimani / AFP (tl). **44-45 Global Volcanism Program (GVP), National Museum of Natural History, Smithsonian Institution:** Global Volcanism Program, 2024. [Database] Volcanoes of the World (v. 5.2.7; 21 Feb 2025). Distributed by Smithsonian Institution, compiled by Venzke, E. https://doi.org/10.5479/si.GVP.VOTW5-2024.5.2 (volcano data). **U.S. Geological Survey:** Earthquake Hazards Program, https://earthquake.usgs.gov/earthquakes/search/ (earthquake data). **46-47 Science Photo Library:** CNES, 2004-2011 Distribution Spot Image. **48 Map from Shipmap.org © Kiln.digital:** (c). **Craig Taylor:** (r). **49 NASA:** Center For International Earth Science Information Network-CIESIN-Columbia University, & Centro Internacional de Agricultura Tropical-CIAT. (2005). Gridded Population of the World, Version 3 (GPWv3): Centroids (Version 3.00) [Data set]. Palisades, NY: NASA Socioeconomic Data and Applications Center (SEDAC). https://doi.org/10.7927/H4TT4NWQ (c). **Earth Resources Observation and Science (EROS) Center** (2020). Landsat 8-9 Operational Land Imager / Thermal Infrared Sensor Level-1, Collection 2 [dataset]. U.S. Geological Survey. https://doi.org/10.5066/P975CC9B. **50-51 NASA:** Center For International Earth Science Information Network-CIESIN-Columbia University, & Centro Internacional De Agricultura Tropical-CIAT (2005). Gridded Population of the World, Version 3 (GPWv3): Centroids (Version 3.00) [dataset]. Palisades, NY: NASA Socioeconomic Data and Applications Center (SEDAC). https://doi.org/10.7927/H4TT4NWQ. **Springer Nature:** Wang, X., Meng, X. & Long, Y. Projecting 1 km-grid population distributions from 2020 to 2100 globally under shared socioeconomic pathways. Sci Data 9, 563 (2022). https://doi.org/10.1038/s41597-022-01675-x. **53 Shutterstock.com:** otto norin (crb). **54 Alamy Stock Photo:** GL Archive (clb). **56 Alamy Stock Photo:** Andriy Blokhin (cl); John Zada (bc). **57 Alamy Stock Photo:** Ian Dagnall (cb); Phil Crean A (br); Richard Newton (tr). **59 Getty Images / iStock:** sansubba (cl). **60 The Washington Post:** Laris Karklis, Weiyi Cai (bc, cl). **61 Made with Natural Earth:** (r/small globes). **The Washington Post:** Laris Karklis, Weiyi Cai. **62 Getty Images:** Benoit Gysembergh / Paris Match Archive (br). **64-65 Illustrated by u/BerryBlue_BlueBerry, a mapmaker on reddit:** (cartograms). **65 UBS:** Data from UBS Global Wealth Report 2024 (bc). **68-69 Craig Taylor:** (Coral Cities). **69 Alamy Stock Photo:** Antiqua Print Gallery (tr). **70-71 Earth Resources Observation and Science (EROS) Center** (2020). Landsat 8-9 Operational Land Imager / Thermal Infrared Sensor Level-1, Collection 2 [dataset]. U.S. Geological Survey. https://doi.org/10.5066/P975CC9B. **72-73 OpenFlights.org:** (data). **74-75 Map from Shipmap.org © Kiln.digital. 74 Prins, B., Gold, A., Phayal, A., & Daxecker, U. (2022, October 19). Maritime Piracy and Foreign Policy. Oxford Research Encyclopedia of Politics.** Retrieved 1 May. 2025, from https://oxfordre.com/politics/view/10.1093/acrefore/9780190228637.001.0001/acrefore-9780190228637-e-522 (fig.3) (tl/adapted from). **75 Shutterstock.com:** AU USAnakul (bl). **76 Library of Congress, Washington, D.C.:** Library of Congress, Geography and Map Division - www.loc.gov/item/2013593218 (br). **Shutterstock.com:** kmls (bl). **76-77 TeleGeography:** submarinecablemap.com. **78 Alamy Stock Photo:** Associated Press (tl). **79 Courtesy of Guinness World Records Limited:** (br). **80-81 Made with Natural Earth:** United States Central Intelligence Agency. **82 The Convention on Migratory Species:** Online maps and species accounts - Franks, S., Fiedler, W., Arizaga, J., Jiguet, F., Nikolov, B., van der Jeugd, H., Ambrosini, R., Aizpurua, O., Bairlein, F., Clark, J., Fattorini, N., Hammond, M., Higgins, D., Levering, H., Skellorn, W., Spina, F., Thorup, K., Walker, J., Woodward, I. and Baillie, S.R.I. (2022). Online Atlas of the movements of Eurasian-African bird populations. EURING/CMS (c). **African Lion Database. Unpublished Data. 2023 2024. Panthera leo. The IUCN Red List of Threatened Species 2024-2**. https://www.iucnredlist.org. Accessed on 14 February 2025 (r). **83 Institute for Health Metrics and Evaluation. Used with permission. All rights reserved.:** (c/data). **Russian Raptor Research and Conservation Network:** Karyakin, Igor & al. (2019). Results of the GPS/GSM-Tracking of Juvenile Steppe Eagles from Russia and Kazakhstan. Raptors Conservation. 71-227. 10.19074/1814-8654-2019-39-71-227 (data). **84 African Lion Database. Unpublished Data. 2023 2024. Panthera leo. The IUCN Red List of Threatened Species 2024-2.** https://www.iucnredlist.org. Accessed on 14 February 2025. **85 Getty Images / iStock:** GlobalP (bl). **IUCN (International Union for Conservation of Nature) 2017.** Bison bison. The IUCN Red List of Threatened Species 2024-2. https://www.iucnredlist.org. Accessed on 14 February 2025 (bl/data - current range, br/data); **IUCN (International Union for Conservation of Nature) 2017.** Vulpes vulpes. The IUCN Red List of Threatened Species 2024-2. https://www.iucnredlist.org. Accessed on 14 February 2025 (bl/data - current range, br/data). **Museum and Institute of Zoology, Polish Academy of Sciences:** Azita Farashi, Morteza Naderi, and Sanaz Safavian "Predicting the potential invasive range of raccoon in the world," Polish Journal of Ecology 64(4), 594-600, (1 December 2016). https://doi.org/10.3161/15052249PJE2016.64.4.014 (fig. 2) (cra/data). **86-87 Worldmapper.org:** data by the Food and Agriculture Organization of the United Nations (FAO) (last accessed March 2018). **87 123RF.com:** Eric Isselee (br). **Dreamstime.com:** Mike_kiev (cra). **Worldmapper.org:** data by the Food and Agriculture Organization of the United Nations (FAO) (last accessed March 2018) (cr, tr, crb). **88-89 The Convention on Migratory Species:** Online maps and species accounts -; Franks, S., Fiedler, W., Arizaga, J., Jiguet, F., Nikolov, B., van der Jeugd, H., Ambrosini, R., Aizpurua, O., Bairlein, F., Clark, J., Fattorini, N., Hammond, M., Higgins, D., Levering, H., Skellorn, W., Spina, F., Thorup, K., Walker, J., Woodward, I. and Baillie, S.R.I. (2022). Online Atlas of the movements of Eurasian-African bird populations. EURING/CMS. **88 Shutterstock.com:** Dennis Jacobsen (tc); Olexandr Panchenko (tl); lovelyday12 (tc/sky). **89 Shutterstock.com:** Mati Kose (tl). **90-91 Russian Raptor Research and Conservation Network:** Karyakin, Igor & al. (2019). Results of the GPS/GSM-Tracking of Juvenile Steppe Eagles from Russia and Kazakhstan. Raptors Conservation. 71-227. 10.19074/1814-8654-2019-39-71-227 (data). **90 Alamy Stock Photo:** imageBROKER / photoholic (cb). **91 Alamy Stock Photo:** Blickwinkel / McPhoto / Mas (br). **92 Alamy Stock Photo:** James Eaton / Agami (fbr); Life on white (bc/alpaca). **Dorling Kindersley:** Twycross Zoo (br/Bactrian camel). **Dreamstime.com:** Vasyl Helevachuk (fbl). **IUCN (International Union for Conservation of Nature) 2008**. Camelus ferus. The IUCN Red List of Threatened Species 2024-2. https://www.iucnredlist.org. Accessed on 14 February 2025 (wild Bactrian camel data). **© Lynx Nature Books:** (dromedary data). **Shutterstock.com:** Ilyas Kalimullin (tc); Fabian Ponce Garcia (bc/vicuña). **Taylor & Francis Group:** Adney, D. R. et al. (2019) 'Bactrian camels shed large quantities of Middle East respiratory syndrome coronavirus (MERS-CoV) after experimental infection', Emerging Microbes & Infections, 8(1), pp. 717-723. doi: 10.1080/22221751.2019.1618687. (Bactrian camel data). **93 IUCN (International Union for Conservation of Nature) 2018**. Lama guanicoe. The IUCN Red List of Threatened Species 2024-2. https://www.iucnredlist.org. Accessed on 14 February 2025 (vicuña); **IUCN (International Union for Conservation of Nature) 2018.** Vicugna vicugna. The IUCN Red List of Threatened Species 2024-2. https://www.iucnredlist.org. Accessed on 14 February 2025 (vicuña data). **© Lynx Nature Books:** (llama & alpaca data). **Shutterstock.com:** Kambiz Pourghanad (bc). **94 Dreamstime.com:** Palex66 (crb). **Shutterstock.com:** buteo (br); Gulf MG (bc). **94-95 Source: Institute for Health Metrics and Evaluation. Used with permission. All rights reserved.:** (data). **96 NASA:** Image taken by the Landsat 7 satellite, operated by the U.S. Geological Survey and NASA (Lena River). **USGS Astrogeology Science Center:** Fortezzo, C.M., Spudis, P. D. and Harrel, S. L. (2020). Release of the Digital Unified Global Geologic Map of the Moon At 1:5,000,000- Scale. Paper presented at the 51st Lunar and Planetary Science Conference, Lunar and Planetary Institute, Houston, TX (r). **97 Pablo Carlos Budassi:** (c). **Eleanor Lutz:** NASA (asteroids). **98 Shutterstock.com:** Anton Balazh. **99 Alamy Stock Photo:** Geopix (cb). **100 Science Photo Library:** Claus Lunau (br). **101 Dorling Kindersley:** NASA Earth Observatory / Reto Stöckli and Robert Simmon. **102-103 NASA:** Planetary Science (map data). **103 Alamy Stock Photo:** Historic Collection (br); Chon Kit Leong (bl). **104 NASA:** (cb); JSC (bl); Neil A. Armstrong (crb). **104-105 NASA:** (c). **105 NASA:** (bl); Neil A. Armstrong (cb); JSC (br). 106-107 USGS **Astrogeology Science Center:** Fortezzo, C.M., Spudis, P. D. and Harrel, S. L. (2020). Release of the Digital Unified Global Geologic Map of the Moon At 1:5,000,000- Scale. Paper presented at the 51st Lunar and Planetary Science Conference, Lunar and Planetary Institute, Houston, TX. **107 ESO:** NASA's Scientific Visualization Studio (br). **108 NASA:** JPL-Caltech / MSSS (tl). **108-109 Eleanor Lutz:** NASA / USGS. **109 NASA:** Jet Propulsion Lab / USGS (bc); JPL-Caltech / MSSS (crb). **110 NASA:** Johns Hopkins APL (crb). **111 Eleanor Lutz:** NASA. **112 Pablo Carlos Budassi:** (bl). **ESA:** NASA, CSA, and STScI (cl). **113 Pablo Carlos Budassi. 114 U.S. Geological Survey:** NASA (t, b). **115 U.S. Geological Survey:** (b); NASA (t). **116 Alamy Stock Photo:** World History Archive (r). **Wien Museum:** Inv.-Nr. 48068, CC0 (https://sammlung.wienmuseum.at/en/object/125187/) (c). **117 Bridgeman Images:** (c). **Getty Images:** Universal History Archive. **118 Alamy Stock Photo:** George Atsametakis (br); Robert Estall photo agency (bl). **© The Trustees of the British Museum. All rights reserved:** (bc). **Coin Hoards of the Roman Empire, https://chre.ashmus.ox.ac.uk:** (data). **119 © The Trustees of the British Museum. All rights reserved:** (fbl, bl). **120-121 Alamy Stock Photo:** Science History Images. **122-123 Bridgeman Images. 124-125 Getty Images:** Universal History Archive. **126 Alamy Stock Photo:** IanDagnall Computing (cla). **126-127 Photo Scala, Florence:** Museo Naval, Ministerio de Marina, Madrid / Album / Oronoz. **127 Alamy Stock Photo:** The History Collection (bl). **128-129 Library of Congress, Washington, D.C.:** Library of Congress, Geography and Map Division - www.loc.gov / item / 2003626426. **129 Alamy Stock Photo:** AF Fotografie (tl). **130-131 Wien Museum:** Inv.-Nr. 48068, CC0 (https://sammlung.wienmuseum.at/en/object/125187/). **130 Shutterstock.com:** Mistervlad (bl). **132-133 Alamy Stock Photo:** World History Archive. **134-135 Paul Heersink. 134 Getty Images / iStock:** ultramarinfoto / E+ (br). **NOAA:** Tane Casserley (cla). **135 Alamy Stock Photo:** Cinematic Collection (br). **Dreamstime.com:** Rob Atherton (cra). **136 Shaded Relief by Sean Conway for Muir Way:** (c). **Visual Wall Maps:** (r). **137 Created by editing the Geological Map of Asia (TERAOKA Yoji, OKUMURA Kimio, 2011), Geological Survey of Japan, AIST** (https://gbank.gsj.jp/geonavi/docdata/data/org_data/wxga_1265_org_1257.jpg, https://gbank.gsj.jp/geonavi/docdata/data/org_data/wxga_1265_org_1258.jpg, https://gbank.gsj.jp/geonavi/docdata/data/pict_data/orgsize_1265_legend_1228.jpg (c). **Shaded Relief by Sean Conway for Muir Way. 138-139 Shaded Relief by Sean Conway for Muir Way. 138 Shutterstock.com:** shipfactory (tc); Gleb Tarro (bc). **139 Shutterstock.com:** Luca Micheli (br). **140-141 Shaded Relief by Sean Conway for Muir Way. 141 Dreamstime.com:** Konstantin Gerasimov (br). **Shutterstock.com:** alejojimenezyt (bl); Nowak Lukasz (cla). **142 Shaded Relief by Sean Conway for Muir Way. 143 Alamy Stock Photo:** Karine Aigner / Nature Picture Library (tl); Michael Runkel / imageBROKER (cra); Michael Cuthbert (bl). **144-145 Visual Wall Maps. 144 Shutterstock.com:** Vadym Lavra (bc); Wead (clb). **145 Shutterstock.com:** Curioso.Photography (tr). **146-147 Visual Wall Maps. 146 Getty Images:** Daniel Grizelj (br). **Shutterstock.com:** Hans Wismeijer (clb). **147 Alamy Stock Photo:** Russotwins (br); Taras Vyshnya (tr). **148-149 Created by editing the Geological Map of Asia (TERAOKA Yoji, OKUMURA Kimio, 2011), Geological Survey of Japan, AIST** (https://gbank.gsj.jp/geonavi/docdata/data/org_data/wxga_1265_org_1257.jpg, https://gbank.gsj.jp/geonavi/docdata/data/org_data/wxga_1265_org_1258.jpg, https://gbank.gsj.jp/geonavi/docdata/data/pict_data/orgsize_1265_legend_1228.jpg **148 U.S. Geological Survey:** (bl/adapted from). **149 Getty Images / iStock:** DanielPrudek (clb). **Shutterstock.com:** Tokareva Irina (tr). **152-153 Science Photo Library:** Copyright 1995, Worldsat International and J. Knighton (crb). **153 Alamy Stock Photo:** IanDagnall Computing (br).

Cover images: *Front & Back:* **Science Photo Library:** Karsten Schneider; *Spine:* **American Geographical Society Library, University of Wisconsin-Milwaukee Libraries:** b/ (Mississippi); **GEBCO:** GEBCO Compilation Group (2024) GEBCO 2024 Grid (doi:10.5285/1c44ce99-0a0d-5f4f-e063-7086abc0ea0f) t/ (Australia); **Shaded Relief by Sean Conway for Muir Way:** t/ (Grand Canyon & Africa); **NASA:** Goddard Space Flight Center Scientific Visualization, Studio b/ (Antarctica); **U.S. Geological Survey:** NASA b/ (Siberia).

Endpapers: Simon Mumford, DK. The coloured lines join areas of equal distance from the coast, revealing the oceans' "poles of inaccessibility" - the places on Earth that are furthest from land.